God Loves Her

365 Devotions
for Women by Women

Our Daily Bread

Our Daily Bread
Publishing™

foreword

My favorite time of day is my morning quiet time with the Lord. But when I'm away from home, it can be hard to carve out the time and space. On a recent trip I stayed at an Airbnb with extended family and eyed the kitchen table as my morning spot. But when I woke early the next day and came to the kitchen with my Bible and colored pencils, someone was already there. A laptop and other remote work essentials covered the table. I hadn't been the only one eyeing it.

I soon discovered that the two living areas wouldn't work either. They both flowed near the kitchen, and the remote worker was taking calls—on speaker.

The following morning when I woke, I prayed, asking the Lord to show me where I could spend extended quiet time with Him and His Word. *Lord, you know I cherish my time with you. And nothing is too hard for you. Could you make a way?*

I walked into the kitchen, greeted by the same scene— family member on a conference call on speaker at the kitchen table. But as I poured a cup of coffee, he ended the call, stood, and stretched.

"I've been up since before dawn," he said. "I'm about to take a nap."

I watched as he cleared the table and returned to his room. Leaning against the counter, I shook my head in wonder and said in my heart, *Lord, you love me. Thank you.*

We've heard that God loves us. For many of us, "For God so loved the world" was seared on our childhood memories. We know that "He gave His only Son, so that everyone who believes in Him will not perish, but have eternal life"—because of His love (John 3:16).

We may also know that we were saved by grace through faith—"because of His great love with which He loved us" (Ephesians 2:4 NASB). If we've learned anything about God, it's probably that He is love, and that He loves *us.*

But do you know that He loves *you*?

Do you know that His love for you is immensely personal?

Hannah wept because she could not bear children and suffered ridicule as a result. Distressed and unable to eat, she poured out her soul before God, asking for a son. And we're told, "the LORD remembered her" (1 Samuel 1:19). *Her.* It was personal. Hannah prayed to her God, and He answered, blessing her with a son. What immense love on display!

What about Mary Magdalene? She had seen her Savior endure the agony of the cross and she came early to the tomb, while it was still dark. When she saw that the stone had been removed, she ran to Peter and John, telling them that Jesus's body was missing. They ran to see for themselves, and after confirming this news, returned to their homes. But Mary stayed, weeping, wanting to know where they had taken her Lord. Moments later she turned—and saw Jesus. She didn't know it was Him until He said her name (John 20:16). And oh, the joy that must have flooded her heart when she realized He'd risen from the dead.

Mary had been weeping, seeking her Lord, and in an amazing show of love, Jesus appeared to *her*.

The devotions in this book highlight the precious truth that God loves us—that God loves *you*. Personally. As you read through this book, I pray you draw near to the Lord. Ask Him to show you daily glimpses of His love. You'll see it in a myriad of ways: an encouraging word from a friend, a random hug, an act of kindness from a stranger, or an unexpected answer to prayer. It's all from our loving and faithful God. Because He loves *you*.

Kim Cash Tate

Author, Bible teacher, speaker,
and singer-songwriter

Forever Love
Psalm 136:1–9

We know and rely on the love God has for us.
God is love. —1 JOHN 4:16

Years ago, my four-year-old son gave me a framed wooden heart mounted on a metal plate with the word *forever* painted in its center. "I love you forever, Mommy," he said.

I thanked him with a hug. "I love you more."

That priceless gift still assures me of my son's never-ending love. On tough days, God uses that sweet present to comfort and encourage me as He affirms I'm deeply loved.

The frame also reminds me of the gift of God's everlasting love, as expressed throughout His Word and confirmed by His Spirit. We can trust God's unchanging goodness and sing grateful praises that confirm His enduring love, as the psalmist does (Psalm 136:1). We can exalt the Lord as greater than and above all (vv. 2–3), as we reflect on His endless wonders and unlimited understanding (vv. 4–5). The God who loves us forever is the conscious and caring Maker of the heavens and earth, who maintains control of time itself (vv. 6–9).

We can rejoice because the everlasting love the psalmist sang about is the same continuing love our all-powerful Creator and Sustainer pours into the lives of His children today. No matter what we're facing, the One who made us and remains with us strengthens us by asserting He loves us unconditionally and completely.

Thank you, God, for the countless reminders of your endless and life-transforming love! *Xochitl*

Flourishing Like a Flower
Psalm 103:13–22

The life of mortals is like grass, they flourish like a flower of the field. —*PSALM 103:15*

It's fun to notice the little changes in my grandchildren as they grow. I remember that when one of my grands was two months old, as I cooed to him, he looked up at me and smiled! Suddenly I began crying. Perhaps it was joy mixed with remembering my own children's first smiles, which I witnessed so long ago, and yet it feels like just yesterday. Some moments are like that—inexplicable.

In Psalm 103, David penned a poetic song that praised God while also reflecting on how quickly the joyful moments of our lives pass by: "The life of mortals is like grass, they flourish like a flower of the field; the wind blows over it and it is gone" (vv. 15–16).

But despite acknowledging the brevity of life, David describes the flower as flourishing, or thriving. Although each individual flower blossoms and blooms swiftly, its fragrance and color and beauty bring great joy in the moment. And even though an individual flower can be quickly forgotten—"its place remembers it no more" (v. 16). By contrast, we have the assurance that "from everlasting to everlasting the LORD's love is with those who fear him" (v. 17).

We, like flowers, can rejoice and flourish in the moment; but we can also celebrate the truth that the moments of our lives are never truly forgotten. God holds every detail of our lives, and His everlasting love is with His children forever! *Alyson*

God Knows Your Story

Psalm 139:1–6, 23–24

Search me, God, and know my heart; test me and know my anxious thoughts. —PSALM 139:23

As I drove home after lunch with my best friend, I thanked God out loud for her. She knows me and loves me in spite of things I don't love about myself. She's one of a small circle of people who accept me as I am—my quirks, habits, and screw-ups. Still, there are parts of my story I resist sharing even with her and others I love—times where I've clearly not been the hero, times I've been judgmental or unkind or unloving.

But God knows my whole story. He's the One I can freely talk to even if I'm reluctant to talk with others.

The familiar words of Psalm 139 describe the intimacy we enjoy with our Sovereign King. He knows us completely! (v. 1). He's "familiar with all [our] ways" (v. 3). He invites us to come to Him with our confusion, our anxious thoughts, and our struggles with temptation. When we're willing to yield completely to Him, He reaches out to restore and rewrite the parts of our story that make us sad because we've wandered from Him.

God knows us better than anyone else ever can, and still . . . He loves us! When we daily surrender ourselves to Him and seek to know Him more fully, He can change our story for His glory. He's the Author who's continuing to write it. *Cindy*

Scar Stories
John 20:24–29

See my hands. Reach out your hand and put it into my side. Stop doubting and believe. —JOHN 20:27

The butterfly flitted in and out of my mother's panda-faced pansies. As a child, I longed to catch it. I raced from our backyard into our kitchen and grabbed a glass jar, but on my hasty return, I tripped and hit the concrete patio hard. The jar smashed under my wrist and left an ugly slash that would require eighteen stitches to close. Today the scar crawls like a caterpillar across my wrist, telling the story of both wounding and healing.

When Jesus appeared to the disciples after His death, He brought His scars. John reports Thomas wanting to see "the nail marks in his hands" and Jesus inviting Thomas to "put your finger here; see my hands. Reach out your hand and put it into my side" (John 20:25, 27). In order to demonstrate He was the same Jesus, He rose from the dead with the scars of His suffering still visible.

The scars of Jesus prove Him to be the Savior and tell the story of our salvation. The pierced marks through His hands and feet, and the hollow in His side reveal a story of pain inflicted, endured, and then healed—for us. He did it so that we might be restored to Him and made whole.

Have you ever considered the story told by Christ's scars? *Elisa*

Welcoming Strangers
Deuteronomy 10:12–19

You are to love those who are foreigners, for you yourselves were foreigners in Egypt. —DEUTERONOMY 10:19

When my friends lived in Moldova, one of the poorest countries in Europe, they were overwhelmed by the warm welcome they received there, especially from other Christians. Once they took some clothes and provisions to a couple from their church who were very poor, yet who were fostering several children. The couple treated my friends like honored guests, giving them sweet tea and, despite their protests, something to eat. As my friends left with gifts of watermelons and other fruits and vegetables, they marveled at the hospitality they experienced.

These believers embody the welcome that God commanded His people, the Old Testament Israelites, to exhibit. He instructed them "to walk in obedience to him, to love him, to serve the LORD your God with all your heart and with all your soul" (Deuteronomy 10:12). How could the Israelites live this out? The answer comes a few verses later: "You are to love those who are foreigners, for you yourselves were foreigners in Egypt" (v. 19). By welcoming strangers, they would be serving and honoring God; and in showing them love and care, they would demonstrate their trust in Him.

Our circumstances might differ from the Moldovans or the Israelites, but we too can live out our love for God through our welcome to others. Whether through opening our homes or smiling a greeting to those we meet, we can extend God's care and hospitality in a lonely, hurting world. *Amy*

God's Storybook
Genesis 1:26–31

God blessed them. . . . God saw all that he had made, and it was very good. —GENESIS 1:28, 31

Wanting to enjoy the beautiful day, I headed out for a walk and soon met a new neighbor. He stopped me and introduced himself: "My name is Genesis, and I'm six and a half years old."

"Genesis is a great name! It's a book in the Bible," I replied.

"What's the Bible?" he asked.

"It's God's storybook about how He made the world and people and how He loves us."

His inquisitive response made me smile: "Why did He make the world and people and cars and houses? And is my picture in His book?"

While there isn't a literal picture of my new friend Genesis or the rest of us in the Scriptures, we're a big part of God's storybook. We see in Genesis 1 that "God created mankind in his own image, in the image of God he created them" (v. 27). God walked with them in the garden, and He then warned about giving in to the temptation to be their own god (chapter 2). Later in His book, God told about how, in love, His Son, Jesus, came to walk with us again and brought about a plan for our forgiveness and the restoration of His creation.

As we look at the Bible, we learn that our Creator wants us to know Him, talk with Him, and even ask Him our questions. He cares for us more than we can imagine. *Anne*

A Time for Beauty
Isaiah 61:1–7

A crown of beauty instead of ashes, the oil of joy instead of mourning. —ISAIAH 61:3

One January morning I woke expecting to see the same dreary midwinter landscape that had greeted me for several weeks: beige grass poking through patches of snow, gray skies, and skeletal trees. Something unusual had happened overnight, though. A frost had coated everything with ice crystals. The lifeless and depressing landscape had become a beautiful scene that glistened in the sun and dazzled me.

Sometimes we view problems without the imagination it takes to have faith. We expect pain, fear, and despair to greet us every morning, but we overlook the possibility of something different ever happening. We don't expect recovery, growth, or victory through God's power. Yet the Bible says God is the one who helps us through difficult times. He repairs broken hearts and liberates people in bondage. He comforts the grieving with "a crown of beauty instead of ashes, the oil of joy instead of mourning, and a garment of praise instead of a spirit of despair" (Isaiah 61:3).

It isn't that God just wants to cheer us up when we have problems. It's that He himself is our hope during trials. Even if we have to wait until we get to heaven to find ultimate relief, God is present with us, encouraging us and often giving us glimpses of himself. In our journey through life, may we come to understand St. Augustine's words: "In my deepest wound I saw your glory, and it dazzled me." *Jennifer*

The Blessing Is Coming
Galatians 6:7–10

*Let us not become weary in doing good, for at the proper
time we will reap a harvest if we do not give up.*
—*GALATIANS 6:9*

A friend and I went for a walk with her grandkids. While
pushing the stroller, she commented that her steps were
being wasted—they weren't being counted on the activity tracker she wore on her wrist because she wasn't
swinging her arm. I reminded her that those steps were
still helping her physical health. "Yeah," she laughed.
"But I really want that electronic gold star!"

I understand how she feels! Working toward something without immediate results is disheartening. But
rewards aren't always immediate or immediately visible.

When that's the case, it's easy to feel that the good
things we do are useless, even if we are helping a friend
or being kind to a stranger. Paul explained to the church
in Galatia, however, that "a man reaps what he sows"
(Galatians 6:7). But we must "not become weary in doing good, for at the proper time we will reap a harvest"
(v. 9). Doing good isn't the way to gain salvation, and the
text doesn't specify whether what we reap will be now
or in heaven, but we can be assured that there will be "a
harvest of blessing" (6:9 NLT).

Doing good is difficult, especially when we don't see
or know what the "harvest" will be. But as with my
friend who still gained the physical benefit from walking, it's worth continuing to do good. Why? The blessing
is coming! *Julie*

Guiding Light
Genesis 1:1–5

God said, "Let there be light," and there was light.
—GENESIS 1:3

The restaurant was lovely but dark. Only one small candle flickered on every table. To create light, diners used their smartphones to read their menus, look to their tablemates, and even to see what they were eating.

Finally, a patron quietly pushed back his chair, walked over to a waiter, and asked a simple question. "Could you turn on the lights?" Before long, a warm ceiling light flashed on and the room erupted with applause. But also with laughter. And happy chatter. And thank-yous. My friend's husband turned off his phone, picked up his utensils, and spoke for us all. "Let there be light! Now, let's eat!"

Our gloomy evening turned festive with the flick of a switch. But how much more important to know the real source of true light. God himself spoke those astonishing words, "Let there be light," on the first day when He created the universe, "and there was light" (Genesis 1:3). Then "God saw that the light was good" (v. 4).

Light expresses God's great love for us. His light points us to Jesus, "the light of the world" (John 8:12), who guides us from the gloom of sin. Walking in His light, we find the bright path to a life that glorifies the Son. He is the world's brightest gift. As He shines, may we walk His way. *Patricia*

The Miracle of White Snow
Isaiah 1:15–20

Though your sins are like scarlet, they shall be as white as snow. —ISAIAH 1:18

In the seventeenth century, Sir Isaac Newton used a prism to study how light helps us see different colors. He found that when light passes through an object, the object appears to possess a specific color. While a single ice crystal looks translucent, snow is made up of many ice crystals smashed together. When light passes through all of the crystals, snow appears to be white.

The Bible mentions something else that has a certain color—sin. Through the prophet Isaiah, God confronted the sins of the people of Judah and described their sin as "like scarlet" and as "red as crimson." But God promised they would "be as white as snow" (Isaiah 1:18). How? Judah needed to turn away from wrongdoing and seek God's forgiveness.

Thanks to Jesus, we have permanent access to God's forgiveness. Jesus called himself "the light of the world" and said whoever follows Him "will never walk in darkness, but will have the light of life" (John 8:12). When we confess our sins, God forgives us and we're seen through the light of Christ's sacrifice on the cross. This means that God sees us as He sees Jesus—blameless.

We don't have to wallow in the guilt and shame of what we've done wrong. Instead, we can hold on to the truth of God's forgiveness, which makes us "white as snow." *Linda*

Biblical Prescription
Proverbs 17:19–20

A cheerful heart is good medicine, but a crushed spirit dries up the bones. —PROVERBS 17:22

Greg and Elizabeth have a regular "Joke Night" with their four school-age children. Each child brings several jokes they've read or heard (or made up themselves!) during the week to tell at the dinner table. This tradition has created joyful memories of fun shared around the table. Greg and Elizabeth even noticed the laughter was healthy for their children, lifting their spirits on difficult days.

The benefit of joyful conversation around the dinner table was observed by C. S. Lewis, who wrote, "The sun looks down on nothing half so good as a household laughing together over a meal."

The wisdom of fostering a joyful heart is found in Proverbs 17:22, where we read, "A cheerful heart is good medicine, but a crushed spirit dries up the bones." The proverb offers a "prescription" to stimulate health and healing—allowing joy to fill our hearts, a medicine that costs little and yields great results.

We all need this biblical prescription. When we bring joy into our conversations, it can put a disagreement into perspective. It can help us to experience peace, even after a stressful test at school or a difficult day at work. Laughter among family and friends can create a safe place where we both know and feel that we're loved.

Do you need to incorporate more laughter into your life as "good medicine" for your spirit? Remember, you have encouragement from Scripture to cultivate a cheerful heart. *Lisa*

Small but Significant

2 Corinthians 1:8–11

On him we have set our hope that he will continue to
deliver us, as you help us by your prayers.
—2 CORINTHIANS 1:10–11

The day started out like any other, but it ended as a nightmare. Esther (not her real name) and several hundred women were kidnapped from their boarding school by a religious militant group. A month later all were released—except for Esther, who refused to deny Christ. As my friend and I read about her and others who are being persecuted for their faith, our hearts were moved. We wanted to do something. But what?

When writing to the Corinthian church, the apostle Paul shared about the trouble he experienced in the province of Asia. The persecution was so severe that he and his companions "despaired of life itself" (2 Corinthians 1:8). However, Paul was helped by the prayers of believers (v. 11). Though the Corinthian church was many miles away from the apostle, their prayers mattered and God heard them. Herein lies an amazing mystery: the sovereign One has chosen to use our prayers to accomplish His purpose. What a privilege!

Today we can continue to remember our brothers and sisters in Christ who are suffering for their faith. There's something we can do. We can pray for those who are marginalized, oppressed, beaten, tortured, and sometimes even killed for their belief in Christ. Let's pray for them to experience God's comfort and encouragement and to be strengthened with hope as they stand firmly with Jesus. *Poh Fang*

"Love You—Whole World"

1 John 4:7–19

Whoever lives in love lives in God, and God in them.
—1 JOHN 4:16

When my niece Jenna was three years old, she had an expression that never failed to melt my heart. When she loved something (really loved it), be it banana cream pie, jumping on the trampoline, or playing Frisbee, she would proclaim, "I love it—whole world!" ("whole world" accompanied with a dramatic sweep of her arms).

Sometimes I wonder, When's the last time I've dared to love like that? With nothing held back, completely unafraid?

"God is love," John wrote, repeatedly (1 John 4:8, 16), perhaps because the truth that God's love—not our anger, fear, or shame—is the deepest foundation of reality, is hard for us grown-ups to "get." The world divides us into camps based on what we're most afraid of—and all too often we join in, ignoring or villainizing the voices that challenge our preferred vision of reality.

Yet amid the deception and power struggles (vv. 5–6), the truth of God's love remains, a light that shines in the darkness, inviting us to learn the path of humility, trust, and love (1:7–9; 3:18). For no matter what painful truths the light uncovers, we can know that we'll still be loved (4:10, 18; Romans 8:1).

When Jenna would lean over and whisper to me, "I love you—whole world!" I would whisper back, "I love you whole world!" And I'm grateful for a gentle reminder that every moment I'm held in limitless love and grace.

Monica

Joy in Hard Places
Habakkuk 3:16–19

Yet I will rejoice in the LORD, I will be joyful in
God my Savior. —HABAKKUK 3:18

Whenever my friend was unable to take my phone call, her voicemail recording invited me to leave her a message. The recording cheerfully concluded, "Make it a great day!" As I reflected on her words, I realized that it's not within our power to make every day "great"—some circumstances truly are devastating. But a closer look might reveal something redeeming and beautiful in my day, whether things are going well or poorly.

Habakkuk wasn't experiencing easy circumstances. As a prophet, he had sensed God showing him coming days when none of the crops or livestock—on which God's people depended—would be fruitful (3:17). It would take more than mere optimism to endure the coming hardships. As a people group, Israel would be in extreme poverty. Habakkuk experienced heart-pounding, lip-quivering, leg-trembling fear (v. 16).

Yet despite that, Habakkuk said he would "rejoice in the Lord" and "be joyful" (v. 18). He proclaimed His hope in the God who provides the strength to walk in difficult places (v. 19).

Sometimes we go through seasons of deep pain and hardship. But no matter what we've lost, or wanted but never had, we can, like Habakkuk, rejoice in our relationship with a loving God. He will never fail or abandon us (Hebrews 13:5). He, the One who "provide[s] for those who grieve," is our ultimate reason for joy (Isaiah 61:3).

Kirsten

Another Chance
Micah 7:1–3, 18–20

Once again you will have compassion on us. You will trample our sins under your feet and throw them into the depths of the ocean! —MICAH 7:19 NLT

At the Second Chance Bike Shop near our neighborhood, volunteers rebuild cast-off bicycles and donate them to needy kids. Shop founder Ernie Clark also donates bikes to needy adults, including the homeless, the disabled, and military veterans struggling to make it in civilian life. Not only do the bicycles get a second chance but sometimes the recipients get a new start too. One veteran used his new bike to get to a job interview.

Second chances can transform a person's life, especially when the second chance comes from God. The prophet Micah extoled such grace during a time the nation of Israel groveled in bribery, fraud, and other despicable sins. As Micah lamented, "Not one honest person is left on the earth" (Micah 7:2 NLT).

God would rightly punish evil, Micah knew. But being loving, He would give those who repented another chance. Humbled by such love, Micah asked, "Where is another God like you, who pardons the guilt of the remnant, overlooking the sins of his special people?" (v. 18 NLT).

We too can rejoice that God doesn't abandon us because of our sins if we ask for forgiveness. As Micah declared of God, "Once again you will have compassion on us. You will trample our sins under your feet and throw them into the depths of the ocean!" (v. 19 NLT).

God's love gives second chances to all who seek Him.
Patricia

Out of Context
John 20:13–16

She turned around and saw Jesus standing there, but she did not realize that it was Jesus. —JOHN 20:14

As I queued up to board my flight, someone tapped my shoulder. I turned and received a warm greeting. "Elisa! Do you remember me? It's Joan!" My mind flipped through various "Joans" I'd known, but I couldn't place her. Was she a previous neighbor? A past coworker? Oh dear . . . I didn't know.

Sensing my struggle, Joan responded, "Elisa, we knew each other in high school." A memory rose: Friday night football games, cheering from the stands. Once the context was clarified, I recognized Joan.

After Jesus's death, Mary Magdalene went to the tomb early in the morning and found the stone rolled away and His body gone (John 20:1–2). She ran to get Peter and John, who returned with her to find the tomb empty (vv. 3–10). But Mary lingered outside in her grief (v. 11). When Jesus appeared there, "she did not realize that it was Jesus" (v. 14), thinking He was the gardener (v. 15).

How could she have not recognized Jesus? Was His resurrected body so changed that it was difficult to recognize Him? Did her grief blind her to His identity? Or, perhaps, like me, was it because Jesus was "out of context," alive in the garden instead of dead in the tomb, that she didn't recognize Him?

How might we too miss Jesus when He comes into our days—during prayer or Bible reading, or by simply whispering in our hearts? *Elisa*

Two Are Better
Ecclesiastes 4:9–11

Two are better than one, because they have a good return for their labor. —ECCLESIASTES 4:9

In the 1997 Ironman Triathlon in Hawaii, two women fought to stay on their feet as they hobbled toward the finish line. Exhausted, the runners persevered on wobbly legs, until Sian Welch bumped into Wendy Ingraham. They both dropped to the ground. Struggling to stand, they stumbled forward, only to fall again about twenty meters from the finish line. When Ingraham began to crawl, the crowd applauded. When her competitor followed suit, they cheered louder. Ingraham crossed the finish line in fourth place, and she slumped into the outstretched arms of her supporters. Then she turned and reached out to her fallen sister. Welch lunged her body forward, stretching her weary arm toward Ingraham's hand and across the finish line. As she completed the race in fifth place, the crowd roared their approval.

This pair's completion of the 140-mile swimming, biking, and running race inspired many. But the image of the weary competitors persevering together remains ingrained in my mind, affirming the life-empowering truth in Ecclesiastes 4:9–11.

There's no shame in admitting we require assistance in life (v. 9), especially since we can't honestly deny our needs or hide them from our all-knowing God. At one time or another, we'll all fall, whether physically or emotionally. Knowing we're not alone can comfort us as we persevere. As our loving Father helps us, He empowers us to reach out to others in need, affirming they too aren't alone. *Xochitl*

Ancient Promises
Numbers 6:22–27

The Lord bless you and keep you. —NUMBERS 6:24

In 1979, Dr. Gabriel Barkay and his team discovered two silver scrolls in a burial ground outside the Old City of Jerusalem. In 2004, after twenty-five years of careful research, scholars confirmed that the scrolls were the oldest biblical text in existence, having been buried in 600 BC. What I find particularly moving is what the scrolls contain—the priestly blessing that God wanted spoken over His people: "The Lord bless you and keep you; the Lord make his face shine on you" (Numbers 6:24–25).

In giving this benediction, God showed Aaron and his sons (through Moses) how to bless the people on His behalf. The leaders were to memorize the words in the form God gave so they would speak to them just as God desired. Note how these words emphasize that God is the one who blesses, for three times they say, "the Lord." And six times He says, "you," reflecting just how much God wants His people to receive His love and favor.

Ponder for a moment that the oldest existing fragments of the Bible tell of God's desire to bless. What a reminder of God's boundless love and how He wants to be in a relationship with us. If you feel far from God today, hold tightly to the promise in these ancient words. May the Lord bless you; may the Lord keep you. *Amy*

Don't Forget!
Acts 1:1–11

He was taken up before their very eyes, and a cloud hid him from their sight. —ACTS 1:9

My niece, her four-year-old daughter Kailyn, and I had a wonderful Saturday afternoon together. We enjoyed blowing bubbles outside, coloring in a princess coloring book, and eating peanut butter and jelly sandwiches. When they got in the car to leave, Kailyn sweetly called out the opened window, "Don't forget me, Auntie Anne." I quickly walked toward the car and whispered, "I could never forget you. I promise I will see you soon."

In Acts 1, the disciples watched as Jesus was "taken up before their very eyes" into the sky (v. 9). I wonder if they thought they might be forgotten by their Master. But He'd just promised to send His Spirit to live in them and empower them to handle the persecution that was to come (v. 8). And He'd taught them He was going away to prepare a place for them and would come back and take them to be with Him (John 14:3). Yet they must have wondered how long they would have to wait. Perhaps they wanted to say, "Don't forget us, Jesus!"

For those of us who have put our faith in Jesus, He lives in us through the Holy Spirit. We still may wonder when He will come again and restore us and His creation fully. But it will happen—He won't forget us. "Therefore encourage one another and build each other up" (1 Thessalonians 5:11). *Anne*

For Such a Time as This
Esther 4:10–17

Who knows but that you have come to your royal position for such a time as this? —ESTHER 4:14

Tammie Jo Shults wasn't scheduled to pilot Southwest Airlines Flight 1380. She had switched flights with her husband, also a pilot for the same airline, so she could attend her son's track meet. She certainly wasn't expecting to implement a rapid descent when one of the two engines blew and broke apart at thirty-two thousand feet, sending shrapnel through a window, and fatally injuring a passenger. Thankfully, Tammie Jo safely landed the plane.

Tammi Jo had no idea that she would be conducting an emergency landing that saved many people. Think of Esther in the Old Testament. She never dreamed she would be instrumental in saving the lives of her fellow Jewish people. God allowed Esther to become queen of Persia. When the time came to intercede for her countrymen, Esther faced the possibility of her own death in order to save the lives of her people. But she persevered in the mission God called her to.

"If I have found favor with you, Your Majesty, and if it pleases you, grant me my life–this is my petition," she said to King Ahasuerus. "And spare my people—this is my request" (Esther 7:3).

The Jews of Esther's day rejoiced at Esther's unexpected rise to royalty. God placed Esther on the throne, "for such a time as this" (Esther 4:14).

We too can trust that God orchestrates the timing and experiences of our lives to help us fulfill His purposes for us. *Lori*

Beyond the Neighborhood
Luke 10:25–37

Love your neighbor as yourself. —*MARK 12:31*

Several years ago, Hurricane Harvey brought devastating losses of life and property to the Gulf Coast of the US. In the aftermath of the storm, many people provided food, water, clothing, and shelter for their fellow citizens in immediate need.

The owner of a piano store in Maryland felt prompted to do something more. He considered how music could bring a special kind of healing and sense of normalcy to people who had lost everything. So he and his staff began to refurbish pre-owned pianos and to make inquiries to see where the need was the greatest. That spring, Dean Kramer and his wife, Lois, began the long trek to Houston, Texas, driving a truck filled with free pianos to give to grateful families, churches, and schools in the ravaged area.

We sometimes assume the word *neighbor* means someone who lives nearby or at least is someone we know. But in Luke 10, Jesus told the parable of the good Samaritan to teach that our love for our neighbors shouldn't have barriers. The man from Samaria freely gave to a wounded stranger, even though the man was a Jew, part of a people group at odds with the Samaritans (vv. 25–37).

When Dean Kramer was asked why he gave away all those pianos, he explained simply: "We're told to love our neighbors." And it was Jesus who said, "There is no commandment greater" (Mark 12:31) than to love God and our neighbor. *Cindy*

Good for You
Proverbs 24:13–14

Wisdom is like honey for you: If you find it, there is a future hope. —PROVERBS 24:14

People the world over spent an estimated $98.2 billion on chocolate in a recent year. The number is staggering, yet at the same time not all that surprising. Chocolate, after all, tastes delicious and we enjoy consuming it. So the world rejoiced collectively when the sweet treat was found to have significant health benefits as well. Chocolate contains flavonoids that help safeguard the body against aging and heart disease. Never has a prescription for health been so well received or heeded (in moderation, of course!).

Solomon suggested there's another "sweet" worthy of our investment: wisdom. He recommended his son eat honey "for it is good" (Proverbs 24:13) and compared its sweetness to wisdom. The person who feeds on God's wisdom in Scripture finds it not only sweet to the soul but also beneficial for teaching and training, equipping us for "every good work" we'll need to accomplish in life (2 Timothy 3:16–17).

Wisdom is what allows us to make smart choices and understand the world around us. And it's worth investing in and sharing with those we love—as Solomon wished to do for his son. We can feel good about feasting on God's wisdom in the Bible. It's a sweet treat that we can enjoy without limit—in fact, we're encouraged to! *God, thank you for the sweetness of your Scriptures!*

　Kirsten

Tongue Tamers
James 3:1–6

*Do not let any unwholesome talk come out of your mouths,
but only what is helpful for building others up. —*
EPHESIANS 4:29

In *West with the Night*, author Beryl Markham detailed her work with Camciscan, a feisty stallion she was tasked with taming. She'd met her match with Camciscan. No matter what strategy she employed, she could never fully tame the proud stallion, chalking up only one victory over his stubborn will.

How many of us feel this way in the battle to tame our tongues? While James compares the tongue to the bit in a horse's mouth or a ship's rudder (James 3:3–5), he also laments, "Out of the same mouth come praise and cursing. My brothers and sisters, this should not be" (v. 10).

So, how can we win the battle over the tongue? The apostle Paul offers tongue-taming advice. The first involves speaking only the truth (Ephesians 4:25). This is not a license to be painfully blunt, however. Paul follows up with "do not let any unwholesome talk come out of your mouths, but only what is helpful for building others up" (v. 29). We can also take out the trash: "Get rid of all bitterness, rage and anger, brawling and slander, along with every form of malice" (v. 31). Is this easy? Not if we attempt to do it on our own. Thankfully, we have the Holy Spirit who helps us as we rely on Him.

As Markham learned, consistency with Camciscan was needed in the battle of wills. Such is the case in the taming of the tongue. *Linda*

Haystack Prayers
2 Corinthians 1:8–11

You help us by your prayers. —*2 CORINTHIANS 1:11*

Samuel Mills and four of his friends often gathered together to pray for God to send more people to share the good news of Jesus. One day in 1806, after returning from their prayer meeting, they got caught in a thunderstorm and took refuge in a haystack. Soon, their weekly prayer gathering became known as the Haystack Prayer Meeting, which resulted in a global mission movement. Today the Haystack Prayer Monument stands at Williams College in the US as a reminder of what God can do through prayer.

Our heavenly Father is delighted when His children approach Him with a common request. It's like a family gathering where they're united in purpose, sharing a common burden.

The apostle Paul acknowledges how God helped him through the prayers of others during a time of severe suffering: "He will continue to deliver us, as you help us by your prayers" (2 Corinthians 1:10–11). God has chosen to use our prayers—especially our prayers together—to accomplish His work in the world. No wonder the verse continues: "Then many will give thanks . . . [for the] answer to the prayers of many."

Let's pray together so we can also rejoice together in God's goodness. Our loving Father is waiting for us to come to Him so He can work through us in ways that reach far beyond anything we could ever imagine.

Poh Fang

Never Forgotten
Isaiah 49:8–16

See, I have engraved you on the palms of my hands!
—ISAIAH 49:16

Egged on by my children to prove that I had endured years mastering the basics of piano, I sat down and started playing the C Major scale. Having played very little piano in nearly two decades, I was surprised I remembered! Feeling brave, I proceeded to play seven different scales by heart one right after the other. I was shocked! Years of practicing had imprinted the notes and technique so deeply in my fingers' "memory" that they instantly knew what to do.

There are some things that can never be forgotten. But God's love for His children is far more deeply imprinted than any of our fading memories—in fact, God can't forget them. This is what the Israelites needed to hear when their exile into Babylon left them feeling abandoned by Him (Isaiah 49:14). His response through Isaiah was unequivocal: "I will not forget you!" (v. 15). God's promise to care for His people was more certain than a mother's love for her child.

To assure them of His unchanging love, He gave them a picture of His commitment: "See, I have engraved you on the palms of my hands" (v. 16). It's a beautiful image of God's constant awareness of His children; their names and faces always before Him.

Still today, we can easily feel overlooked and forgotten. How comforting to remember that we're "etched" on God's hands—always remembered, cared for, and loved by our Father. *Lisa*

Made for Each Other
Genesis 2:18–24

It is not good for the man to be alone. I will make a helper suitable for him. —GENESIS 2:18

"I take care of him. When he's happy, I'm happy," says Stella. Merle replies, "I'm happy when she's around." When Merle and Stella made those statements, they had been married for seventy-nine years. When Merle had to be admitted to a nursing home, he was miserable—so Stella gladly brought him home. He was 101, and she was 95. Though she needed a walker to get around, she lovingly did what she could for her husband, such as preparing the food he likes. But she couldn't do it on her own. Grandchildren and neighbors helped with the things Stella can't manage.

Stella and Merle's life together is an example of Genesis 2, where God said, "It is not good for the man to be alone. I will make a helper suitable for him" (v. 18). None of the creatures God brought before Adam fit that description. Only in Eve, made from the rib of Adam, did Adam find a suitable helper and companion (vv. 19–24).

Eve was the perfect companion for Adam, and through them God instituted marriage. This wasn't only for the mutual aid of individuals but also to begin a family and to care for creation, which includes other people (1:28). From that first family came a community so that, whether married or single, old or young, none of us would be alone. As a community, God has given us the privilege of sharing "each other's burdens" (Galatians 6:2). *Alyson*

Don't Feed the Trolls
Proverbs 26:4–12

Make the most of every opportunity. Let your conversation be always full of grace. —COLOSSIANS 4:5–6

Ever heard the expression, "Don't feed the trolls"? Trolls refers to a new problem in today's digital world—online users who repeatedly post intentionally inflammatory and hurtful comments on news or social media discussion boards. But ignoring such comments—not "feeding" the trolls—makes it harder for them to derail a conversation.

Of course, it's nothing new to encounter people who aren't genuinely interested in productive conversation. "Don't feed the trolls" could almost be a modern equivalent of Proverbs 26:4, which warns that arguing with an arrogant, unreceptive person risks stooping to their level.

And yet . . . even the most seemingly stubborn person is also a priceless image-bearer of God. If we're quick to dismiss others, we may be the ones in danger of being arrogant and becoming unreceptive to God's grace (see Matthew 5:22).

That might, in part, explain why Proverbs 26:5 offers the exact opposite guideline. It takes humble, prayerful dependence on God to discern how best to show love to others in each situation (see Colossians 4:5–6). Sometimes we speak up; other times, it's best to be silent.

But in every situation, we find peace in knowing that the same God who drew us near while we were still in hardened opposition to Him (Romans 5:6) is powerfully at work in each person's heart. Let's rest in His wisdom as we try to share Christ's love. *Monica*

Who Is He?

Psalm 24

Who is he, this King of glory? The LORD Almighty—he is the King of glory. —PSALM 24:10

On our way home from our honeymoon, my husband and I waited to check in our luggage at the airport. I nudged him and pointed to a man standing a few feet away.

My spouse squinted. "Who is he?"

I excitedly rattled off the actor's most notable roles, then walked up and asked him to take a photo with us. Twenty-four years later, I still enjoy sharing the story of the day I met a movie star.

Recognizing a famous actor is one thing, but there's Someone more important I'm thankful to know personally. "Who is this King of glory?" (Psalm 24:8). The psalmist David points to the Lord Almighty as Creator, Sustainer, and Ruler of all. He sings, "The earth is the LORD's, and everything in it, the world, and all who live in it; for he founded it on the seas and established it on the waters" (vv. 1–2). In awestruck wonder, David proclaims God is above all, yet intimately approachable (vv. 3–4). We can know Him, be empowered by Him, and trust Him to fight on our behalf, as we live for Him (v. 8).

God provides opportunities for us to declare Him as the only Famous One truly worth sharing with others. As we reflect His character, those who don't recognize Him can have more reasons to ask, "Who is He?" Like David, we can point to the Lord with awestruck wonder and tell His story! *Xochitl*

Loving the Stranger
Exodus 23:1–9

*Do not mistreat or oppress a foreigner, for you were
foreigners in Egypt. —EXODUS 22:21*

After a member of my family converted to a different religion, Christian friends urged me to "convince" her to return to Jesus. I found myself first seeking to love my family member as Christ would—including in public places where some people frowned at her "foreign-looking" clothes. Others even made rude comments. "Go home!" one man yelled at her from his truck, not knowing or apparently caring that she already is "home."

Moses taught a much kinder way to act toward people whose dress or beliefs feel different. Teaching laws of justice and mercy, Moses instructed the children of Israel, "Do not oppress a foreigner; you yourselves know how it feels to be foreigners, because you were foreigners in Egypt" (Exodus 23:9). The edict expresses God's concern for all strangers, people vulnerable to bias and abuse, and it is repeated in Exodus 22:21 and Leviticus 19:33.

Therefore, when I spend time with my family member—at a restaurant, in a park, taking a walk together or sitting and talking with her on my front porch—I seek first to show her the same kindness and respect that I would want to experience. It's one of the best ways to remind her of the sweet love of Jesus, not by shaming her for rejecting Him, but by loving her as He loves all of us—with amazing grace. *Patricia*

Go-Between Prayer
Romans 8:26–34

The Spirit intercedes for God's people.
—ROMANS 8:27

Late one Saturday afternoon, my family and I stopped at a local restaurant for lunch. As the waiter set crispy fries and thick burgers on our table, my husband glanced up and asked his name. Then he said, "We pray as a family before we eat. Is there something we can pray for you today?" Allen, whose name we now knew, looked at us with a mixture of surprise and anxiety. A short silence followed before he told us that he was sleeping on his friend's couch each night, his car had just quit working, and he was broke.

As my husband quietly asked God to provide for Allen and show him His love, I thought about how our go-between prayer was similar to what happens when the Holy Spirit takes up our cause and connects us with God. In our moments of greatest need—when we realize we're no match to handle life on our own, when we don't know what to say to God, "The Spirit intercedes for God's people" (Romans 8:27). What the Spirit says is a mystery, but we're assured that it always fits with God's will for our lives.

The next time you pray for God's guidance, provision, and protection in someone else's life, let that act of kindness remind you that your spiritual needs are also being lifted to God who knows your name and cares about your problems. *Jennifer*

Sovereign Intervention
Exodus 3:1–9

God looked on the Israelites and was concerned about them.
—EXODUS 2:25

Barbara grew up under the care of the British government in the 1960s, but when she turned sixteen, she and her newborn son, Simon, became homeless. The state was no longer obligated to provide for her at that age. Barbara wrote to the Queen of England for help and received a response! The Queen compassionately arranged for Barbara to be given a house of her own.

The Queen of England had the right resources to help Barbara, and her compassionate assistance can be seen as a small picture of God's help. The King of heaven knows all of our needs and sovereignly works out His plans in our lives. As He does, however, He longs for us to come to Him—sharing our needs and other concerns—as part of our loving relationship with Him.

The Israelites brought their need for deliverance to God. They were suffering under the burden of Egyptian slavery and cried out for help. He heard them and remembered His promise: "God looked on the Israelites and was concerned about them" (Exodus 2:25). He instructed Moses to bring liberty to His people and declared that He would once again release them "into a good and spacious land, a land flowing with milk and honey" (3:8).

Our King loves it when we come to Him! He wisely provides what we need, not necessarily what we want. Let's rest in His sovereign, loving provision. *Ruth*

Precious Departure
Psalm 116:1–19

Precious in the sight of the LORD is the death of his
faithful servants. —PSALM 116:15

Sculptor Liz Shepherd's 2018 exhibition *The Wait* was described by a Boston Globe correspondent as "evok[ing] the precious, exposed, and transcendent in life." Inspired by the time Shepherd spent at her dying father's bedside, the exhibition attempts to convey yearning, the emptiness of loss, and the fragile sense that loved ones are just out of reach.

The idea that death is precious might seem counterintuitive; however, the psalmist declares, "Precious in the sight of the Lord is the death of his faithful servants" (Psalm 116:15). God treasures the death of His people, for in their passing He welcomes them home.

Who are these faithful servants ("saints" NKJV) of God? According to the psalmist, they are those who serve God in gratitude for His deliverance, who call on His name, and who honor the words they speak before Him (Psalm 116:16–18). Such actions represent deliberate choices to walk with God, accept the freedom He offers, and cultivate a relationship with Him.

In so doing, we find ourselves in the company of Jesus, who is "chosen by God and precious to him . . . . For in Scripture it says: 'See, I lay a stone in Zion, a chosen and precious cornerstone, and the one who trusts in him will never be put to shame'" (1 Peter 2:4–6). When our trust is in God, our departure from this life is precious in His sight. *Remi*

Words That Wound
1 Samuel 1:1–8

The words of the reckless pierce like swords, but the tongue
of the wise brings healing. —PROVERBS 12:18

"Skinny bones, skinny bones," the boy taunted. "Stick," another chimed. In return, I could have chanted "sticks and stones may break my bones, but words will never hurt me." But even as a little girl, I knew the popular rhyme wasn't true. Unkind, thoughtless words did hurt—sometimes badly, leaving wounds that went deeper and lasted much longer than a welt from a stone or stick.

Hannah certainly knew the sting of thoughtless words. Her husband, Elkanah, loved her, but she had no children, while his second wife, Peninnah, had many. In a culture where a woman's worth was often based on having children, Peninnah made Hannah's pain worse by continually "provoking her" for being childless. She kept it up until Hannah wept and couldn't eat (1 Samuel 1:6–7).

And Elkanah probably meant well, but his thoughtless response, "Hannah, why are you weeping? . . . Don't I mean more to you than ten sons?" (v. 8) was still hurtful.

Like Hannah, many of us have been left reeling in the wake of hurtful words. And some of us have likely reacted to our own wounds by lashing out and hurting others with our words. But all of us can run to our loving and compassionate God for strength and healing (Psalm 27:5, 12–14). He lovingly rejoices over us—speaking words of love and grace. *Alyson*

The True Nature of Love

2 Corinthians 8:1–9

They gave as much as they were able.
—2 CORINTHIANS 8:3

During the pandemic lockdown, Jerry was forced to close his fitness center and had no income for months. One day he received a text from a friend asking to meet him at his facility at 6:00 p.m. Jerry wasn't sure why but made his way there. Soon cars started streaming into the parking lot. The driver in the first car placed a basket on the sidewalk near the building. Then car after car (maybe fifty of them) came by. Those inside waved at Jerry or hollered out a hello, stopped at the basket, and dropped in a card or cash. Some sacrificed their money; all gave their time to encourage him.

The true nature of love is sacrificial, according to the apostle Paul. He explained to the Corinthians that the Macedonians gave "even beyond their ability" so they could meet the needs of the apostles and others (2 Corinthians 8:3). They even "pleaded" with Paul for the opportunity to give to them and to God's people (v. 4). The basis for their giving was the sacrificial heart of Jesus himself. He left the riches of heaven to come to earth to be a servant and to give His very life. "Though he was rich, yet for [our] sake he became poor" (v. 9).

May we too plead with God so that we might "excel in this grace of giving" (v. 7) in order to lovingly meet the needs of others. *Anne*

Knocking Down Pins
Ecclesiastes 1:3–11

What has been will be again, what has been done will be done again. —ECCLESIASTES 1:9

I was intrigued when I noticed a tattoo of a bowling ball knocking down pins on my friend Erin's ankle. Erin was inspired to get this unique tattoo after listening to Sara Groves's song, "Setting Up the Pins." The clever lyrics encourage listeners to find joy in the repetitive, routine tasks that sometimes feel as pointless as manually setting up bowling pins over and over again, only to have someone knock them down.

Laundry. Cooking. Mowing the lawn. Life seems full of tasks that, once completed, have to be done again—and again. This isn't a new struggle but an old frustration, one wrestled with in the Old Testament book of Ecclesiastes. The book opens with the writer complaining about the endless cycles of daily human life as futile (1:2–3), even meaningless, because "what has been will be again, what has been done will be done again" (v. 9).

Yet, like my friend, the writer was able to regain a sense of joy and meaning by remembering our ultimate fulfillment comes as we "fear [reverence] God and keep his commandments" (12:13). There's comfort in knowing that God values even the ordinary, seemingly mundane aspects of life and will reward our faithfulness (v. 14).

Lisa

A Lasting Legacy
Genesis 4:1–2

[Eve] said, "With the help of the LORD I have brought forth a man." —GENESIS 4:1

Thomas Edison invented the first practical electric light bulb. Jonas Salk developed an effective polio vaccine. Amy Carmichael penned many of the hymns we sing in worship. But what about you? Why were you put on earth? How will you invest your life?

Genesis 4:4 tells us that Eve "became pregnant and gave birth to Cain." After holding Cain for the first time, Eve announced, "With the help of the Lord I have brought forth a man" (v. 1). In an effort to explain the surprising experience of the very first birth, Eve uses a phrase dripping with dependency on the sovereign aid of God: "With the help of the Lord." Eventually, through Eve's seed, God would provide rescue for His people through another Son (John 3:16). What a legacy!

Parenthood is just one of many ways people make lasting contributions to this world. Perhaps your offering will burst forth from a room where you write or knit or paint. You might be an example for another who is deprived of godly influence. Or your investment might even come after your death in ways you could never imagine. It may be the work you leave behind or your reputation for integrity in business. In any case, will your words echo Eve's dependency on God? With the help of the Lord, what will you do for His honor? *Elisa*

Out of the Mouths of Babes
Matthew 21:14–16

Out of the mouth of babies and infants, you have established strength because of your foes. —PSALM 8:2 ESV

After watching ten-year-old Viola using a tree branch as a microphone to mimic a preacher, Michele decided to give Viola the opportunity to "preach" during a village outreach. Viola accepted. Michele, a missionary in South Sudan, wrote, "The crowd was enraptured. . . . A little girl who had been abandoned stood in authority before them as a daughter of the King of kings, powerfully sharing the reality of God's Kingdom. Half the crowd came forward to receive Jesus" (Michele Perry, *Love Has a Face*).

The crowd that day hadn't expected to hear a child preach. This incident brings to mind the phrase "out of the mouths of babes," which comes from Psalm 8. David wrote, "Out of the mouth of babies and infants, you have established strength because of your foes" (v. 2 ESV). Jesus later quoted this verse in Matthew 21:16, after the chief priests and scribes criticized the children calling out praise to Jesus in the temple at Jerusalem. The children were a nuisance to these leaders. By quoting this Scripture, Jesus showed that God took seriously the praise of these children. They did what the leaders were unwilling to do: give glory to the longed-for Messiah.

As Viola and the children in the temple showed, God can use even a child to bring Him glory. Out of their willing hearts came a fountain of praise. *Linda*

Hazardous Materials
Isaiah 6:1–10

See, this [live coal] has touched your lips; your guilt is taken away and your sin atoned for. —ISAIAH 6:7

The sound of a siren increased to an ear-piercing level as an emergency vehicle sped by my car. Its flashing lights glared through my windshield, illuminating the words "hazardous materials" printed on the side of the truck. Later, I learned it had been racing to a science laboratory where a four-hundred-gallon container of sulfuric acid had begun to leak. Emergency workers had to contain the substance immediately because of its ability to damage whatever it came in contact with.

As I thought about this news story, I wondered what would happen if sirens blared every time a harsh or critical word "leaked" out of my mouth? Sadly, it might become rather noisy around our house.

The prophet Isaiah shared this sense of awareness about his sin. When he saw God's glory in a vision, he was overcome by his unworthiness. He recognized that he was "a man of unclean lips" living with people who shared the same problem (Isaiah 6:5). What happened next gives me hope. An angel touched his lips with a red-hot coal, explaining, "your guilt is taken away and your sin atoned for" (v. 7).

We have moment-by-moment choices to make with our words—both written and spoken. Will they be "hazardous" material, or will we allow God's glory to convict us and His grace to heal us so we can honor Him with everything we express? *Jennifer*

Washed in Love
James 2:14–26

You see that a person is considered righteous by what they do and not by faith alone. —*JAMES 2:24*

A small church in Southern California recognized an opportunity to express God's love in a practical way. Believers in Jesus gathered at a local laundromat to give back to their community by washing clothes for those in financial need. They cleaned and folded clothes together, and sometimes provided a hot meal or bags of groceries for recipients.

One volunteer discovered the greatest reward was in the "actual contact with people . . . hearing their stories." Because of their relationship with Jesus, these volunteers wanted to live out their faith through loving words and actions that helped them nurture genuine relationships with others.

The apostle James affirms that every act of a professing believer's loving service is a result of genuine faith. He states that "faith by itself, if it is not accompanied by action, is dead" (James 2:14–17). Declaring we believe makes us children of God, but it's when we serve Him by serving others that we act as believers who trust and follow Jesus (v. 24). Faith and service are as closely interdependent as the body and the spirit (v. 26), a beautiful display of the power of Christ as He works in and through us.

After personally accepting that God's sacrifice on the cross washes us in perfect love, we can respond in authentic faith that overflows into the ways we serve others.

 Xochitl

Strengthened by Song
Psalm 59:1, 14–17

I will sing of your strength, in the morning I will sing of your love; for you are my fortress. —PSALM 59:16

When French villagers helped Jewish refugees hide from the Nazis during World War II, some sang songs in the dense forest surrounding their town—letting the refugees know it was safe to come out from hiding. These brave townspeople of Le Chambon-sur-Lignon had answered the call of local pastor André Trocmé and his wife, Magda, to offer wartime refuge to Jews on their windswept plateau known as "La Montagne Protestante." Their musical signal became just one feature of the villagers' bravery that helped save up to three thousand Jews from almost certain death.

In another dangerous time, David sang when his enemy Saul sent nighttime assassins to his house. His use of music wasn't a signal; rather, it was his song of gratitude to God his refuge. David rejoiced, "I will sing of your strength, in the morning I will sing of your love; for you are my fortress, my refuge in times of trouble" (Psalm 59:16).

Such singing isn't "whistling in the dark" during danger. Instead, David's singing conveyed his trust in almighty God. "You, God, are my fortress, my God on whom I can rely" (v. 17).

David's praise, and the villagers' singing in Le Chambon, offer an invitation to bless God today with our singing, making melody to Him despite the worries of life. His loving presence will respond, strengthening our hearts. *Patricia*

Thoughts of Joy
Philippians 4:4–9

Rejoice in the Lord always. I will say it again: Rejoice!
—*PHILIPPIANS 4:4*

In *What We Keep*, a collection of interviews by Bill Shapiro, each person tells of a single item that holds such importance and joy that he or she would never part with it.

This caused me to reflect on the possessions that mean the most to me and bring me joy. One is a simple forty-year-old recipe card in my mom's handwriting. Another is one of my grandma's pink teacups. Other people may value treasured memories—a compliment that encouraged them, a grandchild's giggle, or a special insight they gleaned from Scripture.

What we often keep stashed away in our hearts, though, are things that have brought us great unhappiness: Anxiety—hidden, but easily retrieved. Anger—below the surface, but ready to strike. Resentment—silently corroding the core of our thoughts.

The apostle Paul addressed a more positive way to "think" in a letter to the church at Philippi. He encouraged the people of the church to always rejoice, to be gentle, and to bring everything to God in prayer (Philippians 4:4–9).

Paul's uplifting words on what to think about helps us see that it's possible to push out dark thoughts and allow the peace of God to guard our hearts and minds in Christ Jesus (v. 7). It's when the thoughts that fill up our minds are true, noble, right, pure, lovely, admirable, and praiseworthy that we keep His peace in our hearts (v. 8).

Cindy

Through a New Lens
Exodus 25:31–40

God's invisible qualities—his eternal power and divine nature—have been clearly seen, being understood from what has been made. —ROMANS 1:20

"It must be amazing to look at a tree and see the individual leaves instead of just a blur of green!" my dad said. I couldn't have said it better. I was eighteen at the time and not a fan of my new need to wear glasses, but they changed the way I saw everything, making the blurry beautiful!

When reading Scripture, I view certain books like I do when I look at trees without my glasses. There doesn't seem to be much to see. But noticing details can reveal the beauty in what might seem to be a boring passage.

This happened to me when I was reading Exodus. God's directions for building the tabernacle—His temporary dwelling place among the Israelites—can seem like a blur of boring details. But I paused at the end of chapter 25 where God gave directions for the lampstand. It was to be hammered out "of pure gold," including its base and shaft and its flowerlike cups, buds, and blossoms (v. 31). The cups were to be "shaped like almond flowers" (v. 34).

Almond trees are breathtaking. And God incorporated that same natural beauty into His tabernacle!

Paul wrote, "God's invisible qualities—his eternal power and divine nature" are seen and understood in creation (Romans 1:20). To see God's beauty, sometimes we have to look at creation, and what might seem like uninteresting passages in the Bible, through a new lens.

Julie

You Have to Relax!
Psalm 116:1–9

Return to your rest, my soul, for the LORD has been good to you. —PSALM 116:7

"You must relax," pronounces a doctor crisply in Disney's *Rescuers Down Under*, while attempting to treat the injured albatross Wilbur, a reluctant patient. "Relax? I am relaxed!" a clearly not relaxed Wilbur responds sarcastically as his panic grows. "If I were any more relaxed, I'd be dead!"

Can you relate? In light of the doctor's dubious methods (such as a chainsaw dubbed an "epidermal tissue disruptor"), Wilbur's misgivings seem justified. But the scene is funny because it captures how we tend to feel when we're panicking—whether or not what we're facing is actually life-threatening.

When we're terrified, encouragement to relax can feel ridiculous. I know when I feel life's terrors piling up around me, and when painful "cords of death" (Psalm 116:3) tighten my stomach into knots, my every instinct is to fight back, not relax.

And yet . . . more often than not, my panicked attempts to fight back only tighten anxiety's vise-grip, leaving me crippled by fear. But when I, albeit reluctantly, allow myself to feel my pain and lift it up to God (v. 4), something surprising happens. The knot inside me relaxes a bit (v. 7), and a peace I can't understand rushes through me.

And as the Spirit's comforting presence surrounds me, I understand a bit more the truth at the heart of the gospel: that we fight best when we surrender into the powerful arms of God (1 Peter 5:6–7). *Monica*

Untying the Rope
Genesis 33:1–11

But Esau ran to meet Jacob and embraced him; he threw his arms around his neck and kissed him. And they wept.
—*GENESIS 33:4*

One Christian organization's mission is to promote the healing nature of forgiveness. One of their activities involves a skit in which a person who has been wronged is strapped back to back with a rope to the wrongdoer. Only the one sinned against can untie the rope. No matter what she does, she's got someone on her back. Without forgiveness—without untying the rope—she cannot escape.

Offering forgiveness to someone who comes to us in sorrow for their wrongdoing begins the process of releasing us and them from the bitterness and pain that can cling to us over wrongs we've suffered. In Genesis, we see two brothers separated for twenty years after Jacob stole Esau's birthright. After this long time, God told Jacob to return to his homeland (Genesis 31:3). He obeyed, but nervously, sending ahead to Esau gifts of herds of animals (32:13–15). When the brothers met, Jacob bowed at Esau's feet seven times in humility (33:3). Imagine his surprise when Esau ran and embraced him, both of them weeping over their reconciliation (v. 4). No longer was Jacob held by the sin he committed against his brother.

Do you feel imprisoned by unforgiveness, saddled with anger, fear, or shame? Know that God through His Son and Spirit can release you when you seek His help. He will enable you to begin the process of untying any ropes and setting you free. *Amy*

God's Love Is Stronger

Song of Songs 8:6–7

Love is as strong as death. —SONG OF SONGS 8:6

In 2020, Alyssa Mendoza received a surprising email from her father in the middle of the night. The message had instructions about what to do for her mother on her parents' twenty-fifth anniversary. Why was this shocking? Alyssa's father had passed away ten months earlier. She discovered that he'd written and scheduled the email while he was sick, knowing he might not be there. He'd also arranged and paid for flowers to be sent to his wife for upcoming years on her birthday, future anniversaries, and Valentine's Day.

This story could stand as an example of the kind of love that's described in detail in Song of Songs. "Love is as strong as death, its jealousy unyielding as the grave" (8:6). Comparing graves and death to love seems odd, but they're strong because they don't give up their captives. However, neither will true love give up the loved one. The book reaches its peak in verses 6–7, describing marital love as one so strong that "many waters cannot quench [it]" (v. 7).

Throughout the Bible, the love of a husband and wife is compared to God's love (Isaiah 54:5; Ephesians 5:25; Revelation 21:2). Jesus is the groom and the church is His bride. God showed His love for us by sending Christ to face death so we wouldn't have to die for our sins (John 3:16). Whether we're married or single, we can remember that God's love is stronger than anything we could imagine. *Julie*

In God's Image
Genesis 1:26–31

God created mankind in his own image, in the image of
God he created them; male and female he created them.
—GENESIS 1:27

When her beautiful brown skin started losing its color, a young woman felt frightened, as if she were disappearing or losing her "self." With heavy makeup, she covered up "my spots," as she called them—patches of lighter skin caused by a condition called vitiligo. It's a loss of skin pigment, melanin, which gives skin its tone.

Then one day, she asked herself: Why hide? Relying on God's strength to accept herself, she stopped wearing heavy makeup. Soon she began gaining attention for her self-confidence. Eventually she became the first spokesmodel with vitiligo for a global cosmetics brand.

"It's such a blessing," she told a TV news host, adding that her faith, family, and friends are the ways she finds encouragement.

This woman's story invites us to remember that we each are created in God's image. "God created mankind in his own image, in the image of God he created them; male and female he created them" (Genesis 1:27). No matter what we look like on the outside, all of us are image-bearers of God. As His created persons, we reflect His glory; and as believers in Jesus we are being transformed to represent Him in the world.

Do you struggle to love the skin you're in? Today, look in the mirror and smile for God. He created you in His image. *Patricia*

Everyone Needs Compassion
Matthew 9:27–38

When he saw the crowds, he had compassion on them,
because they were harassed and helpless, like sheep
without a shepherd. —MATTHEW 9:36

When Jeff was a new believer in Jesus and fresh out of college, he worked for a major oil company. In his role as a salesman, he traveled; and in his travels he heard people's stories—many of them heartbreaking. He realized that what his customers most needed wasn't oil, but compassion. They needed God. This led Jeff to attend seminary to learn more about the heart of God and eventually to become a pastor.

Jeff's compassion had its source in Jesus. In Matthew 9:27–33 we get a glimpse of Christ's compassion in the miraculous healing of two blind men and one demon-possessed man. Throughout His earthly ministry, He went about preaching the gospel and healing "through all the towns and villages" (v. 35). Why? "When he saw the crowds, he had compassion on them, because they were harassed and helpless, like sheep without a shepherd" (v. 36).

The world today is still full of troubled and hurting people who need the Savior's gentle care. Like a shepherd who leads, protects, and cares for his sheep, Jesus extends His compassion to all who come to Him (11:28). No matter where we are in life and what we're experiencing, in Him we find a heart overflowing with tenderness and care. And when we've been a beneficiary of God's loving compassion, we can't help but want to extend it to others. *Alyson*

Celebrating God's Creativity
Romans 12:3–8

We have different gifts, according to the grace given to each of us. —ROMANS 12:6

As music filled the church auditorium, color-blind artist Lance Brown stepped onstage. He stood in front of a large white canvas, with his back to the congregation and dipped his brush into black paint. With smooth swipes, he completed a cross. Stroke after stroke with brushes and his hands, this visual storyteller created images of Christ's crucifixion and resurrection. He covered the large patches of the canvas with black paint and added blue and white to finish a now abstract painting in less than six minutes. He picked up the canvas, turned it upside down, and revealed a hidden image—a compassion-filled face—Jesus.

Brown said he'd been reluctant when a friend suggested he speed-paint during a church service. Yet he now travels internationally to lead people into worship as he paints and shares Christ with others.

The apostle Paul affirms the value and purpose of the diverse gifts God has dispersed to His people. Every member of His family is equipped to glorify the Lord and build others up in love (Romans 12:3–5). Paul encourages us to identify and use our gifts to edify others and point to Jesus, serving diligently and cheerfully (vv. 6–8).

God has given each of us spiritual gifts, talents, skills, and experiences to serve wholeheartedly behind the scenes or in the forefront. As we celebrate His creativity, He uses our uniqueness to spread the gospel and build up other believers in love. *Xochitl*

Do the Next Thing
John 14:15–21

If you love me, keep my commands. —JOHN 14:15

When was the last time you felt compelled to help someone, only to let the moment pass without a response? In his book *The 10-Second Rule*, Clare De Graaf suggests that daily impressions can be one of the ways God calls us to a deeper spiritual walk, a life of obedience prompted by love for Him. The 10-Second Rule encourages you to simply "do the next thing you're reasonably certain Jesus wants you to do," and to do it right away "before you change your mind."

Jesus says, "If you love me, keep my commands" (John 14:15). We might think, I do love Him, but how can I be certain of His will and follow it? In His wisdom, Jesus has provided what we need to better understand and follow the wisdom found in the Bible. He once said, "I will ask the Father, and he will give you another advocate to help you and will be with you forever—the Spirit of truth" (vv. 16–17). It's by the work of the Spirit, who is with us and in us, that we can learn to obey Jesus and "keep [His] commands" (v. 15)—responding to the promptings experienced throughout our day (v. 17).

In the big and little things, the Spirit motivates us to confidently do by faith what will honor God and reveal our love for Him and others (v. 21). *Ruth*

Starting Now
1 Peter 4:7–11

Love each other deeply. —*1 PETER 4:8*

When my oldest sister's biopsy revealed cancer in late February 2017, I remarked to friends, "I need to spend as much time with Carolyn as possible—starting now." Some told me my feelings were an overreaction to the news. But she died within ten months. And even though I had spent hours with her, when we love someone there's never enough time for our hearts to love enough.

The apostle Peter called Jesus's followers in the early church to "love each other deeply" (1 Peter 4:8). They were suffering under persecution and needed the love of their brothers and sisters in their Christian community more than ever. Because God had poured His own love into their hearts, they would then want to love others in return. Their love would be expressed through praying, offering gracious hospitality, and gentle and truthful conversation—all in the strength God provided (vv. 9–11). Through His grace, God had gifted them to sacrificially serve each other for His good purposes, so that "in all things God may be praised through Jesus Christ" (v. 11). This is God's powerful plan that accomplishes His will through us.

We need others and they need us. Let's use whatever time or resources we have received from God to love—starting now. *Anne*

Failure Is Impossible
Nehemiah 6:1–9

This work had been done with the help of our God.
—*NEHEMIAH 6:16*

"Failure is impossible!" These words were spoken by Susan B. Anthony (1820–1906), known for her immovable stance on women's rights in the US. Though she faced constant criticism and later an arrest, trial, and guilty verdict for voting illegally, Anthony vowed to never give up the fight to gain women the right to vote, believing her cause was just. Though she didn't live to see the fruit of her labor, her declaration proved true. In 1920, the nineteenth amendment to the Constitution gave women the right to vote.

Failure wasn't an option for Nehemiah either, mainly because he had a Powerful Helper: God. After asking Him to bless his cause—rebuilding the wall of Jerusalem—Nehemiah and those who had returned to Jerusalem from exile in Babylon worked to make that happen. The wall was needed to keep the people safe from enemies. But opposition to the cause came in the form of deception and threats. Nehemiah refused to let opposition deter him. He informed those who opposed the work, "I am carrying on a great project" (Nehemiah 6:3). After that, he prayed, "Now strengthen my hands" (v. 9). Thanks to perseverance and divine help, the work was completed (v. 15).

God gave Nehemiah the strength to persevere in the face of opposition. Is there a task for which you're tempted to give up? Ask God to provide whatever you need to keep going. *Linda*

Truth: Bitter or Sweet?
Ezekiel 2:4–3:3

*So I ate it, and it tasted as sweet as honey
in my mouth. —EZEKIEL 3:3*

I'd had the spot on my nose for the better part of a year when I went to the doctor. The biopsy results came back days later with words I didn't want to hear: skin cancer. Though the cancer was operable and not life-threatening, it was a bitter pill to swallow.

God commanded Ezekiel to swallow a bitter pill—a scroll containing words of lament and woe (Ezekiel 2:10; 3:1–2). He was "to fill [his] stomach with it" (3:3) and share the words with the people of Israel, whom God considered "obstinate and stubborn" (2:4). One would expect a scroll filled with correction to taste like a bitter pill. Yet Ezekiel describes it being "as sweet as honey" in his mouth (3:3).

Ezekiel seems to have acquired a taste for God's correction. Instead of viewing His rebuke as something to avoid, Ezekiel recognized that what is good for the soul is "sweet." God instructs and corrects us with loving kindness, helping us live in a way that honors and pleases Him.

Some truths are bitter pills to swallow while others taste sweet. If we remember how much God loves us, His truth will taste more like honey. His words are given to us for our good, providing wisdom and strength to forgive others, refrain from gossip, and bear up under mistreatment. *Help us, Lord, to recognize Your wisdom as the sweet counsel it truly is!* Kirsten

Joyful Learning
Romans 12:1–3

Be transformed by the renewing of your mind.
—ROMANS 12:2

In the city of Mysore, India, there's a school made of two refurbished train cars connected end-to-end. Local educators teamed up with the South Western Railway Company to buy and remodel the discarded coaches. The units were essentially large metal boxes, unusable until workers installed stairways, fans, lights, and desks. Workers also painted the walls and added colorful murals inside and out. Now, sixty students attend classes there because of the amazing transformation that took place.

Something even more amazing takes place when we follow the apostle Paul's command to "be transformed by the renewing of your mind" (Romans 12:2). As we allow the Holy Spirit to uncouple us from the world and its ways, our thoughts and attitudes begin to change. We become more loving, more hopeful, and filled with inner peace (8:6).

Something else happens too. Although this transformation process is ongoing, and often has more stops and starts than a train ride, the process helps us understand what God wants for our lives. It takes us to a place where we "will learn to know God's will" (12:2 NLT). Learning His will may or may not involve specifics, but it always involves aligning ourselves with His character and His work in the world.

Nali Kali, the name of the transformed school in India, means "joyful learning" in English. How's God's transforming power leading you to the joyful learning of His will? *Jennifer*

How to Reflect Christ
Colossians 1:25–27

God has chosen to make known . . . the glorious riches of this
mystery, which is Christ in you, the hope of glory.
—COLOSSIANS 1:27

Thérèse of Lisieux was a joyful and carefree child—until her mother died when she was just four years old. She became timid and easily agitated. But many years later on Christmas Eve, all of that changed. After celebrating the birth of Jesus with her church community, she experienced God releasing her from her fear and giving her joy. She attributed the change to the power of God leaving heaven and becoming a man, Jesus, and through His dwelling in her.

What does it mean for Christ to dwell within us? It's a mystery, said Paul to the Colossian church. It's one that God "kept hidden for ages and generations" (Colossians 1:26), but which He disclosed to God's people. To them God revealed "the glorious riches of this mystery, which is Christ in you, the hope of glory" (v. 27). Because Christ now dwelled in the Colossians, they experienced the joy of new life. No longer were they enslaved to the old self of sin.

If we've asked Jesus to be our Savior, we too live out this mystery of His dwelling in us. Through His Spirit, He can release us from fear, as He did Thérèse, and grow within us the fruit of His Spirit, such as joy, peace, and self-control (Galatians 5:22–23).

Let's give thanks for the wonderful mystery of Christ within us. *Amy*

Eat and Repeat
Exodus 16:14–18

We have lost our appetite; we never see anything
but this manna! —NUMBERS 11:6

When Kerry and Paul got married, neither one knew how to cook. But one night Kerry decided to try her hand at spaghetti—making so much that the couple had it for dinner again the next day. On the third day, Paul volunteered to cook, doubling the amount of pasta and sauce, hoping the huge pot would last through the weekend. As the couple sat down for dinner that night, however, it was Kerry who confessed, "I'm sick of spaghetti."

Just imagine eating the same meal as the Israelites did—for forty years. Each morning they gathered the sweet "super food" God supplied and cooked it (no leftovers unless the next day was the Sabbath, Exodus 16:23–26). Sure, they got creative—baking it, boiling it (v. 23). But, oh, how they missed the good food they had enjoyed in Egypt (v. 3; Numbers 11:1–9), even though that nourishment had come at the high cost of cruelty and enslavement!

We too may sometimes resent that our life isn't what it once was. Or perhaps the "sameness" of life has caused us to be discontent. But Exodus 16 tells of God's faithful provision to the Israelites, causing them to trust and depend on His care each day.

God promises to give us everything we need. He satisfies our longings and fills up our soul with "good things" (Psalm 107:9 ESV). *Cindy*

Bear Hug
1 John 4:13–19

We love because he first loved us. —*1 JOHN 4:19*

"Bear" was a gift for my grandchild—a heaping helping of love contained in a giant stuffed animal frame. Baby D's response? First, wonder. Next, an amazed awe. Then, a curiosity that nudged a daring exploration. He poked his pudgy finger at Bear's nose, and when the Bear tumbled forward into his arms he responded with joy joy JOY! Baby D laid his toddler head down on Bear's fluffy chest and hugged him tightly. A dimpled smile spread across his cheeks as he burrowed deeply into Bear's cushiony softness. The child had no idea of Bear's inability to truly love him. Innocently and naturally, he felt love from Bear and returned it with all his heart.

In his first of three letters to early Christians, the apostle John boldly states that God himself is love. "We know and rely on the love God has for us," he writes. "God is love" (1 John 4:16).

God loves. Not in the pillow of a pretend animal but rather with the outstretched arms of a real human body encasing a beating but breaking heart (John 3:16). Through Jesus, God communicated His extravagant and sacrificial love for us.

John goes on, "We love because he first loved us" (1 John 4:19). When we believe we're loved, we love back. God's real love makes it possible for us to love God and others—with all our hearts. *Elisa*

True Friends
1 Samuel 18:1–4; 19:1–6

A friend loves at all times. —PROVERBS 17:17

In middle school, I had a "sometimes friend." We were "buddies" at our small church (where I was nearly the only girl her age), and we occasionally hung out together outside of school. But at school, it was a different story. If she met me by herself, she might say hello; but only if no one else was around. Realizing this, I rarely tried to gain her attention within school walls. I knew the limits of our friendship.

We've probably all experienced the pain of disappointingly one-sided or narrow friendships. But there's another kind of friendship—one that extends beyond all boundaries. It's the kind of friendship we have with kindred spirits who are committed to sharing life's journey with us.

David and Jonathan were such friends. Jonathan was "one in spirit" with David and loved him "as himself" (1 Samuel 18:1–3). Although Jonathan would have been next in line to rule after his father Saul's death, he was loyal to David, God's chosen replacement. Jonathan even helped David to evade two of Saul's plots to kill him (19:1–6; 20:1–42).

Despite all odds, Jonathan and David remained friends—pointing to the truth of Proverbs 17:17: "A friend loves at all times." Their faithful friendship also gives us a glimpse of the loving relationship God has with us (John 3:16; 15:15). Through friendships like theirs, our understanding of God's love is deepened. *Alyson*

Treasure the Moments
Ecclesiastes 3:1–14

[God] has made everything beautiful in its time.
—ECCLESIASTES 3:11

Su Dongpo (also known as Su Shi) was one of China's greatest poets and essayists. While in exile and gazing upon a full moon, he wrote a poem to describe how much he missed his brother. "We rejoice and grieve, gather and leave, while the moon waxes and wanes. Since times of old, nothing remains perfect," he writes. "May our loved ones live long, beholding this beautiful scene together though thousands of miles apart."

His poem carries themes found in the book of Ecclesiastes. The author, known as the Teacher (1:1), observed that there's "a time to weep and a time to laugh . . . a time to embrace and a time to refrain from embracing" (3:4–5). By pairing two contrasting activities, the Teacher, like Su Dongpo, seems to suggest that all good things must inevitably come to an end.

As Su Dongpo saw the waxing and waning of the moon as another sign that nothing remains perfect, the Teacher also saw in creation God's providential ordering of the world He'd made. God oversees the course of events, and "He has made everything beautiful in its time" (v. 11).

Life may be unpredictable and sometimes filled with painful separations, but we can take heart that everything takes place under God's gaze. We can enjoy life and treasure the moments—the good and the bad—for our loving God is with us. *Poh Fang*

I Will Fear No Evil
Psalm 23

Even though I walk through the darkest valley, I will fear no evil, for you are with me. —PSALM 23:4

In 1957, Melba Pattillo Beals was selected to be one of the "Little Rock Nine," a group of nine African American students who first integrated the previously all-white Central High School in Little Rock, Arkansas. In her 2018 memoir, *I Will Not Fear: My Story of a Lifetime of Building Faith under Fire*, Beals gives a heartbreaking account of the injustices and harassment she struggled to face courageously every day as a fifteen-year-old student.

But she also wrote about her deep faith in God. In her darkest moments, when fear almost overwhelmed her, Beals repeated the familiar Bible verses she had learned at an early age from her grandmother. As she recited them, she was reminded of God's presence with her, and Scripture gave her courage to endure.

Beals frequently recited Psalm 23, finding comfort in confessing, "Even though I walk through the darkest valley, I will fear no evil, for you are with me" (v. 4). Her grandmother's encouragement would ring through her ears as well, reassuring her that God "is as close as your skin, and you have only to call on Him for help."

Although our particular situations may vary, we will all likely endure difficult struggles and overwhelming circumstances that could easily cause us to give in to fear. In those moments, may your heart find encouragement in the truth that God's powerful presence is always with us. *Lisa*

Here Be Dragons?
2 Timothy 1:6–14

The Spirit God gave us does not make us timid, but gives us power, love and self-discipline. —*2 TIMOTHY 1:7*

Legend has it that at the edges of medieval maps, marking the boundaries of the world the maps' creators knew at the time, there'd be inscribed the words "Here be dragons"—often alongside vivid illustrations of the terrifying beasts supposedly lurking there.

There's not much evidence medieval cartographers actually wrote these words, but I like to think they could have. Maybe because "here be dragons" sounds like something I might've written at the time—a grim warning that even if I didn't know exactly what would happen if I ventured into the great unknown, it likely wouldn't be good!

But there's one glaring problem with my preferred policy of self-protection and risk-aversion: it's the opposite of the courage to which I'm called as a believer in Jesus (2 Timothy 1:7).

One might even say I'm misguided about what's really dangerous. As Paul explained, in a broken world, bravely following Christ will sometimes be painful (v. 8). But as those brought from death to life and entrusted with the Spirit's life flowing in and through us (vv. 9–10,14), how could we not?

When God gives us a gift this staggering, to fearfully shrink back would be the real tragedy—far worse than anything we might face when we follow Christ's leading into uncharted territory (vv. 6–8, 12). He can be trusted with our hearts and our future (v. 12). *Monica*

Jump Start
John 13:4–17

I have set you an example that you should do as I have done for you. —*JOHN 13:15*

My car sputtered as I turned the key. I was stranded. A man in the parking lot saw me in distress, ducked back inside the restaurant, and emerged with a friend. They jump-started my car so my battery could recharge, and soon I was ready to go. That man had been ready to leave, but he took the time to enlist a friend in order to care for a stranger and her needs.

Although I don't know if either of these men are believers in Jesus, they served in the way Jesus commands us to serve. In John 13:5 we see that Jesus "poured water into a basin and began to wash his disciples' feet." Washing feet filthy from walking the dirt roads of Jerusalem in sandals was a lowly slave's job. When Peter questioned Jesus's actions, Jesus explained that this is how He wants us to treat each another: "I have set you an example that you should do as I have done for you" (v. 15). His washing of the disciples' feet demonstrates how we should humbly serve one another.

Living in the spirit of Jesus could mean baking brownies for a neighbor or listening with compassion to the person next to you in line at the store. It could be cleaning up someone else's mess or taking time to visit a friend who's lonely. Jesus cares for us unconditionally and sacrificially and asks us to do the same for others. The outcome will be revitalized people who feel seen, heard, noticed, and loved. *Laura*

The Greatest Mystery
Colossians 1:15–22

The Son is the image of the invisible God, the firstborn over all creation. —COLOSSIANS 1:15

Before I came to faith in Jesus, I'd heard the gospel preached but wrestled with His identity. How could Jesus offer forgiveness for my sins when the Bible says only God can forgive sins? I discovered I wasn't alone in my struggles after reading J. I. Packer's *Knowing God*. Packer suggests that for many unbelievers the "really staggering Christian claim is that Jesus of Nazareth was God made man . . . as truly and fully divine as He was human." Yet this is the truth that makes salvation possible.

When the apostle Paul refers to Christ as "the image of the invisible God," he's saying Jesus is completely and perfectly God—Creator and Sustainer of all things in heaven and earth—but also fully human (Colossians 1:15–17). Because of this truth, we can be confident that through Christ's death and resurrection, He's not only carried the consequences for our sins but has also redeemed human nature, so that we—and all of creation—can be reconciled to God (vv. 20–22).

In an amazing, initiating act of love, God the Father reveals himself in and through Scripture by the power of God the Holy Spirit and through the life of God the Son. Those who believe in Jesus are saved because He is Emmanuel—God with us. Hallelujah! *Xochitl*

Blue Lines
Proverbs 4:10–17

*I instruct you in the way of wisdom and lead you along
straight paths.* —PROVERBS 4:11

Downhill skiing racecourses are often marked by swaths
of blue paint sprayed across the white, snowy surface. The
crude arcs might be a visual distraction for spectators but
prove to be vital to both the success and safety of the
competitors. The paint serves as a guide for the racers to
visualize the fastest line to the bottom of the hill. Addi-
tionally, the contrast of the paint against the snow offers
racers depth perception, which is critical to their safety
when traveling at such high rates of speed.

Solomon begs his sons to seek wisdom in hopes of
keeping them safe on the racecourse of life. Like the blue
lines, wisdom, he says, will "lead [them] along straight
paths" and keep them from stumbling (Proverbs 4:11–
12). His deepest hope as a father is for his sons to enjoy
a rich life, free from the damaging effects of living apart
from the wisdom of God.

God, as our loving Father, offers us "blue-line" guidance in the Bible. While He's given us the freedom to
"ski" wherever we like, the wisdom He offers in the Scriptures, like racecourse markers, are "life to those who find
them" (v. 22). When we turn from evil and walk instead
with Him, our path will be lit with His righteousness,
keeping our feet from stumbling and guiding us onward
each day (vv. 12, 18). *Kirsten*

The Power of God
Psalm 121

My help comes from the LORD, the Maker of heaven and earth. —PSALM 121:2

Rebecca and Russell's doctors told them they couldn't have children. But God had other ideas—and ten years later Rebecca conceived. The pregnancy was a healthy one; and when the contractions started, the couple excitedly rushed to the hospital. Yet the hours of labor grew long and more intense, and Rebecca's body still wasn't progressing enough for delivery. Finally, the doctor decided she needed to perform an emergency C-section. Fearful, Rebecca sobbed for her baby and herself. The doctor calmly assured her, saying, "I will do my best, but we're going to pray to God because He can do more." She prayed with Rebecca, and fifteen minutes later, Bruce, a healthy baby boy, was born.

That doctor understood her dependence on God and His power. She recognized that although she had the training and skill to do the surgery, she still needed God's wisdom, strength, and help to guide her hands (Psalm 121:1–2).

It's encouraging to hear about highly skilled people, or of anyone, who recognize they need Him—because, honestly, we all do. He's God; we're not. He alone "is able to do immeasurably more than all we ask or imagine" (Ephesians 3:20). Let's have a humble heart to learn from Him and to trust Him in prayer, because He can do more than we ever could. *Anne*

A Light in the Darkness
John 1:5; 16:1–11, 33

In this world you will have trouble. But take heart!
I have overcome the world. —JOHN 16:33

In *These Are the Generations*, Mr. Bae describes God's faithfulness and the power of the gospel to penetrate the darkness. His grandfather, parents, and his own family were all persecuted for sharing their faith in Christ. But an interesting thing happened when Mr. Bae was imprisoned for telling a friend about God: his faith grew. The same was true for his parents when they were sentenced to a concentration camp—they continued to share Christ's love even there. Mr. Bae found the promise of John 1:5 to be true: "The light shines in the darkness, and the darkness has not overcome it."

Before His arrest and crucifixion, Jesus warned His disciples about the trouble they'd face. They would be rejected by people who "will do such things because they have not known the Father or me" (16:3). But Jesus offered words of comfort: "In this world you will have trouble. But take heart! I have overcome the world" (v. 33).

While many believers in Jesus haven't experienced persecution on the level of that endured by the family of Mr. Bae, we can expect to face trouble. But we don't have to give in to discouragement or resentment. We have a Helper—the Holy Spirit, the One Jesus promised to send before He ascended to heaven. We can turn to Him for guidance and comfort (v. 7). The power of God's presence can hold us steady in dark times. *Linda*

God's Provision
Genesis 1:11–13, 29–30

See how the flowers of the field grow. . . . Will [God] not much more clothe you? —*MATTHEW 6:28, 30*

We trekked deeper and deeper into the forest, venturing farther and farther away from the village at Yunnan Province, China. After an hour or so, we heard the deafening roar of the water. Quickening our steps, we soon reached a clearing and were greeted by a beautiful view of a curtain of white water cascading over the gray rocks. Spectacular!

Our hiking companions, who lived in the village we had left an hour earlier, decided that we should have a picnic. Great idea, but where was the food? We hadn't brought any. My friends disappeared into the surrounding forest and returned with an assortment of fruits and vegetables and even some fish. The shuixiangcai looked strange with its small purple flowers, but it tasted heavenly!

I was reminded that creation declares God's extravagant provision. We can see proof of His generosity in "all sorts of seed-bearing plants, and trees with seed-bearing fruit" (Genesis 1:12 NLT). God has made and given us for food "every seed-bearing plant . . . and every tree that has fruit with seed in it" (v. 29).

Do you sometimes find it hard to trust God to meet your needs? Why not take a walk in nature? Let what you see remind you of Jesus's assuring words: "Do not worry, saying, 'What shall we eat?' or 'What shall we drink?' . . . Your heavenly Father knows that you need [all these things]" (Matthew 6:31–32). *Poh Fang*

The Favorite
Genesis 37:2–4, 17–24

As I have loved you, so you must love one another.
—JOHN 13:34

My husband's brother lives about 1,200 miles away in the mountains of Colorado. Despite the distance, Gerrits has always been a beloved family member because of his great sense of humor and kind heart. As long as I can remember, however, his siblings have good-naturedly joked about his favored status in their mother's eyes. Several years ago, they even presented him with a T-shirt sporting the words, "I'm Mom's Favorite." While we all enjoyed the silliness of our siblings, true favoritism is no joking matter.

In Genesis 37, we read about Jacob, who gave his son Joseph an ornate coat—an indication to his other children that Joseph was special (v. 3). Without a hint of subtlety, the coat's message shouted: "Joseph is my favorite son!"

Displaying favoritism can be crippling in a family. Jacob's mother, Rebekah, had favored him over her son Esau, leading to conflict between the two brothers (25:28). The dysfunction was perpetuated when Jacob favored his wife Rachel (Joseph's mother) over his wife Leah, creating discord and heartache (29:30–31). No doubt this pattern was the unhealthy basis for Joseph's brothers to despise their younger brother, even plotting his murder (37:18).

When it comes to our relationships, we may sometimes find it tricky to be objective. But our goal must be to treat everyone without favoritism and to love every person in our life as our Father loves us (John 13:34).

Cindy

Obscured by Clouds
2 Corinthians 4:16–18

We fix our eyes not on what is seen, but on what is unseen.
—2 CORINTHIANS 4:18

A rare supermoon appeared in November 2016—the moon in its orbit reached its closest point to the earth in over sixty years and so appeared bigger and brighter than at other times. But for me that day the skies over my city were shrouded in gray. Although I saw photos of this wonder from friends in other places, as I gazed upward I had to trust that the supermoon was lurking behind the clouds.

The apostle Paul faced many hardships but believed that what is unseen will last forever. He said how his "momentary troubles" achieve "an eternal glory" (2 Corinthians 4:17). Thus he could fix his eyes "not on what is seen, but on what is unseen," because what is unseen is eternal (v. 18). Paul yearned that the Corinthians and our faith would grow, and although we suffer, that we too would trust in God. We might not be able to see Him, but we can believe He is renewing us day by day (v. 16).

I thought about how God is unseen but eternal when I gazed at the clouds that day, knowing that the supermoon was hidden but there. And I hoped the next time I was tempted to believe that God was far from me, I would fix my eyes on what is unseen but real. *Amy*

In Our Weakness
Romans 8:1–2, 10–17

In the same way, the Spirit helps us in our weakness.
—ROMANS 8:26

Although Anne Sheafe Miller died in 1999 at the age of ninety, she nearly passed away fifty-seven years earlier after developing septicemia following a miscarriage, and no treatments were helping. When a patient at the same hospital mentioned his connection to a scientist who'd been working on a new wonder drug, Anne's doctor pressed the government to release a tiny amount for Anne. Within a day, her temperature was back to normal! Penicillin saved Anne's life.

Since the fall, all human beings have experienced a devastating spiritual condition brought about by sin (Romans 5:12). Only the death and resurrection of Jesus and the power of the Holy Spirit has made it possible for us to be healed (8:1–2). The Holy Spirit enables us to enjoy abundant life on earth and for eternity in the presence of God (vv. 3–10). "And if the Spirit of him who raised Jesus from the dead is living in you, he who raised Christ from the dead will also give life to your mortal bodies because of his Spirit who lives in you" (v. 11).

When your sinful nature threatens to drain the life out of you, look to the source of your salvation, Jesus, and be strengthened by the power of His Spirit (vv. 11–17). "The Spirit helps us in our weakness" and "intercedes for God's people in accordance with the will of God" (vv. 26–27). *Ruth*

Watched by God
Psalm 121:5–8

The LORD watches over you. —PSALM 121:5

Our little grandson waved goodbye, then turned back with a question. "Grandma, why do you stand on the porch and watch until we leave?" I smiled at him, finding his question "cute" because he's so young. Seeing his concern, however, I tried to give a good answer. "Well, it's a courtesy," I told him. "If you're my guest, watching until you leave shows I care." He weighed my answer, but still looked perplexed. So, I told him the simple truth. "I watch," I said, "because I love you. When I see your car drive away, I know you're safely heading home." He smiled, giving me a tender hug. Finally, he understood.

His childlike understanding reminded me what all of us should remember—that our heavenly Father is constantly watching over each of us, His precious children. As Psalm 121 says, "The LORD watches over you—the LORD is your shade at your right hand" (v. 5).

What assurance for Israel's pilgrims as they climbed dangerous roads to Jerusalem to worship. "The sun will not harm you by day, nor the moon by night. The LORD will keep you from all harm—he will watch over your life" (vv. 6–7). Likewise, as we each climb our life's road, sometimes facing spiritual threat or harm, "The LORD will watch over [our] coming and going." Why? His love. When? "Now and forevermore" (v. 8). 🕊 *Patricia*

Does What We Do Matter?

Colossians 3:12–17

Whatever you do, do it all for the glory of God.
—1 CORINTHIANS 10:31

I dropped my forehead to my hand with a sigh, "I don't know how I'm going to get it all done." My friend's voice crackled through the phone: "You have to give yourself some credit. You're doing a lot." He then listed the things I was trying to do—maintain a healthy lifestyle, work, do well in graduate school, write, and attend a Bible study. I wanted to do all these things for God, but instead I was more focused on what I was doing than how I was doing it—or that perhaps I was trying to do too much.

Paul reminded the church in Colossae that they were to live in a way that glorified God. Ultimately, what they specifically did on a day-to-day basis was not as important as how they did it. They were to do their work with "compassion, kindness, humility, gentleness and patience" (Colossians 3:12), to be forgiving, and above all to love (vv. 13–14) and to "do it all in the name of the Lord Jesus" (v. 17). Their work wasn't to be separated from Christlike living.

What we do matters, but how we do it, why, and who we do it for matters more. Each day we can choose to work in a stressed-out way or in a way that honors God and seeks out the meaning Jesus adds to our work. When we pursue the latter, we find satisfaction. *Julie*

Beautifully Burdened
Matthew 11:28–30

My yoke is easy and my burden is light.
—MATTHEW 11:30

I awoke to pitch darkness. I hadn't slept more than thirty minutes and my heart sensed that sleep wouldn't return soon. A friend's husband lay in the hospital, having received the dreaded news, "The cancer is back—in the brain and spine now." My whole being hurt for my friends. What a heavy load! And yet, somehow my spirit was lifted through my sacred vigil of prayer. You might say I felt beautifully burdened for them. How could this be?

In Matthew 11:28–30, Jesus promises rest for our weary souls. Strangely, His rest comes as we bend under His yoke and embrace His burden. He clarifies in verse 30, "For my yoke is easy and my burden is light." When we allow Jesus to lift our burden from our backs and then tether ourselves to Jesus's yoke, we become harnessed with Him, in step with Him and all He allows. When we bend under His burden, we share in His sufferings, which ultimately allows us to share in His comfort as well (2 Corinthians 1:5).

My concern for my friends was a heavy burden. Yet I felt grateful that God would allow me to carry them in prayer. Gradually I ebbed back to sleep and awoke—still beautifully burdened but now under the easy yoke and light load of walking with Jesus. *Elisa*

Ministering to "The Least of These"
Matthew 25:31–40

I was in prison and you came to visit me.
—*MATTHEW 25:36*

Frankie San, a native of Japan, worked at a roadside fruit stand to support himself while he attended Bible college. One day a bus full of men in orange jumpsuits passed the produce stand. When he heard they were prisoners from the minimum-security section of the nearby jail, he remembered the words of Christ in Matthew 25:36: "I needed clothes and you clothed me, I was sick and you looked after me, I was in prison and you came to visit me."

He volunteered to serve as the prison librarian, a position that allowed him to visit each prisoner once a week—even the ones on death row.

"I'm Frankie San," he'd say as he passed books through the bar every week. "I love you and Jesus loves you." He demonstrated his love and Christ's love by caring for their needs, praying for them, and treating them with respect.

When Jesus first encouraged His followers to minister to "the least of these" (v. 40), He challenged the thinking of the day. Religious leaders said only the rich, the pious, and the pedigreed deserved God's favor. Jesus urged His disciples to do the opposite—to share God's love with the poor, the sinful, and the outcasts. When we do, we demonstrate our faith and impact those around us.

Our calling hasn't changed in the 2,000 years since Jesus walked the earth. He still calls His disciples to serve Him by serving others, whether they "deserve" it or not. "Whatever you did for one of the least of these brothers and sisters of mine, you did for me" (v. 40). *Lori*

Who Is That?

2 Samuel 12:1–14

David said to Nathan, "I have sinned against the LORD."
Nathan replied, "The LORD has taken away your sin."
—2 SAMUEL 12:13

When a man installed a security camera outside his house, he checked the video feature to ensure that the system was working. He was alarmed to see a broad-shouldered figure in dark clothing wandering around his yard. He watched intently to see what the man would do. The interloper seemed familiar, however. Finally he realized he wasn't watching a stranger roam his property, but a recording of himself in his own backyard!

What might we see if we could step out of our skin and observe ourselves in certain situations? When David's heart was hardened and he needed an outside perspective—a godly perspective—on his involvement with Bathsheba, God sent Nathan to the rescue (2 Samuel 12).

Nathan told David a story about a rich man who robbed a poor man of his only lamb. Though the rich man owned herds of animals, he slaughtered the poor man's lone sheep and made it into a meal. When Nathan revealed that the story illustrated David's actions, David saw how he had harmed Uriah. Nathan explained the consequences, but more important he assured David, "The LORD has taken away your sin" (v. 13).

If God reveals sin in our lives, His ultimate purpose isn't to condemn us, but to restore us and to help us reconcile with those we've hurt. Repentance clears the way for renewed closeness with God through the power of His forgiveness and grace. *Jennifer*

Reunion
Revelation 21:1–7

Look! God's dwelling place is now among the people.
—REVELATION 21:3

The little boy excitedly ripped open a big box from his serviceman daddy, whom he believed wouldn't be home to celebrate his birthday. Inside that box was yet another giftwrapped box, and inside that box was another that simply held a piece of paper saying, "Surprise!" Confused, the boy looked up—just as his dad entered the room. Tearfully the son leapt into his father's arms, exclaiming, "Daddy, I missed you" and "I love you!"

That tearful yet joyful reunion captures the heart of Revelation 21's description of the glorious moment when God's children see their loving Father face to face—in the fully renewed and restored creation. There, "[God] will wipe every tear from [our] eyes." No longer will we experience pain or sorrow, because we'll be with our heavenly Father. As the "loud voice" in Revelation 21 declares, "Look! God's dwelling place is now among the people, and he will dwell with them" (vv. 3–4).

There's a tender love and joy that followers of Jesus already enjoy with God, as 1 Peter 1:8 describes: "Though you have not seen him, you love him; and even though you do not see him now, you believe in him and are filled with an inexpressible and glorious joy." Yet imagine our incredible, overflowing joy when we see the one we've loved and longed for welcoming us into His open arms!

🕊 *Alyson*

The Secret
Philippians 4:10–19

*I have learned the secret of being content in any and
every situation. —PHILIPPIANS 4:12*

Sometimes I suspect that my cat Heathcliff suffers from
a bad case of FOMO (fear of missing out). When I come
home with groceries, Heathcliff rushes over to inspect
the contents. When I'm chopping vegetables, he stands
up on his back paws peering at the produce and begging me to share. But when I actually give Heathcliff
whatever has caught his fancy, he quickly loses interest,
walking away with an air of bored resentment.

But it would be hypocritical for me to be hard on my
little buddy. In comical caricature, he reflects a bit of
my own insatiable hunger for more, my assumption that
"now" is never enough.

According to Paul, contentment isn't natural—it's
learned (Philippians 4:11). On our own, we desperately
pursue whatever we think will satisfy, moving on to the
next thing the minute we realize it won't. Other times,
our discontent takes the form of anxiously shielding ourselves from any and all suspected threats.

Ironically, sometimes it takes experiencing what we'd
feared the most in order to stumble into real joy. Having experienced much of the worst life has to offer, Paul
could testify firsthand to "the secret" of true contentment (vv. 11–12)—the mysterious reality that as we lift
up to God our longings for wholeness, we experience un-
explainable peace (vv. 6–7), carried ever deeper into the
depths of Christ's power, beauty, and grace. *Monica*

Asking God

Psalm 6:4–9

*The LORD has heard my cry for mercy; the LORD accepts
my prayer.* —PSALM 6:9

When my husband, Dan, was diagnosed with cancer, I couldn't find the "right" way to ask God to heal him. In my limited view, other people in the world had such serious problems—war, famine, poverty, natural disasters. Then one day, during our morning prayer time, I heard my husband humbly ask, "Dear Lord, please heal my disease."

It was such a simple but heartfelt plea that it reminded me to stop complicating every prayer request, because God perfectly hears our righteous cries for help. As David simply asked, "Turn, LORD, and deliver me; save me because of your unfailing love" (Psalm 6:4).

That's what David declared during a time of spiritual confusion and despair. His exact situation isn't explained in this psalm. His honest pleas, however, show a deep desire for godly help and restoration. "I am worn out from my groaning," he wrote (v. 6).

Yet, David didn't let his own limits, including sin, stop him from going to God with his need. Thus, even before God answered, David was able to rejoice, "the LORD has heard my weeping. The LORD has heard my cry for mercy; the LORD accepts my prayer" (vv. 8–9).

Despite our own confusion and uncertainty, God hears and accepts the honest pleas of His children. He's ready to hear us, especially when we need Him most.

Patricia

Plight of the Crawdads
1 Thessalonians 5:11–18

Always strive to do what is good for each other and for everyone else. —*1 THESSALONIANS 5:15*

When my cousin invited me to join him to fish for crawdads (crayfish), I couldn't help but be excited. I grinned when he handed me a plastic pail. "No lid?"

"You won't need one," he said, picking up the fishing rods and the small bag of chicken chunks we'd use for bait.

Later, as I watched the small crustaceans climbing over one another in a futile attempt to escape the almost-full bucket, I realized why we wouldn't need a lid. Whenever one crawdad reached the rim, the others would pull it back down.

The plight of the crawdads reminds me how destructive it is to be selfishly concerned about our own gain instead of the benefit of a whole community. Paul understood the need for uplifting, interdependent relationships when he wrote to the believers in Thessalonica. He urged them to "warn those who are idle and disruptive, encourage the disheartened, help the weak," and "be patient with everyone" (1 Thessalonians 5:14).

Commending their caring community (v. 11), Paul spurred them toward even more loving and peaceful relationships (vv. 13-15). By striving to create a culture of forgiveness, kindness, and compassion, their relationships with God and others would be strengthened (vv. 15, 23).

The church can grow and witness for Christ through this kind of loving unity. When believers honor God, committing to lift others up instead of pulling them down with words or actions, we and our communities thrive. *Xochitl*

Adolescent Faith
Deuteronomy 5:28–33

Oh, that their hearts would be inclined to fear me and keep all my commands always. —DEUTERONOMY 5:29

The teenage years are sometimes among the most agonizing seasons in life—for both parent and child. In my adolescent quest to "individuate" from my mother, I openly rejected her values and rebelled against her rules, suspicious their purposes were merely to make me miserable. Though we've since come to agree on those matters, that time in our relationship was riddled with tension. Mom undoubtedly lamented my refusal to heed the wisdom of her instructions, knowing they would spare me unnecessary emotional and physical pain.

God had the same heart for His children, Israel. God imparted His wisdom for living in what we know as the Ten Commandments (Deuteronomy 5:7–21). Though they could be viewed as a list of rules, God's intention is evident in His words to Moses: "so that it might go well with them and their children forever!" (v. 29). Moses recognized God's desire, saying that obedience to the decrees would result in their enjoyment of His ongoing presence with them in the promised land (v. 33).

We all go through a season of "adolescence" with God, not trusting that His guidelines for living are truly meant for our good. May we grow into the realization that He wants what's best for us and learn to heed the wisdom He offers. His guidance is meant to lead us into spiritual maturity as we become more like Jesus (Psalm 119:97–104; Ephesians 4:15; 2 Peter 3:18). *Kirsten*

A Place of Belonging
Ephesians 3:14–21

So that Christ may dwell in your hearts through faith.
—*EPHESIANS 3:17*

Some years after the tragic loss of their first spouses, Robbie and Sabrina fell in love, married, and combined their two families. They built a new home and named it Havilah (a Hebrew word meaning "writhing in pain" and "to bring forth"). It signifies the making of something beautiful through pain. The couple says they didn't build the home to forget their past but "to bring life from the ashes, to celebrate hope." For them, "it is a place of belonging, a place to celebrate life and where we all cling to the promise of a future."

That's a beautiful picture of our life in Jesus. He pulls our lives from the ashes and becomes for us a place of belonging. When we receive Him, He makes His home in our hearts (Ephesians 3:17). God adopts us into His family through Jesus so that we belong to Him (1:5–6). Although we'll go through painful times, He can use even those to bring good purposes in our lives.

Daily we have opportunity to grow in our understanding of God as we enjoy His love and celebrate what He's given us. In Him, there's a fullness to life that we couldn't have without Him (3:19). And we have the promise that this relationship will last forever. Jesus is our place of belonging, our reason to celebrate life, and our hope now and forever. *Anne*

Extending Mercy
Luke 17:1–5

If your brother or sister sins against you, rebuke them; and if they repent, forgive them. —LUKE 17:3

Reflecting on how she forgave Manasseh, the man who killed her husband and some of her children in the Rwandan genocide, Beata said, "My forgiving is based on what Jesus did. He took the punishment for every evil act throughout all time. His cross is the place we find victory—the only place!" Manasseh had written to Beata from prison more than once, begging her—and God—for forgiveness as he detailed the regular nightmares that plagued him. At first she could extend no mercy, saying she hated him for killing her family. But then "Jesus intruded into her thoughts," and with God's help, some two years later, she forgave him.

In this, Beata followed Jesus's instruction to His disciples to forgive those who repent. He said that even if they "sin against you seven times in a day and seven times come back to you saying 'I repent,' you must forgive them" (Luke 17:4). But to forgive can be extremely difficult, as we see by the disciples' reaction: "Increase our faith!" (v. 5).

Beata's faith increased as she wrestled in prayer over her inability to forgive. If, like her, we're struggling to forgive, we can ask God through His Holy Spirit to help us to do so. As our faith increases, He helps us to forgive.

Amy

Intentional Kindness
2 Samuel 9:3–11

I want to show God's kindness to them.
—2 SAMUEL 9:3 NLT

Boarding a plane alone with her children, a young mom tried desperately to calm her three-year-old daughter who began kicking and crying. Then her hungry four-month-old son also began to wail.

A traveler seated next to her quickly offered to hold the baby while Jessica got her daughter buckled in. Then the traveler—recalling his own days as a young dad—began coloring with the toddler while Jessica fed her infant. And on the next connecting flight, the same man offered to assist again if needed.

Jessica recalled, "I [was] blown away by God's hand in this. [We] could have been placed next to anyone, but we were seated next to one of the nicest men I have ever met."

In 2 Samuel 9, we read of another example of what I call intentional kindness. After King Saul and his son Jonathan had been killed, some people expected David to kill off any competition to his claim for the throne. Instead, he asked, "Is there no one still alive from the house of Saul to whom I can show God's kindness?" (v. 3). Mephibosheth, Jonathan's son, was then brought to David. who restored his inheritance and warmly invited him to share his table from then on—just as if he were his own son (v. 11).

As beneficiaries of the immense kindness of God, may we look for opportunities to show intentional kindness toward others (Galatians 6:10). *Cindy*

Divine Escape
John 11:45–53

So from that day on they plotted to take his life.
—JOHN 11:53

Agatha Christie's Hercule Poirot mystery *The Clocks* features antagonists who commit a series of murders. Although their initial plot targeted a single victim, they began taking more lives in order to cover up the original crime. When confronted by Poirot, a conspirator confessed, "It was only supposed to be the one murder."

Like the schemers in the story, the religious authorities of Jesus's day formed a conspiracy of their own. After Jesus raised Lazarus from the dead (John 11:38–44), they called an emergency meeting and plotted to kill Him (vv. 45–53). But they didn't stop there. After Jesus rose from the dead, the religious leaders spread lies about what happened at the grave (Matthew 28:12–15). Then they began a campaign to silence Jesus's followers (Acts 7:57–8:3). What started as a religious plot against one man for the "greater good" of the nation became a web of lies, deceit, and multiple casualties.

Sin plunges us down a road that often has no end in sight, but God always provides a way of escape. When Caiaphas the high priest said, "It is better for you that one man die for the people than that the whole nation perish" (John 11:50), he didn't understand the profound truth of his words. The conspiracy of the religious leaders would help bring about the redemption of mankind.

Jesus saves us from sin's vicious grip. Have you received the freedom He offers? *Remi*

Strengthening Weak Knees
Isaiah 35:1–4

Strengthen the feeble hands, steady the knees
that give way. —ISAIAH 35:3

When I was a kid, I thought the song title "He Looked Beyond My Fault and Saw My Need," written by Dottie Rambo in 1967, was "He Looked Beyond My Faults and Saw My Knees." Employing the logic of a child, I wondered why God would look at knees. Was it because they were weak? I knew that weak-kneed meant "afraid." I later discovered that Dottie had written the song about God's unconditional love in response to her brother Eddie's belief that he was unlovable because of the wrong things he'd done. Dottie assured him that God saw his weakness but loved him anyway.

God's unconditional love is apparent throughout the many weak-kneed moments of the people of Israel and Judah. He sent prophets like Isaiah with messages for His wayward people. In Isaiah 35, the prophet shares the hope of God's restoration. The encouragement that would come as a result of embracing hope would "strengthen the feeble hands, steady the knees that give way" (v. 3). Through the encouragement they received, God's people would in turn be able to encourage others. This is why Isaiah instructs in verse 4, "Say to those with fearful hearts, 'Be strong, do not fear.' "

Feeling weak-kneed? Talk to your heavenly Father. He strengthens weak knees through the truth of the Scriptures and the power of His presence. You'll then be able to encourage others. *Linda*

Clean Containers
1 Peter 4:7–11

Hatred stirs up conflict, but love covers over all wrongs.
—PROVERBS 10:12

"Hatred corrodes the container that carries it." These words were spoken by former Senator Alan Simpson at the funeral of George H. W. Bush. Attempting to describe his dear friend's kindness, Senator Simpson recalled how the forty-first president of the United States embraced humor and love rather than hatred in his professional leadership and personal relationships.

I relate to the senator's quote, don't you? Oh, the damage done to me when I harbor hatred!

Medical research reveals the damage done to our bodies when we cling to the negative or release bursts of anger. Our blood pressure rises. Our hearts pound. Our spirits sag. Our containers corrode.

In Proverbs 10:12, King Solomon observes, "Hatred stirs up conflict, but love covers over all wrongs." The conflict that results from hatred here is a blood feud between rivaling peoples of different tribes and races. Such hatred fuels the drive for revenge so that people who despise each other can't connect.

By contrast, God's way of love covers—draws a veil over, conceals, or forgives—all wrongs. That doesn't mean we overlook errors or enable a wrongdoer. But we don't nurse the wrong when someone is truly remorseful. And if they never apologize, we still release our feelings to God. We who know the Great Lover are to "love each other deeply, because love covers over a multitude of sins" (1 Peter 4:8). *Elisa*

Creator and Sustainer
Hebrews 1:1–45

The Son is the radiance of God's glory . . . sustaining all things by his powerful word. —HEBREWS 1:3

Working with a magnifying glass and tweezers, Swiss watchmaker Phillipe meticulously explained to me how he takes apart, cleans, and reassembles the tiny parts of specialty mechanical watches. Looking at all the intricate pieces, Phillipe showed me the essential component of the timepiece, the mainspring. The mainspring is the component that moves all the gears to allow the watch to keep time. Without it, even the most expertly designed watch will not function.

In a beautiful passage found in the book of Hebrews, the writer eloquently praises Jesus for being the one through whom God created the heavens and the earth. Like the intricacy of a specialty watch, every detail of our universe was created by Jesus (Hebrews 1:2). From the vastness of the solar system to the uniqueness of our fingerprints, all things were made by Him.

But more than the Creator, Jesus, like a clock's mainspring, is essential for the function and flourishing of creation. His presence continually "[sustains] all things by his powerful word" (v. 3), keeping all that He has created working together in all its amazing complexity.

As you have opportunity to experience the beauty of creation today, remember that "in him all things hold together" (Colossians 1:17). May the recognition of Jesus's central role in both creating and sustaining the universe result in a joyful heart and a response of praise as we acknowledge His ongoing provision for us. ❦ *Lisa*

Our New Home
Revelation 22:1–5

No longer will there be any curse. The throne of God and of the Lamb will be in the city. —REVELATION 22:3

As the first immigrant to the US to pass through Ellis Island in New York Harbor in 1892, Annie Moore must have felt incredible excitement at the thought of a new home and a fresh start. Millions would pass through there after her. Just a teenager, Annie had left behind a difficult life in Ireland to start a new one. Carrying only a little bag in her hand, she came with lots of dreams, hopes, and expectations of a land of opportunity.

How much more excitement and awe will God's children experience when we see "a new heaven and a new earth" (Revelation 21:1). We will enter what the book of Revelation calls "the Holy City, the new Jerusalem" (v. 2). The apostle John describes this amazing place with powerful imagery. There will be "the river of the water of life, as clear as crystal, flowing from the throne of God and of the Lamb" (22:1). Water represents life and abundance, and its source will be the eternal God himself. John says that "no longer will there be any curse" (v. 3). The beautiful, pure relationship God intended between himself and humans will be fully restored.

How incredible to know that God, who loves His children and purchased us with the life of His Son, is preparing such an amazing new home—where He will live with us and be our God (21:3). *Estera*

Hungry for God
Jeremiah 15:15–21

*When your words came, I ate them; they were my joy and
my heart's delight. —JEREMIAH 15:16*

A new believer in Jesus was desperate to read the Bible.
However, he'd lost his eyesight and both hands in an ex-
plosion. When he heard about a woman who read Braille
with her lips, he tried to do the same—only to discover
that the nerve endings of his lips had also been destroyed.
Later, he was filled with joy when he discovered that he
could feel the Braille characters with his tongue! He had
found a way to read and enjoy the Scriptures.

Joy and delight were the emotions the prophet Jeremiah experienced when he received God's words. "When
your words came, I ate them," he said. "They were my
joy and my heart's delight" (Jeremiah 15:16). Unlike the
people of Judah who despised His words (8:9), Jeremiah
had been obedient and rejoiced in them. His obedience,
however, also led to the prophet being rejected by his
own people and persecuted unfairly (15:17).

Some of us may have experienced something similar.
We once read the Bible with joy, but obedience to God
led to suffering and rejection from others. Like Jeremiah,
we can bring our confusion to God. He answered Jeremiah by repeating the promise He gave him when He
first called him to be a prophet (vv. 19-21; see 1:18–19).
God reminded him that He never lets His people down.
We can have this same confidence too. He's faithful and
will never abandon us. *Poh Fang*

A Kind Critique
John 4:7–15, 28–29

The law was given through Moses; grace and truth came through Jesus Christ. —JOHN 1:17

During a landscape painting class, the teacher, a highly experienced professional artist, assessed my first assignment. He stood silently in front of my painting, one hand cupping his chin. Here we go, I thought. He's going to say it's terrible.

But he didn't.

He said he liked the color scheme and the feeling of openness. Then he mentioned that the trees in the distance could be lightened. A cluster of weeds needed softer edges. He had the authority to criticize my work based on the rules of perspective and color, yet his critique was truthful and kind.

Jesus, who was perfectly qualified to condemn people for their sin, didn't use the Ten Commandments to crush a Samaritan woman He met at an ancient watering hole. He gently critiqued her life with just a handful of statements. The result was that she saw how her search for satisfaction had led her into sin. Building on this awareness, Jesus revealed himself as the only source of eternal satisfaction (John 4:10–13).

The combination of grace and truth that Jesus used in this situation is what we experience in our relationship with Him (1:17). His grace prevents us from being overwhelmed by our sin, and His truth prevents us from thinking it isn't a serious matter.

Will we invite Jesus to show us areas of our lives where we need to grow so we can become more like Him?

Jennifer

The Lord Will Provide
Genesis 22:2–14

So Abraham called that place The Lord Will Provide.
—GENESIS 22:14

My anxiety increased throughout the summer between my undergraduate and graduate programs. I love to have everything planned out, and the idea of going out of state and entering graduate school without a job made me uncomfortable. However, a few days before I left my summer job, I was asked to continue working for the company remotely. I accepted and had peace that God was taking care of me.

God provided, but it was in His timing, not mine. Abraham went through a far more difficult situation with his son Isaac. He was asked to take his son and sacrifice him on a mountain (Genesis 22:1–2). Without hesitation, Abraham obeyed and took Isaac there. This three-day journey gave Abraham plenty of time to change his mind, but he didn't (vv. 3–4).

When Isaac questioned his father, Abraham replied, "God himself will provide the lamb for the burnt offering" (v. 8). I wonder if Abraham's anxiety grew with each knot he tied as he bound Isaac to the altar and with every inch he raised his knife (vv. 9–10). What a relief it must have been when the angel stopped him! (vv. 11–12). God did indeed provide a sacrifice, a ram, caught in the thicket (v. 13). God tested Abraham's faith, and he proved to be faithful. And at the right time, to the very second, God provided (v. 14). *Julie*

A Future with Forgiveness

Romans 12:9–21

*Do not be overcome by evil, but overcome evil
with good.* —ROMANS 12:21

In 1994, when South Africa made the transition from government by apartheid (imposed racial segregation) to a democracy, it faced the difficult question of how to address the crimes committed under apartheid. The country's leaders couldn't ignore the past, but merely imposing harsh punishments on the guilty risked deepening the country's wounds. As Desmond Tutu, the first black Anglican Archbishop of South Africa, explained in his book *No Future Without Forgiveness*, "We could very well have had justice, retributive justice, and had a South Africa lying in ashes."

Through establishing the Truth and Reconciliation Committee, the new democracy chose the difficult path of pursuing truth, justice, and mercy. Those guilty of crimes were offered a path to restoration—if they were willing to confess their crimes and seek to make restitution. Only by courageously facing the truth could the country begin to find healing.

In a way, South Africa's dilemma mirrors the struggle we all face. We're called to pursue both justice and mercy (Micah 6:8), but mercy is often misunderstood to be a lack of accountability, while pursuing justice can become distorted into pursuing revenge.

Our only path forward is a love that not only "hates what is evil" (Romans 12:9) but also longs for the transformation and good of our "neighbor" (13:10). Through the power of Christ's Spirit, we can learn what it means to have a future of overcoming evil with good (12:21).

Monica

The Only King
Matthew 2:1–12

They bowed down and worshiped him.
—MATTHEW 2:11

As five-year-old Eldon listened to the pastor talk about Jesus leaving heaven and coming to earth, he gasped when the pastor thanked Him in prayer for dying for our sins. "Oh, no! He died?" the boy said in surprise.

From the start of Christ's life on earth, there were people who wanted Him dead. Wise men came to Jerusalem during the reign of King Herod inquiring, "Where is the one who has been born king of the Jews? We saw his star when it rose and have come to worship him" (Matthew 2:2). When the king heard this, he became fearful of one day losing his position to Jesus. So he sent soldiers to kill all the boys two years old and younger around Bethlehem. But God protected His Son and sent an angel to warn His parents to leave the area. They fled, and He was saved (vv. 13–18).

When Jesus completed His ministry, He was crucified for the sins of the world. The sign placed above His cross, though meant in mockery, read, "this is Jesus, the king of the Jews" (27:37). Yet three days later He rose in victory from the grave. After ascending to heaven, He sat down on the throne as King of kings and Lord of lords (Philippians 2:8–11).

The King died for our sins—yours, mine, and Eldon's. Let's allow Him to rule in our hearts. *Anne*

What Comes Next?
2 Timothy 4:1–8

There is in store for me the crown of righteousness,
which the Lord . . . will award to me on that day.
—2 TIMOTHY 4:8

On the night of April 3, 1968, Dr. Martin Luther King gave his final speech, "I've Been to the Mountaintop." In it, he hints that he believed he might not live long. He said, "We've got some difficult days ahead. But it doesn't matter with me now. Because I've been to the mountaintop. And I've looked over. And I've seen the promised land. I may not get there with you. . . . [But] I'm happy tonight. I'm not worried about anything. I'm not fearing any man. Mine eyes have seen the glory of the coming of the Lord." The next day, he was assassinated.

The apostle Paul, shortly before his death, wrote to his protégé Timothy: "I am already being poured out like a drink offering, and the time for my departure is near. . . . Now there is in store for me the crown of righteousness, which the Lord, the righteous Judge, will award to me on that day" (2 Timothy 4:6, 8). Paul knew his time on earth was drawing to a close, as did Dr. King. Both men realized lives of incredible significance, yet never lost sight of the true life ahead. Both men welcomed what came next.

Like them, may we "fix our eyes not on what is seen, but on what is unseen, since what is seen is temporary, but what is unseen is eternal" (2 Corinthians 4:18).

Remi

Led by His Word
Psalm 119:1, 133–136

Direct my footsteps according to your word; let no sin rule over me. —PSALM 119:133

At the BBC in London, Paul Arnold's first broadcasting job was making "walking sounds" in radio dramas. While actors read from scripts during a walking scene, Paul as stage manager made corresponding sounds with his feet—careful to match his pace to the actor's voice and spoken lines. The key challenge, he explained, was yielding to the actor in the story, "so the two of us were working together."

A divine version of such cooperation was sought by the author of Psalm 119, which emphasizes living by the precepts of God's Word. As Psalm 119:1 says, "Blessed are those whose ways are blameless, who walk according to the law of the Lord." Led this way by God and following His instructions, we can remain pure (v. 9), overcome scorn (v. 22), and escape greed (v. 36). He will enable us to resist sin (v. 61), find godly friends (v. 63), and live in joy (v. 111).

Theologian Charles Bridges commented on verse 133: "When I take therefore a step into the world, let me ask—Is it ordered in God's word, which exhibits Christ as my perfect example?"

Walking this way, we show the world Jesus. May He help us walk so closely with Him that people glimpse in us our Leader, Friend, and Savior! *Patricia*

Restored
Joel 2:18–27

I will repay you for the years the locusts have eaten.
—*JOEL 2:25*

A few years ago, an infestation of Mormon crickets caused more than $25 million in lost crops. The crickets came in such numbers that people couldn't so much as take a step without finding one underfoot. The grasshopper-like insect, named for attacking the crops of the Utah pioneers in 1848, can eat an astounding thirty-eight pounds of plant material in their lifetimes, despite being merely two to three inches long. The impact of infestations on farmers' livelihoods—and the overall economy of a state or country—can be devastating.

The Old Testament prophet Joel described a horde of similar insects ravaging the entire nation of Judah as a consequence of their collective disobedience. He foretold an invasion of locusts (a metaphor for a foreign army, in the minds of some Bible scholars) like nothing previous generations had seen (Joel 1:2). The locusts would lay waste to everything in their path, driving the people into famine and poverty. If, however, the people would turn from their sinful ways and ask God for forgiveness, Joel says the Lord would "repay [them] for the years the locusts have eaten" (2:25).

We too can learn from Judah's lesson: like insects, our wrongdoings eat away at the fruitful, fragrant life God intended for us. When we turn toward Him, and away from our past choices, He promises to remove our shame and restore us to an abundant life in Him. ❧ *Kirsten*

Can We Relax?
John 14:25–31

*Do not let your hearts be troubled and
do not be afraid.* —JOHN 14:27

Darnell entered the physical therapist's office knowing
he would experience a lot of pain. The therapist stretched
and bent his arm and held it in positions it hadn't been in
for months since his injury. After holding each uncomfortable position for a few seconds, she gently told him:
"Okay, you can relax." He said later, "I think I heard
that at least fifty times in each therapy session: 'Okay,
you can relax.'"

Thinking of those words, Darnell realized they could
apply to the rest of his life as well. He could relax in
God's goodness and faithfulness instead of worrying.

As Jesus neared His death, He knew His disciples
would need to learn this. They'd soon face a time of up-
heaval and persecution. To encourage them, Jesus said
He would send the Holy Spirit to live with them and
remind them of what He had taught (John 14:26). And
so He could say, "Peace I leave with you; my peace I give
you. . . . Do not let your hearts be troubled and do not
be afraid" (v. 27).

There's plenty we could be uptight about in our everyday lives. But we can grow in our trust in God by
reminding ourselves that His Spirit lives in us—and He
offers us His peace. As we draw on His strength, we can
hear Him in the therapist's words: "Okay, you can relax."

Anne

Relentless Love
1 John 3:16–18

Let us not love with words or speech but with
actions and in truth. —1 JOHN 3:18

Heidi and Jeff came home from an overseas work assignment in a hot climate and settled for several months near family in the state of Michigan—just in time for winter. This would be the first time many of their ten children had seen the natural beauty of snow.

But winter weather in Michigan requires a lot of warm outerwear, including coats, mittens, and boots. For a large family, it would be quite an expensive undertaking just to outfit them for the bitterly cold months ahead. But God provided. First, a neighbor brought over footwear, then snow pants, then hats and gloves. Then, a friend urged others at her church to collect a variety of warm clothes in all twelve sizes for each member of the family. By the time the snow arrived, the family had exactly what they needed.

One of the ways we serve God is by serving those in need. First John 3:16–18 encourages us to help others from the abundance of our own possessions. Serving helps us to be more like Jesus as we begin to love and see people as He does.

God often uses His children to fulfill needs and to answer prayers. And as we serve others, our own hearts are encouraged as we encourage those we serve. As a result, our own faith will grow as God equips us for service in new ways (v. 18). *Cindy*

Praying for Eyes to See
Psalm 119:11–19

Open my eyes that I may see wonderful things in your law.
—PSALM 119:18

One of the most popular videos on social media recently featured Tommy, a visually impaired toddler, sitting on his father's lap in a doctor's office. While a half million viewers and I watched, an ophthalmologist fitted Tommy with special lenses to improve his limited eyesight.

When his doctor rested the tiny pair of glasses on his nose, Tommy's eyes flew open. He pointed to the light in the ceiling, then at a toy on the floor. Finally, he turned to face his father. When their eyes met for the first time, Tommy's little mouth dropped open, and he sucked in a breath. "Dada!" he exclaimed.

I'm not physically blind like Tommy, but my spiritual vision often needs improvement. Sometimes I jump into my Bible reading with eyes clouded by apathy, impatience, or boredom. When I approach Scripture this way, I don't see everything good God has for me.

But when I pray the psalmist's prayer, "Open my eyes that I may see wonderful things in your law," (Psalm 119:18) He often sends insight and understanding. He helps me see the wisdom of hiding His word in my heart to protect myself from sin (v. 11) and brings me joy through my Bible study (v. 16). Best of all, I catch glimpses of my Father's face on every page.

Tommy needed a doctor's help to see with his physical eyes. We need God's help, every day, to see with spiritual eyes the wonders He has provided in the Scriptures.

Lori

"Just the Office"
Ephesians 1:15–23

I pray that the eyes of your heart may be enlightened in order that you may know the hope to which he has called you. —EPHESIANS 1:18

I gazed out at the rolling, green hills in Lancashire in northern England, noticing the stone fences enclosing some sheep dotted around the hills. Puffy clouds moved across the bright sky, and I inhaled deeply, drinking in the sight. When I remarked about the beautiful scene to the woman working at the retreat center I was visiting, she said, "You know, I never used to notice it before our guests would point it out. We've lived here for years; and when we were farmers, this was just the office!"

We can easily miss the gift of what's right in front of us, especially beauty that's part of our everyday lives. We can also easily miss the beautiful ways God works in and around us daily. But believers in Jesus can ask God's Spirit to open our spiritual eyes so we can understand how He's at work, as the apostle Paul wrote in his letter to the Ephesian believers. Paul yearned that God would give them the wisdom and revelation to know Him better (Ephesians 1:17). He prayed that their hearts would be enlightened so they'd know God's hope, promised future, and power (vv. 18–19).

God's gift of the Spirit of Christ can awaken us to His work in us and through us. With Him, what may have once seemed like "just the office" can be understood as a place that displays His light and glory. *Amy*

Watch Me!
Matthew 21:12–17

From the lips of children and infants you, Lord, have
called forth your praise. —*MATTHEW 21:16*

"Watch my fairy princess dance, Grandma!" my three-year-old granddaughter gleefully called as she raced around the yard of our cabin, a big grin on her face. Her "dancing" brought a smile; and her big brother's glum, "She's not dancing, just running," didn't squelch her joy at being on vacation with family.

The first Palm Sunday was a day of highs and lows. When Jesus rode into Jerusalem on a donkey, the crowds enthusiastically shouted, "Hosanna! . . . Blessed is he who comes in the name of the Lord!" (Matthew 21:9). Yet many in the crowd were expecting a Messiah to free them from Rome, not a Savior who would die for their sins that same week.

Later that day, despite the anger of the chief priests who questioned Jesus's authority, children in the temple expressed their joy by shouting, "Hosanna to the Son of David" (v. 15), perhaps leaping and waving palm branches as they ran around the courtyard. They couldn't help but worship Him, Jesus told the indignant leaders, for "from the lips of children and infants [God has] called forth [His] praise" (v. 16). They were in the presence of the Savior!

Jesus invites us to also see Him for who He is. When we do, like a child overflowing with joy, we can't help but revel in His presence. *Alyson*

The Faith to Endure
Acts 27:27–38

Suffering produces endurance. —ROMANS 5:3 ESV

Ernest Shackleton (1874–1922) led an unsuccessful expedition to cross Antarctica in 1914. When his ship, aptly named Endurance, became trapped in heavy ice in the Weddell Sea, it became an endurance race just to survive. With no means of communicating with the rest of the world, Shackleton and his crew used lifeboats to make the journey to the nearest shore—Elephant Island. While most of the crew stayed behind on the island, Shackleton and five crewmen spent two weeks traveling eight hundred miles across the ocean to South Georgia to get help for those left behind. The "failed" expedition became a victorious entry in the history books when all of Shackleton's men survived, thanks to their courage and endurance.

The apostle Paul knew what it meant to endure. During a stormy sea voyage to Rome to face trial for his belief in Jesus, Paul learned from an angel of God that the ship would sink. But the apostle kept the men aboard encouraged, thanks to God's promise that all would survive, despite the loss of the ship (Acts 27:23–24).

When disaster strikes, we tend to want God to immediately make everything better. But God gives us the faith to endure and grow. As Paul wrote to the Romans, "Suffering produces endurance" (Romans 5:3 ESV). Knowing that, we can encourage each other to keep trusting God in hard times. *Linda*

Unity
Ephesians 4:1–6

Make every effort to keep the unity of the Spirit through the bond of peace. —EPHESIANS 4:3

In 1722 a small group of Moravian Christians, who lived in what is now the Czech Republic, found refuge from persecution on the estate of a generous German count. Within four years, more than three hundred people had come. But instead of an ideal community for persecuted refugees, the settlement became filled with discord. Different perspectives on Christianity brought division. What they did next may seem like a small choice, but it launched an incredible revival: They began to focus on what they agreed on rather than on what they disagreed on. The result was unity.

The apostle Paul strongly encouraged the believers in the church in Ephesus to live in unity. Sin would always bring trouble, selfish desires, and conflict in relationships. But as those who were made "alive with Christ" (Ephesians 2:5), the believers were called to live out their new identity in practical ways. Primarily, they were to "make every effort to keep the unity of the Spirit through the bond of peace" (4:3).

This unity isn't just simple camaraderie achieved through human strength. We are to "be completely humble and gentle; be patient, bearing with one another in love" (v. 2). From a human perspective, it's impossible to act in this way. We can't reach unity through our own power but through God's perfect power "that is at work within us" (3:20). *Estera*

Who Knows?
Ecclesiastes 6:12; 7:13–14

When times are good, be happy; but when times are bad,
consider this: God has made the one as well as the other.
—*ECCLESIASTES 7:14*

According to Chinese legend, when Sai Weng lost track of one of his prized horses, his neighbor expressed sorrow for missing animal. But Sai Weng was unconcerned. He said, "Who knows if it may be a good thing for me?" Surprisingly, the lost horse returned home with another horse. As the neighbor congratulated him, Sai Weng said, "Who knows if it may be a bad thing for me?" As it turned out, his son broke his leg when he rode on the new horse. This seemed like a misfortune, until the army arrived at the village to recruit all able-bodied men to fight in the war. Because of the son's injury, he wasn't recruited, which ultimately could have spared him from death.

This is the story behind the Chinese proverb that teaches this truth: a difficulty can be a blessing in disguise and vice versa. This ancient wisdom has a close parallel in Ecclesiastes 6:12, where the author observes: "Who knows what is good for a person in life?" Indeed, none of us know what the future holds. An adversity might have positive benefits, and prosperity might have ill effects.

Each day offers new opportunities, joys, struggles, and suffering. As God's beloved children, we can rest in His sovereignty and trust Him through the good and bad times alike. God has "made the one as well as the other" (7:14). He's with us in all the events in our lives and promises His loving care. *Poh Fang*

In Living Color
Revelation 4:1–6

*The one who sat there had the appearance of jasper
and ruby. A rainbow that shone like emerald
encircled the throne.* —REVELATION 4:3

When Xavier McCoury put on the glasses Aunt Celena
sent for his tenth birthday, he burst into tears. Born col-
orblind, Xavier had only seen the world in shades of gray,
white, and black. With his new EnChroma glasses, however, Xavier saw color for the first time. His euphoria at
witnessing the beauty around him made his family feel
like they'd beheld a miracle.

Witnessing God's colorfully radiant brilliance also
evoked a powerful reaction in the apostle John (Revelation 1:17). After encountering the full glory of the resurrected Christ, John glimpsed "a throne in heaven with
someone sitting on it. And the one who sat there had the
appearance of jasper and ruby. A rainbow that shone like
an emerald encircled the throne. . . . From the throne
came flashes of lightning" (Revelation 4:2–5).

In a different time, Ezekiel had a similar vision, seeing
"what looked like a throne of lapis lazuli," with a figure
above the throne who "looked like glowing metal, as if
full of fire" (Ezekiel 1:26–27). This magnificent figure
was surrounded with rainbow-like radiance (v. 28).

One day we will meet the resurrected Christ face-to-
face. These visions mentioned in Scripture give us just a
tiny hint of the magnificence that awaits us then. As we
celebrate the beauty of God's creation here and now, may
we live in anticipation of the glory yet to be revealed.

Remi

Valiant Actions
John 10:7–18

*I am the good shepherd; I know my sheep and my sheep
know me . . . and I lay down my life for the sheep.*
—*JOHN 10:14–15*

John Harper had no idea what was about to unfold as he
and his six-year-old daughter embarked on the Titanic.
But one thing he knew: he loved Jesus and he was passionate that others know Him too. As soon as the ship hit an
iceberg and water started pouring in, Harper, a widower,
put his little girl on a lifeboat and headed into the chaos
to save as many people as possible. As he distributed life
jackets he reportedly shouted, "Let the women, children,
and the unsaved into the lifeboats." Until his last breath,
Harper shared about Jesus with anyone who was around
him. John willingly gave his life away so others could live.

There was One who laid down His life freely two
thousand years ago so you and I can live not only in this
life but also for all eternity. Jesus didn't just wake up one
day and decide He would pay the penalty of death for
humanity's sin. This was His life's mission. At one point
when He was talking with the Jewish religious leaders
He repeatedly acknowledged that He was going to lay
down His life (John 10:11, 15, 17, 18). He didn't just
say these words but also lived them by actually dying
a horrific death on the cross. He came to earth so the
Pharisees, John Harper, and we "may have life, and have
it to the full" (v. 10). *Estera*

This Is Me
James 3:7–12

Out of the same mouth come praise and cursing. My brothers and sisters, this should not be. —JAMES 3:10

The powerful song "This Is Me" is an unforgettable show tune featured in *The Greatest Showman*, the smash movie musical loosely based on the life of P. T. Barnum and his traveling circus. The lyrics, sung by characters in the film who'd suffered verbal taunts and abuse for failing to conform to societal norms, describe words as destructive bullets and knives that leave scars.

The song's popularity points to how many people bear the invisible but real scars caused by weaponized words.

New Testament writer James understood the potential danger of our words to cause destructive and long-lasting harm, calling the tongue "a restless evil, full of deadly poison" (James 3:8). By using this surprisingly strong comparison, James emphasized the urgent need for believers to recognize the immense power of their words. Even more, he highlighted the inconsistency of praising God with one breath and then injuring people who are made in God's image with the next (vv. 9–10).

The song "This Is Me" similarly challenges the truth of verbal attacks by insisting that we're all glorious—a truth the Bible affirms. The Bible establishes the unique dignity and beauty of each human being, not because of outward appearance or anything we have done, but because we are each beautifully designed by God—His unique masterpieces (Psalm 139:14). And our words to each other and about each other have the power to reinforce that reassuring reality. ✦ *Lisa*

When Sharks Won't Bite
Proverbs 27:1–10

One who is full loathes honey from the comb.
—*PROVERBS 27:7*

My children were thrilled, but I felt uneasy. During a vacation, we visited an aquarium where people could pet small sharks kept in a special tank. When I asked the attendant if the creatures ever snapped at fingers, she explained that the sharks had recently been fed and then given extra food. They wouldn't bite because they weren't hungry.

What I learned about shark petting makes sense according to a proverb: "One who is full loathes honey from the comb, but to the hungry even what is bitter tastes sweet" (Proverbs 27:7). Hunger—that sense of inner emptiness—can weaken our discernment as we make decisions. It convinces us that it's okay to settle for anything that fills us up, even if it causes us to take a bite out of someone.

God wants more for us than a life lived at the mercy of our appetites. He wants us to be filled with Christ's love so that everything we do flows from the peace and stability He provides. The constant awareness that we're unconditionally loved gives us confidence. It enables us to be selective as we consider the "sweet" things in life—achievements, possessions, and relationships.

Only a relationship with Jesus gives true satisfaction. May we grasp His incredible love for us so we can be "filled to the measure [with] all the fullness of God" (Ephesians 3:19) for our sake—and the sake of others.

Jennifer

Never Too Sinful
Nehemiah 9:17, 27–31

You are a forgiving God . . . abounding in love.
—NEHEMIAH 9:17

"If I touched a Bible, it would catch fire in my hands," said my community college English professor. My heart sank. The novel we'd been reading that morning referenced a Bible verse, and when I pulled out my Bible to look it up, she noticed and commented. My professor seemed to think she was too sinful to be forgiven. Yet I wasn't bold enough to tell her about God's love—and that the Bible tells us we can always seek God's forgiveness.

There's an example of repentance and forgiveness in Nehemiah. The Israelites had been exiled because of their sin, but now they were allowed to return to Jerusalem. When they'd "settled in," Ezra the scribe read the law to them (Nehemiah 7:73–8:3). They confessed their sins, remembering that despite their sin God "did not desert" or "abandon them" (9:17, 19). He "heard them" when they cried out; and in compassion and mercy, He was patient with them (vv. 27–31).

In a similar way, God is patient with us. He won't abandon us if we choose to confess our sin and turn to Him. I wish I could go back and tell my professor that, no matter her past, Jesus loves her and wants her to be part of His family. He feels the same way about you and me. We can approach Him seeking forgiveness—and He will give it! *Julie*

Pierced Love
Isaiah 53:1–6

But he was pierced for our transgressions, he was crushed
for our iniquities. —ISAIAH 53:5

She had called. She had texted. Now Carla stood outside her brother's gated entry, unable to rouse him to answer. Burdened with depression and fighting addiction, her brother had hidden himself away in his home. In a desperate attempt to penetrate his isolation, Carla gathered several of his favorite foods along with encouraging Scriptures and lowered the bundle over the fence.

But as the package left her grip, it snagged on one of the gate spikes, tearing an opening and sending its contents onto the gravel below. Her well-intended, love-filled offering spilled out in seeming waste. Would her brother even notice her gift? Would it accomplish the mission of hope she'd intended? She can only hope and pray as she waits for his healing.

God so loved the world that—in essence—He lowered His one and only Son over the wall of our sin, bringing gifts of love and healing into our weary and withdrawn world (John 3:16). The prophet Isaiah predicted the cost of this act of love in Isaiah 53:5. This very Son would be "pierced for our transgressions, . . . crushed for our iniquities." His wounds would bring the hope of ultimate healing. He took on Himself "the iniquity of us all" (v. 6).

Pierced by spikes for our sin and need, God's gift of Jesus enters our days today with fresh power and perspective. What does His gift mean to you? *Elisa*

In Tune with the Spirit
Galatians 5:16–26

Since we live by the Spirit, let us keep in step with the Spirit. —GALATIANS 5:25

As I listened to the piano tuner work on the elegant grand piano, I thought about the times when I'd heard that very same piano pour out the incredible sound of the Warsaw Concerto and the rich melody of "How Great Thou Art." But now the instrument desperately needed to be tuned. While some notes were right on pitch, others were sharp or flat, creating an unpleasant sound. The piano tuner's responsibility wasn't to make each of the keys play the same sound but to assure that each note's unique sound combined with others to create a pleasing harmonious whole.

Even within the church, we can observe notes of discord. People with unique ambitions or talents can create a jarring dissonance when they're joined together. In Galatians 5, Paul pleaded with believers to do away with "discord, jealousy, fits of rage, [and] selfish ambition," which would destroy fellowship with God or relationships with others. Paul went on to encourage us to embrace the fruit of the Spirit: "love, joy, peace, forbearance, kindness, goodness, faithfulness, gentleness and self-control" (vv. 20, 22–23).

When we live by the Spirit, we'll find it easier to avoid unnecessary conflict on nonessential matters. Our shared sense of purpose can be greater than our differences. And with God's help, each of us can grow in grace and unity as we keep our hearts in tune with Him.

❦ *Cindy*

Unseen Realities
2 Kings 6:8–17

Elisha prayed, "Open his eyes, LORD, so that he may see."
—2 KINGS 6:17

Stephen Cass, an editor at Discover magazine, was determined to investigate some of the invisible things that are part of his daily life. As he walked toward his office in New York City, he thought: "If I could see radio waves, the top of the Empire State Building [with its host of radio and TV antennas] would be lit like a kaleidoscopic flare, illuminating the entire city." He realized he was surrounded by an invisible electromagnetic field of radio and TV signals, Wi-Fi, and more.

Elisha's servant learned about another kind of unseen reality one morning—the invisible spiritual world. He awoke to find himself and his master surrounded by the armies of Aram. As far as his eyes could see, there were soldiers mounted on powerful warhorses (2 Kings 6:15)! The servant was afraid, but Elisha was confident because he saw the army of angels that surrounded them. He said: "Those who are with us are more than those who are with them" (v. 16). Then he asked the Lord to open his servant's eyes so he too could see that the Lord had surrounded their enemy and He was in control (v. 17).

Do you feel overpowered and helpless? Remember that God is in control and fights for you. He "will command his angels concerning you to guard you in all your ways" (Psalm 91:11). *Poh Fang*

How to Find Peace
Colossians 3:12–17

*Let the peace of Christ rule in your hearts, since as
members of one body you were called to peace.*
—COLOSSIANS 3:15

"What do you think about peace?" my friend asked as
we ate lunch together. "Peace?" I said, puzzled. "I'm not
sure—why do you ask?" He answered, "Well, as you jig-
gled your foot during the church service I wondered if
you're agitated about something. Have you considered
the peace God gives to those who love Him?"

That day some years ago, I was a bit hurt by my friend's
question, but it started me on a journey. I began exploring the Bible to see how God's people embraced this gift
of well-being, of peace, even in the midst of hardship. As
I read Paul's letter to the Colossians, I chewed over the
apostle's command to let the peace of Christ rule in their
hearts (Colossians 3:15).

Paul was writing to a church he'd never visited but had
heard about from his friend Epaphras. He was concerned
that as they encountered false teaching, they were losing
the peace of Christ. But instead of admonishing them,
Paul encouraged them to trust Jesus, who would give
them assurance and hope (v. 15).

We all will encounter times when we can choose to
embrace or refuse the rule of Christ's peace in our hearts.
As we turn to Him, asking Jesus to dwell in us, He will
gently release us from the anxiety and cares that weigh us
down. As we seek His peace, we trust that He will meet
us with His love. *Amy*

Being Cared For
Psalm 46

The LORD Almighty is with us. —PSALM 46:11

Debbie, the owner of a housecleaning service, was always searching for more clients to build up her business. On one call she talked with a woman whose response was, "I won't be able to afford that now; I'm undergoing cancer treatment." Right then Debbie decided that "no woman undergoing cancer treatment would ever be turned away. They would even be offered a free housecleaning service." So she started a nonprofit organization where companies donated their cleaning services to women battling cancer. One such woman felt a rush of confidence when she came home to a clean house. She said, "For the first time, I actually believed I could beat cancer."

A feeling of being cared for and supported can help sustain us when we're facing a challenge. An awareness of God's presence and support can especially bring hope to encourage our spirit. Psalm 46, a favorite of many people going through trials, reminds us: "God is our refuge and strength, an ever-present help in trouble" and "Be still, and know that I am God; . . . I will be exalted in the earth. The LORD Almighty is with us" (vv. 1, 10–11).

Reminding ourselves of God's promises and His presence with us can be a means to help renew our hearts and give us the courage and confidence to go through hard times. *Anne*

A Legacy of Faith
2 Timothy 1:5–14

*I am reminded of your sincere faith, which first lived
in your grandmother Lois and in your mother Eunice.*
—2 TIMOTHY 1:5

Long before the decisive moment when Billy Graham
came to faith in Christ at age sixteen, his parents' devotion to Jesus was evident. They'd both come to faith
while growing up within a family of believers. After
their marriage, Billy's parents continued that legacy by
lovingly nurturing their children, including praying and
reading Scripture and attending church faithfully with
them. The solid foundation Graham's parents laid for
Billy was part of the soil God used to bring him to faith
and, eventually, to his calling as a bold evangelist.

The apostle Paul's young protégé Timothy also benefited from a strong spiritual foundation. Paul wrote,
"Your sincere faith . . . first lived in your grandmother
Lois and in your mother Eunice" (2 Timothy 1:5). This
legacy helped prepare and steer Timothy's heart toward
faith in Christ.

Now Paul urged Timothy to carry on this faith tradition (v. 5), to "fan into flame the gift of God" within him
through the Holy Spirit, who "gives us power" (vv. 6–7).
Because of the power of the Spirit, Timothy could fear-
lessly live for the gospel (v. 8). A strong spiritual legacy
doesn't guarantee we'll come to faith, but the example
and mentoring of others can help prepare the way. And
after we receive Jesus as Savior, the Spirit will guide us
in service, in living for Him, and even in nurturing the
faith of others. *Alyson*

Join the Street Team
Mark 2:13–17

I have not come to call the righteous, but sinners.
—*MARK 2:17*

City health workers in one major US city are taking medical care to the streets to supply the homeless who are suffering from opioid addiction with medicine to treat their addiction. The program began in response to the rising number of homeless who are injecting. Customarily, doctors wait for patients to come to a clinic. By taking medical care to the afflicted instead, patients don't have to overcome the challenges of transportation or needing to remember the appointment.

The health workers' willingness to go to those in need of care reminds me of the way Jesus has come to us in our need. In His ministry, Jesus sought out those who the religious elite were quick to ignore: He ate with "sinners and tax collectors" (v. 16). When asked why He would do that, Jesus replied, "It is not the healthy who need a doctor, but the sick" (v. 17). He went on to say that His intention was to call sinners, not the righteous, into relationship with Him.

When we realize that we're all "sick" and in need of a doctor (Romans 3:10), we can better appreciate Jesus's willingness to eat with the "sinners and tax collectors"—us. In turn, like the health care workers in San Francisco, Jesus appointed us as His "street team" to take His saving message to others in need. ❦ *Kirsten*

Seeking God's Help
2 Chronicles 20:5–12, 15

We will stand in your presence . . . and will cry out to you in our distress. —2 CHRONICLES 20:9

For five years in the late 1800s, grasshoppers descended on Minnesota, destroying the crops. Farmers tried trapping the grasshoppers in tar and burning their fields to kill the eggs. Feeling desperate, and on the brink of starvation, many people sought a statewide day of prayer, yearning to seek God's help together. The governor relented, setting aside April 26 to pray.

In the days after the collective prayer, the weather warmed and the eggs started to come to life. But then four days later a drop in temperature surprised and delighted many, for the freezing temperatures killed the larvae. Minnesotans once again would harvest their crops of corn, wheat, and oats.

Prayer was also behind the saving of God's people during the reign of King Jehoshaphat. When the king learned that a vast army was coming against him, he called God's people to pray and fast. The people reminded God how He'd saved them in times past. And Jehoshaphat said that if calamity came upon them, "whether the sword of judgment, or plague or famine," they would cry out to God knowing that He would hear and save them (2 Chronicles 20:9).

God rescued His people from the invading armies, and He hears us when we cry out to Him in distress. Whatever your concern—whether a relationship issue or something threatening from the natural world—lift it to God in prayer. Nothing is too hard for Him. *Amy*

Delight in the Book
Joshua 1:1–9

Keep this Book of the Law always on your lips; meditate on it day and night. —JOSHUA 1:8

Tsundoku. It's the word I've always needed! A Japanese term, it refers to the stack of books on a bedside table waiting to be read. Books offer the potential for learning or an escape to a different time or place, and I long for the delights and insights found within their pages. So, the stack remains.

The idea that we can find enjoyment and help in a book is even more true for the book of books—the Bible. I see the encouragement to immerse oneself in Scripture in God's instructions to Joshua, the newly appointed leader of Israel, commissioned to lead them into the land promised to the Israelites (Joshua 1:8).

Knowing the difficulty ahead, God assured Joshua, "I will be with you" (v. 5). His help would come, in part, through Joshua's obedience to God's commands. So God instructed him to "Keep this Book of the Law always on your lips; meditate on it day and night, so that you may be careful to do everything written in it" (v. 8). Although Joshua had the Book of the Law, he needed to regularly search it to gain insight and understanding into who God is and His will for His people.

Do you need instruction, truth, or encouragement for your day? As we take time to read, obey, and find nourishment through Scripture, we can savor all that's contained in its pages (2 Timothy 3:16). *Lisa*

Indestructible Love
Song of Songs 8:6–7

*Many waters cannot quench love; rivers cannot
sweep it away.* —SONG OF SONGS 8:7

When we first saw the stream in our backyard, it was
just a thin vein of water trickling through a bed of rocks
in the heat of the summer. Heavy wooden planks served
as a bridge we could easily cross. Months later, torrents
of rain pounded our area for several days in a row. Our
tame little creek swelled into a quick-moving river four-
feet deep and ten-feet wide! The force of this water
heaved the bridgeboards up and deposited them several
feet away.

Rushing water has the potential to overwhelm almost
anything that stands in its path. Yet there's something
that's indestructible in the face of a flood or other forces
that might threaten to destroy it—love. "Many waters
cannot quench love; rivers cannot sweep it away" (Song
of Songs 8:7). Love's persistent strength and intensity is
often present in romantic relationships, but it's only fully
expressed in the love God has for people through His
Son, Jesus Christ.

When the things we consider to be sturdy and depend-
able are swept away, our disappointment can open the
door to a new understanding of God's love for us. His
affection is higher and deeper and stronger and longer-
lasting than anything on earth. Whatever we face, we
face with Him beside us—holding us up, helping us
along, and reminding us that we're loved. *Jennifer*

Live. Pray. Love.
Romans 12:9–21

Hate what is evil; cling to what is good.
—ROMANS 12:9

Influenced by parents who were strong believers in Jesus, track star Jesse Owens lived as a courageous man of faith. During the 1936 Olympic Games in Berlin, Owens, one of the few African Americans on the US team, received four gold medals in the presence of hate-filled Nazis and their leader, Hitler. He also befriended fellow athlete Luz Long, a German. Surrounded by Nazi propaganda, Owens's simple act of living out his faith impacted Luz's life. Later, Long wrote to Owens: "That hour in Berlin when I first spoke to you, when you had your knee upon the ground, I knew you were in prayer . . . I think I might believe in God."

Owens demonstrated how believers can answer the apostle Paul's charge to "hate what is evil" and be "devoted to one another in love" (Romans 12:9–10). Though he could have responded to the evil around him with hate, Owens chose to live by faith and show love to a man who would later become his friend and eventually consider belief in God.

As God's people commit to being "faithful in prayer" (v. 12), He empowers us to "live in harmony with one another" (v. 16).

When we depend on prayer, we can commit to living out our faith and loving all who are made in God's image. As we cry out to God, He'll help us break down barriers and build bridges of peace with our neighbors.

Xochitl

Carefully Crafted
Ephesians 4:11–14

Christ himself gave the apostles, the prophets, the evangelists, the pastors and teachers, to equip his people.
—EPHESIANS 4:11–12

In a YouTube video, Alan Glustoff, a cheese farmer in Goshen, New York, described his process for aging cheese, a process that adds to a cheese's flavor and texture. Before it can be sent out to a market, each block of cheese remains on a shelf in an underground cave for six to twelve months. In this humid environment the cheese is carefully tended. "We do our best to give it the right environment to thrive . . . [and] to develop to its truest potential," Glustoff explained.

Glustoff's passion for developing the potential of the cheese he produces reminded me of God's passion for developing the "truest potential" of His children so they will become fruitful and mature. In Ephesians 4, the apostle Paul describes the people involved in this process: apostles, prophets, evangelists, pastors, and teachers (v. 11). People with these gifts help to stimulate the growth of each believer as well as to encourage acts of service (the "works" mentioned in verse 12). The goal is that we "become mature, attaining to the whole measure of the fullness of Christ" (v. 13).

Spiritual growth comes about through the power of the Holy Spirit as we submit to His maturing process. As we follow the guidance of the people He places in our lives, we become more effective as He sends us out to serve. *Linda*

The One Who Calms the Storms
Matthew 14:23–33

*But Jesus immediately said to them: "Take courage! It is I.
Don't be afraid." —MATTHEW 14:27*

Jim was frantically sharing about problems he was encountering with his work team: division, judgmental attitudes, and misunderstandings. After an hour of patiently listening to his concerns, I suggested, "Let's ask Jesus what He would have us do in this situation." We sat quietly for five minutes. Then something amazing happened. We both felt God's peace cover us like a blanket. We were more relaxed as we experienced His presence and guidance, and we felt confident to wade back into the difficulties.

Peter, one of Jesus's disciples, needed God's comforting presence. One night he and the other disciples were sailing across the Sea of Galilee when a strong storm arose. All of a sudden, Jesus showed up walking on water! Naturally, this took the disciples by surprise. He reassured them: "Take courage! It is I. Don't be afraid" (Matthew 14:27). Peter impulsively asked Jesus if he could join Him. He stepped out of the boat and walked toward Jesus. But he soon lost focus, became aware of the dangerous and humanly impossible circumstance he was in, and started sinking. He cried out, "Lord, save me!" and Jesus lovingly rescued him (vv. 30–31).

Like Peter, we can learn that Jesus, the Son of God, is with us even in the storms of life! *Estera*

Never Alone
John 14:15–18

He will give you another advocate to help you and be with you forever—the Spirit of truth. —JOHN 14:16–17

While writing a Bible guide for pastors in Indonesia, a writer friend grew fascinated with that nation's culture of togetherness. Called gotong royong—meaning "mutual assistance"—the concept is practiced in villages, where neighbors may work together to repair someone's roof or rebuild a bridge or path. In cities too my friend said, "People always go places with someone else—to a doctor's appointment, for example. It's the cultural norm. So you're never alone."

Worldwide, believers in Jesus rejoice in knowing we also are never alone. Our constant and forever companion is the Holy Spirit, the third person of the Trinity. Far more than a loyal friend, the Spirit of God is given to every follower of Christ by our heavenly Father to "help you and be with you forever" (John 14:16).

Jesus promised God's Spirit would come after His own time on Earth ended. "I will not leave you as orphans," Jesus said (v. 18). Instead, the Holy Spirit—"the Spirit of Truth" who "lives with you and will be in you"—indwells each of us who receives Christ as Savior (v. 17).

The Holy Spirit is our Helper, Comforter, Encourager, and Counselor—a constant companion in a world where loneliness can afflict even connected people. May we forever abide in His comforting love and help. *Patricia*

The Joy God Provides
Proverbs 15:13–15, 30

A cheerful heart is good medicine. —*PROVERBS 17:22*

When Marcia is out in public, she always tries to smile at others. It's her way of reaching out to people who might need to see a friendly face. Most of the time, she gets a genuine smile in return. But during a time when Marcia was mandated to wear a facemask, she realized that people could no longer see her mouth, thus no one could see her smile. It's sad, she thought, but I'm not going to stop. Maybe they'll see in my eyes that I'm smiling.

There's actually a bit of science behind that idea. The muscles for the corners of the mouth and the ones that make the eyes crinkle can work in tandem. It's called a Duchenne smile, and it has been described as "smiling with the eyes."

Proverbs reminds us that "a cheerful look brings joy to the heart" and "a cheerful heart is good medicine" (15:30 NLT; 17:22). Quite often, the smiles of God's children stem from the supernatural joy we possess. It's a gift from God that regularly spills out into our lives as we encourage people who are carrying heavy burdens or share with those who are looking for answers to life's questions. Even when we experience suffering, our joy can still shine through.

When life seems dark, choose joy. Let your smile be a window of hope reflecting God's love and the light of His presence in your life. *Cindy*

Prayer Eggs
Habakkuk 2:1–3

Though it linger, wait for it; it will certainly come and will not delay. —HABAKKUK 2:3

Just outside my kitchen window, a robin built her nest under the eaves of our patio roof. I loved watching her tuck grasses into a safe spot and then hunker down to incubate the eggs. Each morning I checked her progress; but each morning, there was nothing. Robin eggs take two weeks to hatch.

Such impatience isn't new for me. I've always strained against the work of waiting, especially in prayer. My husband and I waited nearly five years to adopt our first child. Decades ago, author Catherine Marshall wrote, "Prayers, like eggs, don't hatch as soon as we lay them."

The prophet Habakkuk wrestled with waiting in prayer. Frustrated at God's silence with Babylon's brutal mistreatment of the southern kingdom of Judah, Habakkuk commits to "stand at my watch and station myself on the ramparts," to "look to see what he will say to me" (Habakkuk 2:1). God replies that Habakkuk is to wait for the "appointed time" (v. 3) and directs Habakkuk to "write down the revelation" so the word can be spread as soon as it's given (v. 2).

What God doesn't mention is that the "appointed time" when Babylon falls is six decades away, creating a long gap between promise and fulfillment. Like eggs, prayers often don't hatch immediately but rather incubate in God's overarching purposes for our world and our lives. *Elisa*

Braided Together
Ecclesiastes 4:9–12

A cord of three strands is not quickly broken.
—ECCLESIASTES 4:12

A friend gave me a houseplant she'd owned for more than forty years. The plant was equal to my height, and it produced large leaves from three separate spindly trunks. Over time, the weight of the leaves had caused all three of the stalks to curve down toward the floor. To straighten them, I put a wedge under the plant's pot and placed it near a window so the sunlight could draw the leaves upward and help cure its bad posture.

Shortly after receiving the plant, I saw one just like it in a waiting room at a local business. It also grew from three long skinny stalks, but they'd been braided together to form a larger, more solid core. This plant stood upright without any help.

Any two people may stay in the same "pot" for years, yet grow apart and experience fewer of the benefits God wants them to enjoy. When their lives are woven together with God, however, there is a greater sense of stability and closeness. Their relationship will grow stronger. "A cord of three strands is not quickly broken" (Ecclesiastes 4:12).

Like houseplants, marriages and friendships require some nurturing. Tending to these relationships involves merging spiritually so that God is present at the center of each important bond. He's an endless supply of love and grace—the things we need most to stay happily united with each other. *Jennifer*

Whack-a-Mole
Philippians 4:10–20

Godliness with contentment is great gain.
—*1 TIMOTHY 6:6*

You might know what it's like. The bills keep arriving after a medical procedure—from the anesthesiologist, the surgeon, the lab, the facility. Jason experienced this after an emergency surgery. He complained, "We owe thousands of dollars after insurance. If only we can get these bills paid, then life will be good and I'll be content! I feel like I'm playing the arcade game Whack-a-Mole"—where plastic moles pop up from their holes, and the player hits them wildly with a mallet.

Life comes at us like that at times. The apostle Paul certainly could relate. He said, "I know what it is to be in need," yet he'd "learned the secret of being content in any and every situation" (Philippians 4:12). His secret? "I can do all this through him who gives me strength" (v. 13). When I was going through a particularly discontented time, I read this on a greeting card: "If it isn't here, where is it?" That was a powerful reminder that if I'm not content here and now, what makes me think I'd be if only I were in another situation?

How do we learn to rest in Jesus? Maybe it's a matter of focus. Of enjoying and being thankful for the good. Of learning more about a faithful Father. Of growing in trust and patience. Of recognizing that life is about God and not me. Of asking Him to teach me contentment in Him. *Anne*

In Need of Rescue
Luke 10:30–37

A Samaritan, as he traveled, came where the man was; and
when he saw him, he took pity on him. —LUKE 10:33

A teenager named Aldi was working alone on a fishing hut anchored about one hundred twenty-five kilometers (about seventy-eight miles) off Indonesia's Sulawesi Island when heavy winds knocked the hut off its mooring and sent it out to sea. For forty-nine days, Aldi drifted in the ocean. Every time he spotted a ship, he turned on his lamp to try and get the sailors' attention, only to be disappointed. About ten ships passed the malnourished teen before he was rescued.

Jesus told a parable to an "expert in the law" (Luke 10:25) about someone who needed to be rescued. Two men—a priest and a Levite—saw an injured man as they were traveling. But rather than help him, both "passed by on the other side" (vv. 31–32). We aren't told why. Both were religious men and would have been familiar with God's law to love their neighbor (Leviticus 19:17–18). They may have thought it was too dangerous. Or perhaps they didn't want to break Jewish laws about touching dead bodies, making them ceremonially unclean and unable to serve in the temple. In contrast, a Samaritan—who was despised by the Jews—acted nobly. He saw the man in need and selflessly took care of him.

Jesus wrapped up His teaching with the command that His followers should "go and do likewise" (Luke 10:37). May God give us the willingness to risk reaching out in love to help others. *Poh Fang*

Secret Delivery
Matthew 6:1–4

When you give to the needy, do not let your left hand know what your right hand is doing. —MATTHEW 6:3

A clear, glass vase with bell-shaped lilies of the valley, pink tulips, and yellow daffodils greeted Kim at her front door. For seven months, an anonymous believer in Jesus sent Kim beautiful bouquets from a local flower shop. Each monthly gift arrived with a note filled with scriptural encouragement and signed with these words: "Love, Jesus."

Kim shared photos of these secret deliveries on Facebook. The flowers gave her the opportunity to celebrate an individual's kindness and to acknowledge the way God expressed His love to her through His people. Month after month, each secret delivery caused her friends to be grateful for the priceless gift of time the Lord gave Kim. As she trusted Him through her battle with a terminal disease, every colorful blossom and handwritten note affirmed God's loving compassion for her.

The sender's anonymity reflects the heart motive Jesus encourages His people to adopt when giving. The Lord warns against practicing righteous acts "to be seen" by others (Matthew 6:1). Good deeds are intended to be expressions of worship overflowing from hearts grateful for all God's done for us. Highlighting our own generosity with the hope or expectation of being honored can take the focus off the Giver of all good things—Jesus.

God knows when we give with good intentions (v. 4)—anonymously or not. He simply wants our generosity motivated by love as we give Him the glory, the honor, and the praise. *Xochitl*

But a Breath
Psalm 39:1–13

My hope is in you. —PSALM 39:7

Bobby's sudden death brought home to me the stark reality of death and the brevity of life. My childhood friend was only twenty-four when a tragic accident on an icy road claimed her life. After growing up in a dysfunctional family, Bobby had just recently seemed to be moving forward. A new believer in Jesus, how could her life end so soon?

Sometimes life seems far too short and full of sorrow. In Psalm 39 the psalmist David bemoans his own suffering and exclaims: "Show me, LORD, my life's end and the number of my days; let me know how fleeting my life is. You have made my days a mere handbreadth; the span of my years is as nothing before you. Everyone is but a breath, even those who seem secure" (vv. 4–5). Life is indeed short. Even if we live to see a century, our earthly life is but a drop in all of time.

Yet, along with David, we can say, "My hope is in [the Lord]" (v. 7). We can trust that our lives do have meaning. Though our bodies waste away, as believers we have confidence that "inwardly we are being renewed day by day"—and one day we'll enjoy eternal life with Him (2 Corinthians 4:16–5:1). We know this because God "has given us the Spirit . . . guaranteeing what is to come"! (5:5). *Alyson*

Eyes Tightly Shut
Genesis 3:1–10

*They hid from the LORD God among the trees
of the garden. —GENESIS 3:8*

He knew he shouldn't have done it. I could clearly see he knew it was wrong: it was written all over his face! As I sat down to discuss his wrongdoing with him, my nephew quickly squeezed his eyes shut. There he sat, thinking–with three-year-old logic–that if he couldn't see me, then I must not be able to see him. And if he was invisible to me, then he could avoid the conversation (and consequences) he anticipated.

I'm so glad I could see him in that moment. While I couldn't condone his actions, and we needed to talk about it, I really didn't want anything to come between us. I wanted him to look fully into my face and see how much I love him and was eager to forgive him! In that moment, I caught a glimmer of how God might have felt when Adam and Eve broke His trust in the garden of Eden. Realizing their guilt, they tried to hide from God (Genesis 3:10), who could "see" them as plainly as I could see my nephew.

When we realize we've done something wrong, we often want to avoid the consequences. We run from it, conceal it, or close our eyes to the truth. While God will hold us accountable to His righteous standard, He sees us (and seeks us!) because He loves us and offers forgiveness through Jesus Christ. *Kirsten*

Victory Parade
2 Corinthians 2:14–17

But thanks be to God, who always leads us as captives in Christ's triumphal procession. —2 CORINTHIANS 2:14

In 2016, after the Chicago Cubs won baseball's World Series for the first time in more than a century, some sources said that five million people lined the parade route and gathered at a downtown rally to celebrate the championship.

Victory parades are not a modern invention. A famous ancient parade was the Roman Triumph, in which victorious generals led a procession of their armies and captives through crowded streets. Such parade imagery was likely in Paul's mind when he wrote to the Corinthian church thanking God for leading believers "as captives in Christ's triumphal procession" (2 Corinthians 2:14). I find it fascinating that in this imagery, followers of Christ are the captives. However, as believers we're not forced to participate but are willing "captives," willingly part of the parade led by the victorious, resurrected Christ. As Christians, we celebrate that through Christ's victory, He is building His kingdom and the gates of hell will not prevail against it (Matthew 16:18).

When we talk about Jesus's victory on the cross and the freedom it gives believers, we help spread the "aroma of the knowledge of him everywhere" (2 Corinthians 2:14). And whether people find the aroma to be the pleasing reassurance of salvation or the odor of their defeat, this unseen but powerful fragrance is present everywhere we go.

As we follow Christ, we declare His resurrection victory, the victory that makes salvation available to the world.

Lisa

In the Vine
John 15:1–8

*No branch can bear fruit by itself; it must remain in the vine.
Neither can you bear fruit unless you remain in me.*
—*JOHN 15:4*

One spring after a particularly dreary winter during which she helped a family member through a long illness, Emma found encouragement each time she walked past a cherry tree near her home in Cambridge, England. Bursting out at the top of the pink blossoms were blossoms of white. A clever gardener had grafted into the tree a branch of white flowers. When Emma passed the unusual tree, she thought of Jesus's words about being the Vine and His followers the branches (John 15:1–8).

By calling himself the Vine, Jesus was speaking of an image familiar to the Israelites in the Old Testament, for there the vine symbolized God's people (Psalm 80:8–9; Hosea 10:1). Jesus extended this symbolism to himself, saying He was the Vine and His followers were grafted into Him as branches. And as they remained in Him, receiving His nourishment and strength, they would bear fruit (John 15:5).

As Emma supported her family member, she needed the reminder that she was connected to Jesus. Seeing the white flowers among the pink ones gave her a visual prompt of the truth that as she remained in the Vine, she gained nourishment through Him.

When we who believe in Jesus embrace the idea of being as close to Him as a branch is to a vine, our faith is strengthened and enriched. *Amy*

Refined in the Fire
1 Peter 1:6–9

These trials will show that your faith is genuine.
—1 PETER 1:7 NLT

Twenty-four karat gold is nearly one hundred percent gold with few impurities. But that percentage is difficult to achieve. Refiners most commonly use one of two methods for the purification process. The Miller process is the quickest and least expensive, but the resulting gold is only about 99.95 percent pure. The Wohlwill process takes a little more time and costs more, but the gold produced is 99.99 percent pure.

In Bible times, refiners used fire as a gold purifier. Fire caused impurities to rise to the surface for easier removal. In his first letter to believers in Jesus who lived in Asia Minor (northern Turkey), the apostle Peter used the gold-refining process as a metaphor for the way trials work in the life of a believer. At that time, many believers were being persecuted by the Romans for their faith in Christ. Peter knew what that was like firsthand. But persecution, Peter explained, brings out the "genuineness of [our] faith" (1 Peter 1:7).

Perhaps you feel as if you're in a refiner's fire—feeling the heat of setbacks, illness, or other challenges. But hardship is often the process by which God purifies the gold of our faith. In our pain we might beg God to quickly end the process, but He knows what's best for us, even when life hurts. Keep connected to the Savior, seeking His comfort and peace. *Linda*

Our Guiding Light
2 Samuel 22:26–30

You, Lord, are my lamp; the Lord turns my darkness into light. —2 SAMUEL 22:29

At a museum, I lingered near a display of ancient lamps. A sign revealed they were from Israel. Decorated with carved designs, these oval-shaped clay vessels had two openings—one for fuel, and one for a wick. Although the Israelites commonly used them in wall alcoves, each was small enough to fit in the palm of a person's hand.

Perhaps a little light like this inspired King David to write a praise song in which he said, "You Lord are my lamp; the Lord turns my darkness into light" (2 Samuel 22:29). David sang these words after God gave him victory in battle. Rivals from both inside and outside his own nation had been stalking him, intending to kill him. Because of his relationship with God, David didn't cower in the shadows. He moved forward into enemy confrontations with the confidence that comes from God's presence. With God helping him, he could see things clearly so he could make good decisions for himself, his troops, and his nation.

The darkness David mentioned in his song likely involved fear of weakness, defeat, and death. Many of us live with similar worries, which produce anxiety and stress. When the darkness presses in on us, we can find peace because we know God is with us too. The divine flame of the Holy Spirit lives in us to light our path until we meet Jesus face to face. *Jennifer*

Peace in the Chaos
Psalm 121

*[Our] help comes from the LORD, the Maker of heaven
and earth. —PSALM 121:2*

Something that sounded like firecrackers roused Joanne
from sleep. Glass shattered. Wishing she didn't live
alone, she got up to see what was going on. The dark
streets were empty and the house seemed to be okay—
then she saw the broken mirror.

Investigators found a bullet only a half-inch from the
gas line. If it had struck the line, she probably wouldn't
have made it out alive. Later they discovered it was a
stray bullet from nearby apartments, but now Joanne
was afraid to be at home. She prayed for peace, and once
the glass was cleaned up, her heart calmed.

Psalm 121 is a reminder for us to look to God in times
of trouble. Here, we see that we can have peace and calm
because our "help comes from the LORD, the Maker of
heaven and earth" (v. 2). The God who created the universe helps us and watches over us (v. 3)—even while we
sleep—but He himself never sleeps (v. 4). He watches
over us day and night (v. 6), "both now and forevermore"
(v. 8).

No matter what kind of situations we find ourselves
in, God sees. And He's waiting for us to turn to Him.
When we do, our circumstances may not always change,
but He's promised His peace in the midst of it all.

Julie

Doing What Matters
2 Timothy 4:1–8

I am already being poured out like a drink offering, and the time for my departure is near. —2 TIMOTHY 4:6

My mother-in-law knew her time on earth was drawing to a close. Her physical body was failing, but her spirit was growing stronger every day. She spent weeks preceding her death witnessing to her nurses and doctors, calling friends and family, and sharing final words of wisdom with her adult children.

"Take care of David," she said of my husband—her son—one day as I spooned tiny bits of watermelon into her mouth. "This is going to be hard on him, but God will carry him through."

The apostle Paul had a similar awareness of his impending death when he wrote, "The time of for my departure is near" (2 Timothy 4:6). In the days preceding his death, he urged his protégé Timothy to "preach the word, be prepared in season and out of season; correct, rebuke and encourage—with great patience and careful instruction" (4:2). Paul maximized his time on earth by sharing his faith and investing in other believers.

One day our lives will end. May we spend them in ways that matter for eternity. Paul did. He pointed people to God, shared His wisdom, and helped others grow in their faith. As the Lord helps us follow Paul's example, we can look forward to receiving the same reward he received: "the crown of righteousness, which the Lord, the righteous Judge, will award to me on that day—and not only to me, but also to all who have longed for his appearing (4:8).

Lori

Unimaginable Promises
2 Peter 1:2–8

He has given us his very great and precious promises.
—2 PETER 1:4

In our moments of greatest failure, it can be easy to believe it's too late for us, that we've lost our chance at a life of purpose and worth. That's how Elias, a former inmate at a maximum-security prison in New York, described feeling as a prisoner. "I had broken . . . promises, the promise of my own future, the promise of what I could be."

It was Bard College's "Prison Initiative" college degree program that began to transform Elias's life. While in the program, he participated on a debate team, which one year debated a team from Harvard—and won. For Elias, being "part of the team . . . [was] a way of proving that these promises weren't completely lost."

A similar transformation happens in our hearts when we begin to understand that the good news of God's love in Jesus is good news for us too. It's not too late, we begin to realize with wonder. God still has a future for me.

And it's a future that can neither be earned nor forfeited, dependent only on God's extravagant grace and power (2 Peter 1:2–3). A future where we're set free from the despair in the world and in our hearts into one filled with His "glory and goodness" (v. 3). A future secure in Christ's unimaginable promises (v. 4); and a future transformed into the "freedom and glory of the children of God" (Romans 8:21). *Monica*

The Illusion of Control
James 4:13–17

You do not even know what will happen tomorrow.
—JAMES 4:14

Ellen Langer's 1975 study titled The Illusion of Control examined the level of influence we exert over life's events. She found that we overestimate our degree of control in most situations. The study also demonstrated how reality nearly always shatters our illusion.

Langer's conclusions are supported by experiments carried out by others since the study was published. However, James identified the phenomenon long before she named it. In James 4, he wrote, "Now listen, you who say, 'Today or tomorrow we will go to this or that city, spend a year there, carry on business and make money.' Why, you do not even know what will happen tomorrow. What is your life? You are a mist that appears for a little while and then vanishes" (vv. 13–14).

Then James provides a cure for the delusion, pointing to the One who's in absolute control: "Instead, you ought to say, 'If it is the Lord's will, we will live and do this or that'" (v. 15). In these few verses, James summarized both a key failing of the human condition and its antidote.

May we understand that our fate doesn't rest in our own hands. Because God holds all things in His capable hands, we can trust His plans! *Remi*

Transformed and Transforming

2 Chronicles 33:9–17

Then he restored the altar of the LORD . . . and
told Judah to serve the LORD, the God of Israel.
—*2 CHRONICLES 33:16*

Tani and Modupe grew up in Nigeria and went to the UK to study in the 1970s. Having been personally transformed by God's grace, they never imagined that they would be used to transform one of the most deprived and segregated communities in England-Anfield in Liverpool. As Drs. Tani and Modupe Omideyi faithfully sought God and served their community, God restored hope to many. They lead a vibrant church and continue to run numerous community projects that have led to the transformation of countless lives.

Manasseh changed his community, first for evil and then for good. Crowned king of Judah at the age of twelve, he led his people astray and they did great evil for many years (2 Chronicles 33:1–9). They paid no attention to God's warnings, so He allowed Manasseh to be taken prisoner to Babylon (vv. 10–11).

In his distress, the king humbly cried out to God who heard his plea and restored him to his kingdom (vv. 12–13). The now reformed king rebuilt the city walls and got rid of the foreign gods (vv. 14–15). "He restored the altar of the LORD and . . . told Judah to serve the LORD, the God of Israel" (v. 16). As the people observed the radical transformation of Manasseh, so too were they transformed (v. 17).

As we seek God, may He transform us and so impact our communities through us. ❧ *Ruth*

Big Enough
Luke 18:15–17

Let the little children come to me, and do not hinder them, for the kingdom of God belongs to such as these.
—*LUKE 18:16*

My grandson ran to the roller coaster line and stood with his back against the height-requirement sign to see if he was big enough to ride. He squealed with joy when his head exceeded the mark.

So much of life is about being "big" enough, isn't it? To move from car seat to seatbelt and from the back seat to the front. To take a driver's test. To vote. To get married. Like my grandson, we can spend our lives longing to grow up.

In New Testament times, children were loved but not highly valued in society until they "became of age" and could contribute to the home and enter the synagogue with adult privileges. Jesus shattered the standards of His day by welcoming the impoverished, the diseased, and even children. Three gospels (Matthew, Mark, and Luke) tell of parents bringing little children to Jesus so He might lay hands on them and pray for them (Matthew 19:13; Mark 10:16).

The disciples rebuked the adults for what they saw as an inconvenience. At this, Jesus was "indignant" (Mark 10:14) and opened His arms to the little ones. He elevated their value in His kingdom and challenged all to become like children themselves—to embrace their vulnerability and need for Him in order to know Him (Luke 18:17). It's our childlike need that makes us "big" enough to receive His love. *Elisa*

The Door of Reconciliation
2 Corinthians 5:14–21

All this is from God, who reconciled us to himself
through Christ and gave us the ministry of reconciliation.
—*2 CORINTHIANS 5:18*

Inside St. Patrick's Cathedral in Dublin, Ireland, there's a door that tells a five-century-old tale. In 1492 two families, the Butlers and the FitzGeralds, began fighting over a high-level position in the region. The fight escalated, and the Butlers took refuge in the cathedral. When the FitzGeralds came to ask for a truce, the Butlers were afraid to open the door. So the FitzGeralds cut a hole in it, and their leader offered his hand in peace. The two families then reconciled, and adversaries became friends.

God has a door of reconciliation that the apostle Paul wrote passionately about in his letter to the church in Corinth. At His initiative and because of His infinite love, God exchanged the broken relationship with humans for a restored relationship through Christ's death on the cross. We were far away from God, but in His mercy He didn't leave us there. He offers us restoration with himself—"not counting people's sins against them" (2 Corinthians 5:19). Justice was fulfilled when "God made [Jesus] who had no sin to be sin for us," so that in Him we could be at peace with God (v. 21).

Once we accept God's hand in peace, we're given the important task of bringing that message to others. We represent the amazing, loving God who offers complete forgiveness and restoration to everyone who believes.

Estera

Open Arms
2 Samuel 22:1–7, 17–20

*In my distress I called to the LORD. . . . My cry
came to his ears.* —2 SAMUEL 22:7

Saydee and his family have an "open arms and open
home" philosophy. People are always welcome in their
home, "especially those who are in distress," he says.
That's the kind of household he had growing up in Li-
beria with his nine siblings. Their parents always welcomed others into their family. He says, "We grew up
as a community. We loved one another. Everybody was
responsible for everybody. My dad taught us to love each
other, care for each other, protect each other."

When King David was in need, he found this type of
loving care in God. Second Samuel 22 (and Psalm 18) re-
cords his song of praise to God for the ways He had been
a refuge for him throughout his life. He recalled, "In
my distress I called to the Lord; I called out to my God.
From his temple he heard my voice; my cry came to his
ears" (2 Samuel 22:7). God had delivered him from his
enemies, including King Saul, many times. He praised
God for being his fortress and deliverer in whom he took
refuge (vv. 2–3).

While our distresses may be small in comparison to
David's, God welcomes us to run to Him to find the
shelter we long for. His arms are always open. Therefore
we "sing the praises of [His] name" (v. 50). *Anne*

Giving Credit
Jeremiah 9:23–26

Let the one who boasts boast in the Lord.
—*1 CORINTHIANS 1:31*

In the early 1960s, a collection of unusual paintings featuring a person or animal with huge, sad eyes became popular. Some considered the work "kitschy"—or tacky—but others delighted in it. As the artist's husband began to promote his wife's creations, the couple grew quite prosperous. But the artist's signature, Margaret Keane, didn't appear on her work. Instead, Margaret's husband presented his wife's work as his own. Margaret fearfully remained silent about the fraud for twenty years until the couple's marriage ended. It took a courtroom "paint-off" between them to prove the true artist's identity.

The man's deception was clearly wrong, but even as followers of Jesus, we may find it easy to take credit when we shouldn't. Often we think we should take credit for talents we possess, leadership skills we display, or even for our kind deeds to others. But those qualities are possible only because of God's grace. In Jeremiah 9, we find the prophet lamenting the lack of humility and the unrepentant hearts of the people. He wrote that the Lord says we shouldn't boast of our wisdom, our strength, or our riches, but only that we might understand and know that He is the Lord "who exercises kindness, justice and righteousness on earth" (v. 24).

Our hearts fill with gratitude as we realize the identity of the true Artist. "Every good and perfect gift is . . . from the Father" (James 1:17). All of the credit, all of the praise belongs to the Giver of good gifts. *Cindy*

Walk Like a Warrior
Judges 6:1, 11–16

When the angel of the LORD appeared to Gideon, he said,
"The LORD is with you, mighty warrior." —JUDGES 6:12

Eighteen-year-old Emma faithfully talks about Jesus on social media, even though bullies have criticized her joy and enthusiastic love for Christ. Some have attacked her with remarks about her physical appearance. Others have suggested a lack of intelligence because of her devotion to God. Though the unkind words cut deep into Emma's heart, she continues to spread the gospel with bold faith and love for Jesus and others. Sometimes, though, she's tempted to believe her identity and worth are determined by the criticism of others. When that happens, she asks God for help, prays for her persecutors, meditates on the words of Scripture, and perseveres with Spirit-empowered courage and confidence.

Gideon faced fierce tormentors—the Midianites (Judges 6:1–10). Though God called him a "mighty warrior," Gideon struggled to let go of his doubt, self-imposed limitations, and insecurities (vv. 11–15). On more than one occasion, he questioned the Lord's presence and his own qualifications, but eventually surrendered in faith.

When we trust God, we can live in a way that shows we believe what He says about us is true. Even when persecution tempts us to doubt our identity, our loving Father confirms His presence and fights on our behalf. He affirms we can walk like mighty warriors armed with His absolute love, guarded by His endless grace, and secured in His reliable truth. *Xochitl*

Shelter from the Storm
Exodus 33:12–23

*When my glory passes by, I will put you in a cleft in the rock
and cover you with my hand until I have passed by.*
—EXODUS 33:22

As the story goes, in 1763, a young minister, traveling on
a cliffside road in Somerset, England, ducked into a cave
to escape the flashes of lightning and pounding rain. As
he looked out at a valley called Burrington Combe, he
pondered the gift of finding shelter and peace in God.
Waiting there, he began to write a hymn, "Rock of
Ages," with its memorable opening lines: "Rock of Ages,
cleft for me, let me hide myself in thee."

We don't know if Augustus Toplady thought about
Moses's experience in the cleft of a rock while writing the
hymn (Exodus 33:22), but perhaps he did. The Exodus
account tells of Moses seeking God's reassurance and
God's response. When Moses asked God to reveal His
glory to him, God answered graciously, knowing that
"no one may see me and live" (v. 20). He tucked Moses
into the rocks when He passed by, letting Moses only
see His back. And Moses knew that God was with him.

We can trust that just as God said to Moses, "My Presence will go with you" (v. 14), so too we can find refuge
in Him. We may experience many storms in our lives,
as did Moses and the English minister in the story, but
when we cry out to Him, He will give us the peace of His
presence. *Amy*

How to Stay on Track
1 John 2:18–27

*The Spirit teaches you everything you need to
know, and what he teaches is true—it is not a lie.*
—*1 JOHN 2:27* NLT

As the world's fastest blind runner, David Brown of
the US Paralympic Team credits his wins to God, his
mother's early advice ("no sitting around"), and his running guide—veteran sprinter Jerome Avery. Tethered
to Brown by a string tied to their fingers, Avery guides
Brown's winning races with words and touches.

"It's all about listening to his cues," says Brown, who
says he could "swing out wide" on 200-meter races where
the track curves. "Day in and day out, we're going over
race strategies," Brown says, "communicating with each
other—not only verbal cues, but physical cues."

In our own life's race, we're blessed with a Divine
Guide. Our Helper, the Holy Spirit, leads our steps when
we follow Him. "I am writing these things to you about
those who are trying to lead you astray," wrote John
(1 John 2:26). "But you have received the Holy Spirit,
and he lives within you, so you don't need anyone to
teach you what is true. For the Spirit teaches you everything you need to know" (v. 27 NLT).

John stressed this wisdom to the believers of his day
who faced "antichrists" who denied the Father and that
Jesus is the Messiah (v. 22). We face such deniers today as
well. But the Holy Spirit, our Guide, leads us in following Jesus. We can trust His guidance to touch us with
truth, keeping us on track. *Patricia*

Aiming for the Prize
1 Corinthians 9:19–27

Run in such a way as to get the prize.
—1 CORINTHIANS 9:24

In the 1994 fictional movie Forrest Gump, Forrest becomes famous for running. What began as a jog "to the end of the road" continued for three years, two months, fourteen days, and sixteen hours. Each time he arrived at his destination, he set another one and continued to run, zig-zagging across the United States, until one day when he no longer felt like it. "Feeling like it" was the way his running began. Forrest says, "That day, for no particular reason, I decided to go for a little run."

In contrast to Forrest's seemingly whimsical running, the apostle Paul asks his readers to follow his example and "run in such a way as to get the prize" (1 Corinthians 9:24). Like disciplined athletes, our running—the way we live our lives—might mean saying no to some of our pleasures. Being willing to forgo our rights might help us reach others with the good news of our rescue from sin and death.

With our hearts and minds trained on the goal of inviting others to run the race alongside us, we are also assured of the ultimate prize—eternal fellowship with God. The victor's crown God bestows will last forever; we win it by running our lives with the aim of making Him known while relying on His strength to do so. What a reason to run! *Kirsten*

He Knows All About It
Mark 12:41–44

His understanding has no limit. —PSALM 147:5

Finn, a Siamese fighting fish, lived at our house for two years. My young daughter would often bend down to talk with him after dropping food into his tank. When the topic of pets came up in kindergarten, she proudly claimed him as her own. Eventually, Finn passed away, and my daughter was heartbroken.

My mother advised me to listen closely to my daughter's feelings and tell her, "God knows all about it." I agreed that God knows everything, yet wondered, *How will that be comforting?* Then it occurred to me that God isn't simply aware of the events in our lives—He compassionately sees into our souls and knows how situations affect us. He understands that "little things" can feel like big things—depending on our age, past wounds, or lack of resources.

Jesus saw the real size of a widow's gift—and heart—as she dropped two coins into a temple collection box. He described what it meant for her as He said, "This poor widow has put more into the treasury than all the others. . . . [She put in] all she had to live on" (Mark 12:43–44).

The widow kept quiet about her situation, but Jesus recognized that what others considered a tiny donation was a sacrifice to her. He sees our lives in the same way. May we find comfort in His limitless understanding.

Jennifer

Remembering
John 15:9–17

*Greater love has no one than this: to lay down one's life
for one's friends. —JOHN 15:13*

On Memorial Day, I think of many former servicemen but especially my dad and uncles, who served in the military during World War II. They made it home, but in that war hundreds of thousands of families tragically lost loved ones in service to their country. Yet, when asked, my dad and most soldiers from that era would say they were willing to give up their lives to protect their loved ones and stand for what they believed to be right.

When someone dies in defense of their country, John 15:13—"Greater love has no one than this: to lay down one's life for one's friends"—is often recited during the funeral service to honor their sacrifice. But what were the circumstances behind this verse?

When Jesus spoke those words to His disciples during the Last Supper, He was about to die. And, in fact, one of His small group of disciples, Judas, had already left to betray Him (13:18–30). Yet Christ knew all of this and still chose to sacrifice His life for His friends and enemies.

Jesus was willing and ready to die for those who'd one day believe in Him, even for those who were still His enemies (Romans 5:10). In return, He asks His disciples (then and now) to "love each other" as He has loved them (John 15:12). His great love compels us to sacrificially love others—friend and foe alike. *Alyson*

Grief Overturned
John 20:11–18

I have seen the Lord! —JOHN 20:18

Jim and Jamie Dutcher, filmmakers known for their knowledge of wolves, say that when those animals are happy, they wag their tails and romp about. But after the death of a pack member, they grieve for weeks. They visit the place where the pack member died, showing grief by their drooping tails and mournful howls.

Grief is a powerful emotion we've all experienced, particularly at the death of a loved one or of a treasured hope. Mary Magdalene experienced it. She had traveled with and helped support Jesus and His disciples (Luke 8:1–3). But His cruel death on a cross separated them. The only thing left for Mary to do for Jesus was to finish anointing His body for burial—a task the Sabbath had interrupted. But imagine how Mary felt when she found not a lifeless, broken body but a living Savior! Though she hadn't at first recognized the man standing before her, when He spoke her name, she knew who He was— Jesus! Instantly, grief turned to joy. Mary now had joyful news to share: "I have seen the Lord!" (John 20:18).

Jesus entered our dark world to bring freedom and life. His resurrection celebrates the reality that He accomplished what He set out to do. We too can celebrate His resurrection and share the good news: He is alive!

🍃 *Linda*

Eclipse
Amos 8:9–12; 9:11–12

*I will restore David's fallen shelter—I will repair its
broken walls and restore its ruins—and will rebuild it
as it used to be. —AMOS 9:11*

I was prepared with eye protection, an ideal viewing location, and homemade moon pie desserts. Along with millions of people in the US, my family watched the rare occurrence of a total solar eclipse—the moon covering the entire disk of the sun.

The eclipse caused an unusual darkness to come over the typically bright summer afternoon. Although for us this eclipse was a fun celebration and a reminder of God's incredible power over creation (Psalm 135:6–7), throughout history darkness during the day has been seen as abnormal and foreboding (Exodus 10:21; Matthew 27:45), a sign that everything is not as it should be.

This is what darkness signified for Amos, a prophet during the time of the divided monarchy in ancient Israel. Amos warned the northern kingdom that destruction would come if they continued to turn away from God. As a sign, God would "make the sun go down at noon and darken the earth in broad daylight" (Amos 8:9).

But God's ultimate desire and purpose was—and is—to make all things right. Even when the people were taken into exile, God promised to one day bring a remnant back to Jerusalem and "repair its broken walls and restore its ruins" (9:11).

Even when life is at its darkest, we can—as did Israel—find comfort in knowing that God is at work to bring light and hope back to all people who seek Him (Acts 15:14–18). *Lisa*

Found on the Edges
Luke 19:1–10

For the Son of Man came to seek and to save the lost.
—LUKE 19:10

In the middle of the crowd at a motorcycle demonstration where riders performed breathtaking tricks, I found myself needing to stand on my tiptoes to see. Glancing around, I noticed three children perched in a nearby tree, apparently because they too were unable to get to the front of the crowd to see the action.

Watching the kids peer out from their lofty location, I couldn't help but think of Zacchaeus, who Luke identifies as a wealthy tax collector (Luke 19:2). Jews often viewed tax collectors as traitors for working for the Roman government collecting taxes from fellow Israelites. What's worse, they frequently demanded additional money to pad their personal bank accounts. So Zacchaeus was likely shunned by his community.

As Jesus passed through Jericho, Zacchaeus longed to see Him but was unable to see over the crowd. So, perhaps feeling both desperate and lonely, he climbed into a sycamore tree to catch a glimpse (vv. 3–4). And it was there, on the outskirts of the crowd, that Jesus searched him out and announced His intention to be a guest at his home (v. 5).

Zacchaeus's story reminds us that Jesus came to "seek and to save the lost," offering His friendship and the gift of salvation (vv. 9–10). Even if we feel on the edges of our communities, pushed to the "back of the crowd," we can be assured that, even there, Jesus finds us. ❧ *Lisa*

The Right Words
Ephesians 6:10–20

*Pray for me, too. Ask God to give me the right words so I
can boldly explain God's mysterious plan.*
—*EPHESIANS 6:19* NLT

Recently, a number of authors have urged believers to
take a fresh look at the "vocabulary" of our faith. One
writer, for example, emphasized that even theologically
rich words of faith can lose their impact when, through
overfamiliarity and overuse, we lose touch with the
depths of the gospel and our need for God. When that
happens, he suggested, we may need to relearn the language of faith "from scratch," letting go of our assumptions until we can see the good news for the first time.

The invitation to learn to "speak God from scratch"
reminds me of Paul, who devoted his life to "[becoming]
all things to all people . . . for the sake of the gospel"
(1 Corinthians 9:22–23). He never assumed he knew
best how to communicate what Jesus had done. Instead,
he relied on constant prayer and pleaded for fellow believers to pray for him as well—to help him find "the
right words" (Ephesians 6:19 NLT) to share the good
news.

The apostle also knew the need for each believer in
Christ to remain humble and receptive each day to their
need for deeper roots in His love (3:16–17). It's only as
we deepen our roots in God's love, each day becoming
more aware of our dependence on His grace, that we can
begin to find the right words to share the incredible news
of what He's done for us. *Monica*

When We Praise
Acts 16:25–34

At once all the prison doors flew open, and everyone's chains came loose. —ACTS 16:26

When nine-year-old Willie was abducted from his front yard, he sang his favorite gospel song "Every Praise" over and over again. During the three-hour ordeal, Willie ignored the kidnapper's repeated orders to keep silent as they drove around. Eventually, the kidnapper let Willie out of the car unharmed. Later, Willie described the encounter, saying that while he felt his fear give way to faith, the abductor seemed agitated by the song.

Willie's response to his dire situation is reminiscent of the experience shared by Paul and Silas. After being flogged and thrown into jail, they reacted by "praying and singing hymns to God, and the other prisoners were listening to them. Suddenly there was such a violent earthquake that the foundations of the prison were shaken. At once all the prison doors flew open, and everyone's chains came loose" (Acts 16:25–26).

Upon witnessing this awesome demonstration of power, the jailer believed in the God of Paul and Silas, and his entire household was baptized along with him (vv. 27–34). Through the avenue of praise, both physical and spiritual chains were broken that night.

We may not always experience a visibly dramatic rescue like Paul and Silas, or like Willie. But we know that God responds to the praises of His people! When He moves, chains fall apart. *Remi*

On the Bubble
1 Peter 2:4–10

You are a chosen people, a royal priesthood, a holy nation,
God's special possession, that you may declare the praises
of him who called you . . . into his wonderful light.
—*1 PETER 2:9*

A news article in May 1970 contained one of the first uses of the idiom "on the bubble." Referring to a state of uncertainty, the expression was used in relation to rookie race car driver Steve Krisiloff. He'd been "on the bubble," having posted a slow qualifying lap for the Indianapolis 500. Later, it was confirmed that his time—though the slowest of those who qualified—allowed him to compete in the race.

We can feel at times that we're "on the bubble," uncertain we have what it takes to compete in or finish the race of life. When we're feeling that way, it's important to remember that in Jesus we're never "on the bubble." As children of God, our place in His kingdom is secure (John 14:3). Our confidence flows from Him who chose Jesus to be the "cornerstone" on which our lives are built, and He chose us to be "living stones" filled with the Spirit of God, capable of being the people God created us to be (1 Peter 2:5–6).

In Christ, our future is secure as we hope in and follow Him (v. 6). For "[we] are a chosen people, a royal priesthood, a holy nation, God's special possession, that [we] may declare the praises of him who called [us] out of darkness into his wonderful light" (v. 9).

In Jesus's eyes we're not "on the bubble." We're precious and loved (v. 4). *Ruth*

Walk in the Present with God
Psalm 102:11–13, 18–28

The children of your servants will live in your presence;
their descendants will be established before you.
—PSALM 102:28

In *Mere Christianity*, C. S. Lewis wrote: "Almost certainly God is not in time. His life does not consist of moments one following another. . . . Ten-thirty—and every other moment from the beginning of the world—is always present for Him." Still, waiting seasons often feel endless. But as we learn to trust God, the eternal Maker of time, we can accept the reality that our fragile existence is secure in His hands.

The psalmist, lamenting in Psalm 102, admits his days are as fleeting as "the evening shadow" and withering grass, while God "endures through all generations" (vv. 11–12). The writer, weary from suffering, proclaims that God sits "enthroned forever" (v. 12). He affirms that God's power and consistent compassion reach beyond his personal space (vv. 13–18). Even in his despair (vv. 19–24), the psalmist turns his focus on the power of God as Creator (v. 25). Though His creations will perish, He will remain the same for eternity (vv. 26–27).

Whether time seems to be standing still or dragging on, it's tempting to accuse God of being late or nonresponsive. We can grow impatient and frustrated with remaining still. We can forget He's chosen every single cobblestone on the path He's planned for us. But He never leaves us to fend for ourselves. As we live by faith in the presence of God, we can walk in the present with God. *Xochitl*

Inheritance Isn't Earned

Ephesians 1:3–14

He predestined us for adoption to sonship through Jesus Christ, in accordance with his pleasure and will.
—*EPHESIANS 1:5*

"Thanks for dinner, Dad," I said as I set my napkin on the restaurant table. I was home on a break from college and, after being gone for a while, it felt strange to have my parents pay for me. "You're welcome, Julie," my dad replied, "but you don't have to thank me for everything all the time. I know you've been off on your own, but you're still my daughter and a part of the family." I smiled. "Thanks, Dad."

In my family, I haven't done anything to earn my parents' love or what they do for me. But my dad's comment reminds me that I haven't done anything to deserve to be a part of God's family either.

In the book of Ephesians, Paul tells his readers that God chose them "to be holy and blameless in his sight" (1:4), or to stand without blemish before Him (5:25–27). But this is only possible through Jesus, in whom "we have redemption through his blood, the forgiveness of sins, in accordance with the riches of God's grace" (1:7). We don't have to earn God's grace, forgiveness, or entrance into His family. We simply accept His free gift.

When we turn our lives over to Jesus, we become children of God, which means we receive eternal life and have an inheritance waiting for us in heaven. Praise God for offering such a wonderful, undeserved gift!

Julie

Praying Like Jesus
Luke 22:39–44

Father, if you are willing, take this cup from me; yet not my will, but yours be done. —LUKE 22:42

Every coin has two sides. The front is called "heads" and, from early Roman times, usually depicts a country's head of state. The back is called "tails," a term possibly originating from the British ten pence depicting the raised tail of a heraldic lion.

Like a coin, Christ's prayer in the garden of Gethsemane possesses two sides. In the deepest hours of His life, on the night before He died on a cross, Jesus prayed, "Father, if you are willing, take this cup from me; yet not my will, but yours be done" (Luke 22:42). When Christ says, "take this cup," that's the raw honesty of prayer. He reveals His personal desire, "This is what I want."

Then Jesus turns the coin, praying "not my will." That's the side of abandonment. Abandoning ourselves to God begins when we simply say, "But what do you want, God?"

This two-sided prayer is also included in Matthew 26 and Mark 14 and is mentioned in John 18. Jesus prayed both sides of prayer: take this cup (what I want, God), yet not My will (what do you want, God?), pivoting between them.

Two sides of Jesus. Two sides of prayer. *Elisa*

Letting Go
John 11:21–36

Jesus said . . . , "I am the resurrection and the life. The one who believes in me will live, even though they die."
—*JOHN 11:25*

"Your father is actively dying," said the hospice nurse. "Actively dying" refers to the final phase of the dying process and was a new term to me, one that felt strangely like traveling down a lonely one-way street. On my dad's last day, not knowing if he could still hear us, my sister and I sat by his bed. We kissed the top of his beautiful bald head. We whispered God's promises to him. We sang "Great Is Thy Faithfulness" and quoted the 23rd Psalm. We told him we loved him and thanked him for being our dad. We knew his heart longed to be with Jesus, and we told him he could go. Speaking those words was the first painful step in letting go. A few minutes later, our dad was joyously welcomed into his eternal home.

The final release of a loved one is painful. Even Jesus's tears flowed when His good friend Lazarus died (John 11:35). But because of God's promises, we have hope beyond physical death. Psalm 116:15 says that God's "faithful servants"—those who belong to Him—are "precious" to Him. Though they die, they'll be alive again.

Jesus promises, "I am the resurrection and the life. The one who believes in me will live, even though they die; and whoever lives by believing in me will never die" (John 11:25–26). What comfort it brings to know we'll be in God's presence forever. *Cindy*

Faithful in Captivity
Genesis 39:6–12, 20–23

While Joseph was there in the prison, the LORD was with him.
—GENESIS 39:20–21

Haralan Popov had no idea what turn his life would take when the doorbell rang early one morning in 1948. Without any warning, the Bulgarian police took Haralan away to prison because of his faith. He spent the next thirteen years behind bars, praying for strength and courage. Despite horrible treatment, he knew God was with him, and he shared the good news of Jesus with fellow prisoners—and many believed.

In the account of Joseph's life beginning in Genesis 37, Jacob's son had no idea what would happen to him after he was mercilessly sold by his angry brothers. Traveling merchants took him to Egypt and sold him to Potiphar, an Egyptian official. He found himself in a culture surrounded by people who believed in thousands of gods. To make things worse, Potiphar's wife tried to seduce Joseph. When Joseph refused repeatedly, she falsely accused him, leading to his being sent to prison (39:16–20). Yet God did not abandon him. Not only was He with Joseph (v. 21, 23) but He also "gave him success in everything he did" and even "showed him kindness and granted him favor" with those in authority (vv. 3, 21).

Imagine the fear Joseph must have felt. But he remained faithful and kept his integrity. God was with Joseph in his difficult journey and had a master plan for him. He has a plan in mind for you too. Take heart and walk in faith, trusting that He sees and He knows.

🌿 *Estera*

Demonstrating Grace
Micah 7:18–20

You will tread our sins underfoot and hurl all our iniquities into the depths of the sea. —MICAH 7:19

"In moments where tragedy happens or even hurt, there are opportunities to demonstrate grace or to exact vengeance," the recently bereaved man remarked. "I chose to demonstrate grace." Pastor Erik Fitzgerald's wife had been killed in a car accident caused by an exhausted firefighter who fell asleep while driving home, and legal prosecutors wanted to know whether he would seek the maximum sentence. The pastor chose to practice the forgiveness he often preached about. To the surprise of both him and the firefighter, the men eventually became friends.

Pastor Erik was living out of the grace he had received from God, who'd forgiven him all of his sins. Through his actions he echoed the words of the prophet Micah, who praised God for pardoning sin and forgiving when we do wrong (Micah 7:18). The prophet uses wonderfully visual language to show just how far God goes in forgiving His people, saying that He will "tread our sins underfoot" and hurl our wrongdoings into the deep sea (v. 19). The firefighter received a gift of freedom that day, which brought him closer to God.

Whatever difficulty we face, we know that God reaches out to us with loving, open arms, welcoming us into His safe embrace. He delights "to show mercy" (v. 18). As we receive His love and grace, He gives us the strength to forgive those who hurt us—even as Pastor Erik did. *Amy*

Fruit Juice
John 15:5–8

Apart from me you can do nothing. —JOHN 15:5

A thrift-store bargain, the lamp seemed perfect for my home office—the right color, size, and price. Back at home, however, when I plugged in the cord, nothing happened. No light. No power. No juice.

No problem, my husband assured me. "I can fix that. Easy." As he took the lamp apart, he saw the trouble immediately. The plug wasn't connected to anything. Without wiring to a source of power, the "perfect" pretty lamp was useless.

The same is true for us. Jesus told His disciples, "I am the vine; you are the branches. If you remain in me and I in you, you will bear much fruit." But then he added this reminder: "Apart from me you can do nothing" (John 15:5).

This teaching was given in a grape-growing region, so His disciples readily understood it. Grapevines are hardy plants, and their branches tolerate vigorous pruning. Cut off from their life source, however, the branches are worthless deadwood. So it is with us.

As we remain in Jesus and let His words dwell in us, we're wired to our life source—Christ himself. "This is to my Father's glory," said Jesus, "that you bear much fruit, showing yourselves to be my disciples" (v. 8). Such a fruitful outcome needs daily nourishment, however. Freely, God provides it through the Scriptures and His love. So plug in and let the juice flow! *Patricia*

On Our Hearts
Deuteronomy 6:1–9

These commandments . . . are to be on your hearts. Impress them on your children. —DEUTERONOMY 6:6–7

After a young boy faced some challenges in school, his dad began to teach him a pledge to recite each morning before school: "I thank God for waking me up today. I am going to school so I can learn . . . and be the leader that God has created me to be." The pledge is one way the father hopes to help his son apply himself and deal with life's inevitable challenges.

In a way, by helping his son to commit this pledge to memory, the father is doing something similar to what God commanded the Israelites in the desert: "These commandments . . . are to be on your hearts. Impress them on your children" (Deuteronomy 6:6–7).

After wandering in the wilderness for forty years, the next generation of Israelites was about to enter the Promised Land. God knew it wouldn't be easy for them to succeed—unless they kept their focus on Him. So, through Moses, He urged them to remember Him and be obedient to Him—and to help their children to know and love God by talking about His Word "when you sit at home and when you walk along the road, when you lie down and when you get up" (v. 7).

Each new day, we too can commit to allowing Scripture to guide our hearts and minds as we live in gratitude to Him. *Alyson*

Talking Bananas
Acts 11:19–26

[Barnabas] encouraged them all to remain true to the Lord with all their hearts. —ACTS 11:23

Never give up. Be the reason someone smiles. You're amazing. It isn't where you came from—it's where you're going that counts. Some schoolchildren in Virginia Beach, Virginia, found these messages and more written on bananas in their lunchroom. Cafeteria manager Stacey Truman took the time to write the encouraging notes on the fruit, which the kids dubbed "talking bananas."

This caring outreach reminds me of Barnabas's heart for the "spiritual youngsters" in the ancient city of Antioch (Acts 11:22–24). Barnabas was famous for his ability to inspire people. Known as a good man, full of faith and the Holy Spirit, he prompted the new believers to "remain true to the Lord with all their hearts" (v. 23). I imagine he spent time with those he wanted to help, saying things like: Keep praying. Trust the Lord. Stay close to God when life is hard.

New believers, like children, need encouragement. They're full of potential. They're discovering what they're good at. They may not fully realize what God wants to do in them and through them, and often the enemy works overtime to prevent their faith from flourishing.

Those of us who've walked with Jesus for a while understand how hard living for Jesus can be. May all of us seek to give and receive encouragement as God's Spirit guides us and reminds us of spiritual truth. *Jennifer*

"Ask the Man Who Owns One"

Psalm 66:1, 8–20

Let me tell you what [God] has done for me.
—PSALM 66:16

In the early 1900s, the Packard Motor Car Company generated a slogan to entice buyers. "Ask the man who owns one" became a powerful tagline, one that contributed to the company's reputation as manufacturing the dominant luxury vehicle in that era. What Packard seemed to understand is that personal testimony is compelling to the hearer: A friend's satisfaction with a product is a powerful endorsement.

Sharing with others our personal experiences of God's goodness to us also makes an impact. God invites us to declare our gratitude and joy not only to Him but also to those around us (Psalm 66:1). The psalmist eagerly shared in his song the forgiveness God granted him when he turned from his sins (vv. 18–20)

God has done amazing works in the course of history, such as parting the waters of the Red Sea (v. 6). He also does amazing work in each of our personal lives: giving us hope in the midst of suffering, giving us the Holy Spirit to understand His Word, and providing for our daily needs. When we share with others our personal experiences of God's work in our lives, we're giving something of much greater value than an endorsement of a particular purchase—we're acknowledging God's goodness and encouraging one another along the journey of life. *Kirsten*

A Wise Builder
Proverbs 14:1–3, 26-27, 33

The wise woman builds her house, but with her own hands the foolish one tears hers down. —PROVERBS 14:1

Sojourner Truth, whose birth name was Isabella Baumfree, was born a slave in 1797 in Esopus, New York. Though nearly all her children were sold as slaves, she escaped to freedom in 1826 with one daughter and lived with a family who paid the money for her freedom. Instead of allowing an unjust system to keep her family apart, she took legal action to regain her small son Peter—an amazing feat for an African American woman in that day. Knowing she couldn't raise her children without God's help, she became a believer in Christ and later changed her name to Sojourner Truth to show that her life was built on the foundation of God's truth.

King Solomon, the writer of Proverbs 14, declares, "The wise woman builds her house" (v. 1). In contrast, one without wisdom "tears hers down." This building metaphor shows the wisdom God provides to those willing to listen. How does one build a house with wisdom? By saying "only what is helpful for building others up" (Ephesians 4:29; see also 1 Thessalonians 5:11). How does one tear down? Proverbs 14 gives the answer: "A fool's mouth lashes out with pride" (v. 3).

Sojourner had a "secure fortress" (v. 26) in a turbulent time, thanks to the wisdom of God. You may never have to rescue your children from an injustice, but you can build your house on the same foundation Sojourner did—the wisdom of God. 🌿 *Linda*

Doubt and Faith
Job 1:20–22; 27–10

The LORD gave and the LORD has taken away; may the name of the LORD be praised. —JOB 1:21

MingTeck woke up with a severe headache and thought it was another migraine. But when he got out of bed, he collapsed onto the floor. He was admitted to the hospital where the doctors discovered he'd had a stroke. After four months of rehabilitation, he recovered his ability to think and talk but still walks with a painful limp. He often struggles with despair, but he finds great comfort from the book of Job.

Job lost all his wealth and his children overnight. Despite the harrowing news, he at first looked to God in hope and praised Him for being the source of everything. He acknowledged God's sovereign hand even in times of calamity (Job 1:21). We marvel at his strong faith, but Job also struggled with despair. After he lost his health too (2:7), he cursed the day he was born (3:1). He was honest with his friends and God about his pain. Eventually, however, he came to accept that both good and bad come from God's hand (13:15; 19:25–27).

In our sufferings, we too may find ourselves vacillating between despair and hope, doubt and faith. God doesn't require us to be dauntless in the face of adversity but instead invites us to come to Him with our questions. Though our faith may fail at times, we can trust God to always be faithful. *Poh Fang*

Betrayed
John 13:18–22; Psalm 41:9–12

Even my close friend, someone I trusted, one who shared my bread, has turned against me. —PSALM 41:9

In 2019, art exhibitions worldwide commemorated the five hundredth anniversary of the death of Leonardo da Vinci. While many of his drawings and scientific discoveries were showcased, there are only five finished paintings universally credited to da Vinci, including *The Last Supper.*

This intricate mural depicts the final meal Jesus ate with His disciples, as described in each of the gospels. The painting captures the disciples' confusion at Jesus' statement, "One of you is going to betray me" (John 13:21). Perplexed, the disciples discussed who the betrayer might be—while Judas quietly slipped out into the night to alert the authorities of Jesus's whereabouts.

Betrayed. The pain of Judas's treachery is evident in Jesus's words, "He who shared my bread has turned against me" (v. 18). A friend close enough to share a meal used that connection to harm Jesus.

Each of us has likely experienced a friend's betrayal. How can we respond to such pain? Psalm 41:9, which Jesus quoted to indicate His betrayer was present during the shared meal (John 13:18), offers hope. After David poured out his anguish at a close friend's duplicity, he took solace in God's love and presence that would uphold and set him in God's presence forever (Psalm 41:11–12).

When friends disappoint, we can find comfort knowing God's sustaining and empowering presence will help us endure even the most devastating pain. *Lisa*

At Our Worst
Ephesians 4:20–32

Be completely humble and gentle; be patient, bearing with one another in love. —EPHESIANS 4:2

"She is tolerable, but not handsome enough to tempt me." This sentence, pronounced by Mr. Darcy in Jane Austen's classic *Pride and Prejudice*, is the reason I'll never forget that novel and its impact on me. After reading that one sentence, I firmly decided I would never like Mr. Darcy.

But I was wrong. Like Austen's character Elizabeth Bennet, I had the humbling experience of slowly—and quite reluctantly—changing my mind. Like her, I'd been unwilling to get to know Darcy's character as a whole; I preferred to hang on to my reaction to one of his worst moments. After finishing the novel, I wondered who I'd made that same mistake with in the real world. What friendships had I missed because I wouldn't let go of a snap judgment?

At the heart of faith in Jesus is the experience of being seen, loved, and embraced by our Savior—at our worst (Romans 5:8; 1 John 4:19). It's the wonder of realizing we can surrender our old, false selves for who we truly are in Christ (Ephesians 4:23–24). And it's the joy of understanding that we are no longer alone but part of a family, a "body" of those learning to walk the "way of love"— real, unconditional love (5:2).

When we remember what Christ has done for us (v. 2), how can we not long to see others the way He sees us?

Monica

When Life Is Hard

Psalm 16

*I say to the Lord, "You are my Lord; apart from you
I have no good thing." —PSALM 16:2*

Physically, mentally, and emotionally exhausted, I curled up in my recliner. Our family had followed God's leading and had moved from California to Wisconsin. After we arrived, our car broke down and left us without a vehicle for two months. Meanwhile, my husband's limited mobility after an unexpected back surgery and my chronic pain complicated our unpacking. We uncovered costly problems with our new-to-us but older home. Our senior dog suffered with health issues. And though our new pup brought great joy, raising a furry ball of energy was far more work than anticipated. My attitude soured. How was I supposed to have unshakable faith while traveling on a bumpy road of hardships?

As I prayed, God reminded me of the psalmist, whose praise didn't depend on circumstances. David poured out his emotions, often with great vulnerability, and he sought refuge in the presence of God (Psalm 16:1). Acknowledging God as provider and protector (vv. 5–6), David praised Him and followed His counsel (v. 7). David affirmed that he would "not be shaken" because he kept his eyes "always on the Lord" (v. 8). So, he rejoiced and rested secure in the joy of God's presence (vv. 9–11).

We too can delight in knowing our peace doesn't depend on our present situation. As we thank our unchanging God for who He is and always will be, His presence will fuel our steadfast faith. — *Xochitl*

Perspectives from Above
Isaiah 48:5–11, 17

I will not yield my glory to another. —ISAIAH 48:11

When Peter Welch was a young boy in the 1970s, using a metal detector was just a hobby. But since 1990, he's been leading people from around the world on metal-detecting excursions. They've made thousands of discoveries—swords, ancient jewelry, coins. Using Google Earth, they look for patterns in the landscape on farmland in the United Kingdom. It shows them where roads, buildings, and other structures may have been centuries ago. Peter says, "To have a perspective from above opens a whole new world."

God's people in Isaiah's day needed "a perspective from above." They prided themselves on being His people yet were disobedient and refused to give up their idols. God had another perspective. Despite their rebellion, He would rescue them from captivity to Babylon. Why? "For my own sake, . . . I will not yield my glory to another" (Isaiah 48:11). God's perspective from above is that life is for His glory and purpose—not ours. Our attention is to be given to Him and His plans and to pointing others to praise Him too.

Having God's glory as our own life's perspective opens a whole new world. Only He knows what we will discover about Him and what He has for us. God will teach us what is good for us and lead us along the paths we should follow (v. 17). *Anne*

Life Changes
Ephesians 4:20–24

Put on the new self, created to be like God in true
righteousness and holiness. —EPHESIANS 4:24

Stephen grew up in a rough part of East London and
fell into crime by the age of ten. He said, "If everyone's
selling drugs and doing robberies and fraud, then you're
going to get involved. It's just a way of life." But when
he was twenty, he had a dream that changed him: "I
heard God saying, 'Stephen, you're going to prison for
murder.'" This vivid dream served as a warning, and he
turned to God and received Jesus as his Savior—and the
Holy Spirit transformed his life.

Stephen set up an organization that teaches inner-city
kids discipline, morality, and respect through sports. He
credits God with the success he has seen as he prays with
and trains the kids. "Rebuilding misguided dreams," he
says.

In pursuing God and leaving behind our past, we—
like Stephen—follow Paul's charge to the Ephesians to
embrace a new way of life. Although our old self is "cor-
rupted by its deceitful desires," we can daily seek to "put
on the new self" that's created to be like God (Ephesians
4:22, 24). All believers embrace this continual process as
we ask God through His Holy Spirit to make us more
like Him.

Stephen said, "Faith was a crucial foundation for me
changing my life around." How has this been true for
you? 🌿 *Amy*

God's Retirement Plan
Exodus 3:1–10

The angel of the LORD appeared to [Moses] in flames of fire from within a bush. —EXODUS 3:2

Archaeologist Dr. Warwick Rodwell was preparing to retire when he made an extraordinary discovery at Lichfield Cathedral in England. As builders carefully excavated part of the floor of the church to make way for a retractable base, they discovered a sculpture of the archangel Gabriel, thought to be 1,200 years old. Dr. Rodwell's retirement plans were put on hold as this find launched him into an exciting and busy new season.

Moses was eighty years old when he made a fiery discovery that would forever alter his life. Though the adopted son of an Egyptian princess, he never forgot his Hebrew lineage and raged at the injustice he witnessed against his kinsmen (Exodus 2:11–12). When Pharaoh learned that Moses had killed an Egyptian who was beating a Hebrew, he planned to have him killed, forcing Moses to flee to Midian, where he settled (vv. 13–15).

Forty years later, when he was eighty, Moses was tending his father-in-law's flock when "the angel of the LORD appeared to him in flames of fire from within a bush. Moses saw that though the bush was on fire it did not burn up" (3:2). In that moment, God called Moses to lead the Israelites out of Egyptian slavery (vv. 3–22).

At this moment in your life, what might God be calling you to do for His greater purpose? What new plans has He placed in your path? *Ruth*

Quarantined by Fear
Luke 12:22–34

Seek his kingdom. —LUKE 12:31

In 2020, an outbreak of the coronavirus left the world in fear. People were quarantined, countries were put under lockdown, flights and large events were canceled. Those living in areas with no known cases still feared they might get the virus. Graham Davey, an expert in anxiety, believes that negative news broadcasts are "likely to make you sadder and more anxious." A meme that circulated on social media showed a man watching the news on TV, and he asked how to stop worrying. In response, another person in the room reached over and flipped off the TV, suggesting that the answer might be a shift in focus!

Luke 12 gives us some advice to help us stop worrying: "Seek his kingdom" (v. 31). We seek God's kingdom when we focus on the promise that His followers have an inheritance in heaven. When we face difficulty, we can shift our focus and remember that God sees us and knows our needs (vv. 24–30).

Jesus encourages His disciples: "Do not be afraid, little flock, for your Father has been pleased to give you the kingdom" (v. 32). God enjoys blessing us! Let's worship Him, knowing He cares for us more than the birds of the air and the flowers of the field (vv. 22–29). Even in difficult times, we can read the Scriptures, pray for God's peace, and trust in our good and faithful God. *Julie*

Wandering Off
Luke 15:1–7

Rejoice with me; I have found my lost sheep.
—*LUKE 15:6*

Living near cattle ranches as he did, humorist Michael Yaconelli noticed how cows were prone to wander while grazing. A cow would keep moving, always looking for the fabled "greener pastures." Near the edge of the property, the cow might discover some cool fresh grass under a shade tree. Just beyond a broken-down part of the fence was a tasty clump of foliage. Then the cow might push far beyond the fence and out to the road. It slowly "nibbled" its way into being lost.

Cows aren't alone in their roaming problem. Sheep wander too. But it's likely that people have the biggest tendency of all to stray.

Perhaps that's one of the reasons God compares us to sheep in the Bible. It can be easy to meander and "nibble our way" through reckless compromises and foolish decisions, never noticing how far away from the truth we've strayed.

Jesus told the Pharisees the story of a lost sheep. The sheep was of such value to the shepherd that he left his other sheep behind while he searched for the wandering one. And when he found the one that had strayed, He celebrated! (Luke 15:1–7).

Such is the happiness of God over those who turn back to Him. Jesus said, "Rejoice with me; I have found my lost sheep" (v. 6). God has sent us a Savior to rescue us and bring us home. *Cindy*

Compassion on the Job
Matthew 14:1–14

[Jesus] had compassion on them and healed their sick.
—MATTHEW 14:14

My friend Ellen calculates payroll for an accounting firm. This may sound like a straightforward job, but there are times when employers submit their information later than requested. Ellen often makes up for this by working long hours so employees can receive their money without delay. She does this out of consideration for the families that depend on those funds to buy groceries, purchase medicine, and pay for housing.

Ellen's compassionate approach to her job points me to Jesus. On earth, He sometimes ministered to people when it was inconvenient for Him. For instance, Christ wanted some alone time after He heard that John the Baptist had been killed, so He boarded a boat in search of an isolated place (Matthew 14:13). Perhaps He needed to grieve for His relative and pray through His sorrow.

There was just one problem. Crowds of people tagged along behind Him. This group had various physical needs. It would have been much easier to send the people away, but "when Jesus landed and saw [them], he had compassion on them and healed their sick" (v. 14).

Although it was part of Jesus's calling to teach people and cure their diseases as He ministered on earth, His empathy affected the way in which He carried out His responsibilities. May God help us to recognize His compassion in our lives and give us the strength to pass it on to others. *Jennifer*

From Pity to Praise
2 Timothy 4:9–18

But the Lord stood at my side and gave me strength.
—2 TIMOTHY 4:17

At a coat drive for children, excited kids searched gratefully for their favorite colors and proper sizes. They also gained self-esteem, an organizer said, with new coats boosting their acceptance by peers and school attendance on winter days.

The apostle Paul seemed to need a coat, as well, when he wrote Timothy, "Bring the cloak that I left with Carpus at Troas" (2 Timothy 4:13). Held in a cold Roman prison, Paul needed both warmth and companionship. "No one came to my support, but everyone deserted me," he lamented, when he faced a Roman judge (v. 16). His words pierce our hearts with the honesty of this great missionary's pain.

Yet in these final words of Paul's last recorded letter—his closing thoughts after an astounding ministry—he moves from pity to praise. "But the Lord stood at my side," he adds (v. 17), and his words rally our hearts. As Paul declared, "[God] gave me strength so that I might preach the Good News in its entirety for all the Gentiles to hear. And he rescued me from certain death" (v. 17 NLT).

If you're facing a crisis, lacking even the right clothing for warmth or close friends to help, remember God. He's faithful to revive, provide, and deliver. Why? For His glory and for our purpose in His kingdom. *Patricia*

Stick-Figure Lesson
2 Corinthians 10:1–11

*What we are in our letters when we are absent,
we will be in our actions when we are present.*
—2 CORINTHIANS 10:11

A friend of mine—okay, it was my counselor—drew a stick figure on a sheet of paper. She labeled this the "private" self. Then she drew an outline around the figure, about a half-inch larger, and named it the "public" self. The difference between the two figures, between the private and public selves, represents the degree to which we have integrity.

I paused at her lesson and wondered, *Am I the same person in public that I am in private? Do I have integrity?*

Paul wrote letters to the church in Corinth, weaving love and discipline into his admonitions to be like Jesus. As he neared the end of this letter (2 Corinthians), he addressed accusers who challenged his integrity by saying he was bold in his letters but weak in person (10:10). These critics used professional oratory to take money from their listeners. While Paul possessed academic prowess, he spoke simply and plainly. "My message and my preaching were not with wise and persuasive words," he had written in an earlier letter, "but with a demonstration of the Spirit's power" (1 Corinthians 2:4). His later letter revealed his integrity: "Such people should realize that what we are in our letters when we are absent, we will be in our actions when we are present" (2 Corinthians 10:11).

Paul presented himself as the same person in public that he was in private. How about us? *Elisa*

Water into Hope
John 4:4–14

Let anyone who is thirsty come to me and drink.
—JOHN 7:37

Tom and Mark's ministry refreshes lives. This is clear in the video they share of a group of fully clad children laughing and dancing in the refreshing water of an open shower—their first ever. The men work with indigenous churches to install water filtration systems on wells in Haiti, easing and lengthening lives as diseases connected to contaminated water are prevented. Access to clean, fresh water gives the people hope for their future.

Jesus referred to "living water" in John 4:10–11 to capture a similar idea of a continual source of refreshment. Tired and thirsty, Jesus had asked a Samaritan woman for a drink (vv. 4–8). This request led to a conversation in which Jesus offered the woman "living water" (vv. 9–15)—water that would become a source of life and hope within them, like "a spring of water welling up to eternal life" (v. 14).

We discover what this living water is later in John, when Jesus said, "Let anyone who is thirsty come to me and drink," declaring that whoever believed in Him would have "rivers of living water [flowing] from within them." John explains, "By this he meant the Spirit" (7:37–39).

Through the Spirit, believers are united to Christ and have access to the boundless power, hope, and joy found in God. Like living water, the Spirit lives inside believers, refreshing and renewing us. *Alyson*

Nearby Neighbors
Proverbs 27:1–10

Better a neighbor nearby than a relative far away.
—PROVERBS 27:10

Our neighborhood, like many others, uses a website to help neighbors connect immediately with those surrounding them. In my community, members warn one another of mountain lion sightings and wildfire evacuation orders, as well as supply one another with child care when the need arises. It has even proven to be a resource for locating runaway pets. By leveraging the power of the internet, those living near one another are connecting again in ways that are often lost in today's fast-paced world.

Being in relationship with those who live nearby was also important long ago in the days of King Solomon. While family relationships are truly important and can be a source of great support, Solomon indicates that the role of a friend is vital—especially when "disaster strikes" (Proverbs 27:10). Relatives might care deeply for their family members and desire to be of help in such circumstances. But if they're far away, there's little they can do in the moments when calamity strikes. Neighbors, however, because they're close by, are likely to know of the need quickly and can assist more readily.

Because technology has made it easier than ever to remain connected with loved ones across the globe, we may be tempted to overlook those living nearby. *Jesus, help us invest in relationships with the people you've placed around us!* Kirsten

Rescue the Weak
Psalm 82:3–4

Rescue the weak and the needy; deliver them from the hand of the wicked. —PSALM 82:4

Which would you choose—a skiing holiday in Switzerland or rescuing children from danger in Prague? Nicholas Winton, just an ordinary man, chose the latter. In 1938, war between Czechoslovakia and Germany seemed on the horizon. After Nicholas visited refugee camps in Prague, where many Jewish citizens lived in horrible conditions, he felt compelled to come up with a plan to help. He raised money to transport hundreds of children safely out of Prague to Great Britain to be cared for by British families before the onset of World War II.

His actions exemplified the calling set forth in Psalm 82: "Uphold the cause of the poor and the oppressed" (v. 3). Asaph, the writer of this psalm, wanted to stir his people to champion the cause of others in need: "Rescue the weak and the needy; deliver them from the hand of the wicked" (v. 4). The psalmist spoke for those who couldn't speak for themselves—like the children Nicholas worked tirelessly to rescue—the poor and the widowed who needed justice and protection.

Everywhere we look we see people in need due to war, storms, disease, poverty, and other hardships. Although we can't solve every problem, we can prayerfully consider what we can do to help in the situations God brings into our lives. *Linda*

Faith-Stand
John 19:38–42

Taking Jesus' body, the two of them wrapped it, with the spices, in strips of linen. —JOHN 19:40

Desmond Doss was enlisted to serve in World War II as a non-combatant. Though his religious beliefs prevented him from carrying a gun, Doss ably served as a combat medic. In one battle, he withstood intense and repeated enemy fire to pull seventy-five soldiers in his unit to safety after they had been injured. His story is told in the documentary *The Conscientious Objector* and dramatized in the movie *Hacksaw Ridge*.

A roll call of the heroes of Christian faith includes such courageous characters as Abraham, Moses, David, Elijah, Peter, and Paul. Yet there are some unsung heroes like Joseph of Arimathea and Nicodemus, who risked their standing with the Jewish leaders to take Christ's crucified body and give Him a decent burial (John 19:40–42). This was a bold move from a fearful, secret disciple of Jesus and another, Nicodemus, who had previously dared to visit Him only at night (vv. 38–39). Even more impressive is that they took their faith-stand before Jesus rose victorious from the grave. Why?

Perhaps the manner of Jesus's death and the events that immediately followed (Matthew 27:50–54) crystallized the fledgling faith of these fearful followers. Maybe they learned to focus on who God is rather than what man could do to them. Whatever the inspiration, may we follow their example and exhibit courage to take risks of faith in our God—for others today. *Remi*

An Ordinary Man
1 Samuel 16:1–7

People look at the outward appearance, but the LORD looks at the heart. —1 SAMUEL 16:7

William Carey was a sickly boy, born to a humble family near Northampton, England. His future didn't look too bright. But God had plans for him. Against all odds, he moved to India, where he brought incredible social reforms and translated the Bible into several Indian languages. He loved God and people, and accomplished many things for God.

David, son of Jesse, was an ordinary young man, the youngest in his family. He was seemingly an insignificant shepherd on the hills of Bethlehem (1 Samuel 16:11–12). Yet God saw David's heart and had a plan for him. King Saul had been rejected by God for disobedience. While the prophet Samuel mourned Saul's choices, God called Samuel to anoint a different king, one of Jesse's sons.

When Samuel saw the handsome, tall Eliab, he naturally thought, "surely the LORD's anointed stands here before the LORD " (v. 6). However, God's strategy to select a king was much different from Samuel's. In fact, God said no to each of Jesse's sons—except the youngest one. Selecting David as king was definitely not a strategic move on God's part, or so it seemed at first glance. What would a young shepherd have to offer his community, let alone his country?

How comforting to know that the Lord knows our hearts and has His plans for us. *Estera*

Small but Mighty
Ephesians 2:4–10

We are God's handiwork, created in Christ Jesus
to do good works. —EPHESIANS 2:10

There are times late at night in North America's harsh Sonoran Desert where one can hear a faint, high-pitched howl. But you probably wouldn't suspect the source of the sound—the small yet mighty grasshopper mouse, howling at the moon to establish its territory.

This unique rodent (dubbed the "werewolf mouse") is also carnivorous. In fact, it preys on creatures few would dare mess with, such as the scorpion. But the werewolf mouse is uniquely equipped for that particular battle. It not only has a resistance to scorpion venom but it can also convert the toxins into a painkiller!

There's something inspiring about the way this resilient little mouse seems custom-made to survive and even thrive in its harsh environment. As Paul explains in Ephesians 2:10, that kind of marvelous craftsmanship characterizes God's designs for His people as well. Each of us is "God's handiwork" in Jesus, uniquely equipped to contribute to His kingdom. No matter how God has gifted you, you have much to offer. As you embrace with confidence who He's made you to be, you'll be a living witness to the hope and joy of life in Him.

So as you face whatever feels most menacing in your own life, take courage. You may feel small, but through the gifting and empowerment of the Spirit, God can use you to do mighty things. *Monica*

Free at Last
John 8:31–36

If the Son sets you free, you will be free indeed.
—JOHN 8:36

Twenty long years passed before British journalist John McCarthy—a five-year hostage during Lebanon's grueling civil war—met the man who negotiated his release. When McCarthy finally met UN envoy Giandomenico Picco, McCarthy simply said, "Thank you for my freedom!" His heartfelt words carried great weight because Picco had risked his own life during dangerous negotiations to secure freedom for McCarthy and others.

We as believers can relate to such hard-won freedom. Jesus gave up His life—enduring death on a Roman cross—to secure spiritual freedom for all people, including each of us. Now as His children, we know "it is for freedom that Christ has set us free," the apostle Paul boldly declared (Galatians 5:1).

The gospel of John also teaches of freedom in Christ, noting, "If the Son sets you free, you will be free indeed" (John 8:36).

But free in what ways? In Jesus, we experience freedom not only from sin and its hold on us but also from guilt, shame, worry, Satan's lies, superstitions, false teaching, and eternal death. No longer hostages, we have freedom to show love to enemies, walk in kindness, live with hope, and love our neighbors. As we follow the Holy Spirit's leading, we can forgive as we've been forgiven.

For all of this, let's thank God today. Then let's love so others will know the power of His freedom too.

Patricia

Named by God
Ruth 1:19–22

*"Don't call me Naomi," she told them. "Call me Mara,
because the Almighty has made my life very bitter."*
—RUTH 1:20

Riptide. Batgirl. Jumpstart. These are a few names given to counselors at the summer camp our family attends every year. Created by their peers, the camp nicknames usually derive from an embarrassing incident, a funny habit, or a favorite hobby.

Nicknames aren't limited to camp—we even find them used in the Bible. For example, Jesus dubs the apostles James and John the "sons of thunder" (Mark 3:17). It is rare in Scripture for someone to give themselves a nickname, yet it happens when a woman named Naomi asks people to call her "Mara," which means "bitterness" (Ruth 1:20), because both her husband and two sons had died. She felt that God had made her life bitter (v. 21).

The new name Naomi gave herself didn't stick, however, because those devastating losses were not the end of her story. In the midst of her sorrow, God had blessed her with a loving daughter-in-law, Ruth, who eventually remarried and had a son, creating a family for Naomi again.

Although we might sometimes be tempted to give ourselves bitter nicknames, like "failure" or "unloved," based on difficulties we've experienced or mistakes we've made, those names are not the end of our stories. We can replace those labels with the name God has given each of us, "loved one" (Romans 9:25), and look for the ways He's providing for us in even the most challenging of times. ❦ *Lisa*

The Bill Is Paid
Deuteronomy 26:12–15

*You shall give it to the Levite, the foreigner, the fatherless
and the widow.* —DEUTERONOMY 26:12

"What happened to you?" asked Zeal, a Nigerian businessman, as he bent over a hospital bed in Lagos. "Someone shot me," replied the young man, his thigh bandaged. Although the injured man was well enough to return home, he wouldn't be released until he settled his bill—a policy that many government hospitals in the region follow. After consulting with a social worker, Zeal anonymously covered the bill through the charitable fund he'd earlier set up as a way to express his Christian faith. In return, he hopes that those receiving the gift of release will one day give to others too.

The theme of giving from God's bounty pulses throughout the Bible. For instance, when Moses instructed the Israelites on how to live in the Promised Land, he told them to give back to God first (see Deuteronomy 26:1–3) and to care for those in need—the foreigners, orphans, and widows (v. 12). Because they dwelled in a "land flowing with milk and honey" (v. 15), they were to express God's love to the needy.

We too can spread God's love through sharing our material goods, whether big or small. We might not have the opportunity to personally give exactly like Zeal did, but we can ask God to show us how to give or who needs our help. *Amy*

It's Up to God
Matthew 6:5–15

Your will be done. —MATTHEW 6:10

Nate and Sherilyn enjoyed their stop at an omakase restaurant while visiting New York City. Omakase is a Japanese word that translates, "I will leave it up to you," which means customers at such restaurants let the chef choose their meal. Even though it was their first time to try this type of cuisine and it sounded risky, they loved the food the chef chose and prepared for them.

That idea could carry over to our attitude toward God with our prayer requests: "I will leave it up to you." The disciples saw that Jesus "often withdrew to lonely places" to pray (Luke 5:16), so they asked Him one day to teach them how to pray. He told them to ask for their daily needs, forgiveness, and the way out of temptation. Part of His response also suggested an attitude of surrender: "Your will be done, on earth as it is in heaven" (Matthew 6:10).

We can pour out our needs to God because He wants to hear what's on our hearts—and He delights to give. But being human and finite, we don't always know what's best, so it only makes sense to ask with a humble spirit, in submission to Him. We can leave the answer to Him, confident that He's trustworthy and will choose to prepare what's good for us. *Anne*

It's Time to Pray . . . Again
Ephesians 6:10–20

Pray in the Spirit on all occasions with all kinds of prayers and requests. —EPHESIANS 6:18

I pulled into my driveway, waving at my neighbor Myriam and her little girl Elizabeth. Over the years, Elizabeth had grown accustomed to our spontaneous chats lasting longer than the promised "few minutes" and morphing into prayer meetings. She climbed the tree planted in the center of their front yard, dangled her legs over a branch, and busied herself while her mother and I spoke. After a while, Elizabeth hopped down from her roost and ran to where we stood. Grabbing our hands, she smiled and almost sang, "It's time to pray . . . again." Even at an early age, Elizabeth seemed to understand how important prayer was in our friendship.

After encouraging believers to "be strong in the Lord and in his mighty power" (Ephesians 6:10), the apostle Paul offered special insight on the crucial role of continual prayer. He described the necessary armor God's people would need during their spiritual walk with the Lord, who provides protection, discernment, and confidence in His truth (vv. 11–17). However, the apostle emphasized this God-given strength grew from deliberate immersion in the life-giving gift of prayer (vv. 18–20).

God hears and cares about our concerns, whether they're spoken boldly, sobbed silently, or secured deep in a hurting heart. He's always ready to make us strong in His power, as He invites us to pray again and again and again. *Xochitl*

Easily Entangled
Hebrews 2:17–18; 12:1–2

*Throw off everything that hinders and the sin
that so easily entangles.* —HEBREWS 12:1

Soldiers fighting in a sweltering jungle many years ago encountered a frustrating problem. Without warning, a pervasive prickly vine would attach itself to the soldiers' bodies and gear, causing them to be trapped. As they struggled to get free, even more of the plant's tentacles entangled them. The soldiers dubbed the weed the "wait-a-minute" vine because, once entwined and unable to move forward, they were forced to shout out to other members of their team, "Hey, wait a minute, I'm stuck!"

In a similar way, it's hard for us as followers of Jesus to move forward when we're ensnared by sin. Hebrews 12:1 tells us to "throw off everything that hinders and the sin that so easily entangles" and "run with perseverance." But how do we throw off the sin weighing us down?

Jesus is the only one who can free us from pervasive sin in our lives. May we learn to fix our eyes on Him, our Savior (12:2). Because the Son of God became "fully human in every way," He knows what it's like to be tempted—yet not sin (2:17–18; 4:15). Alone, we may be desperately entwined by our own sin, but God wants us to overcome temptation. It's not through our own strength, but His, that we can "throw off" entangling sin and run after His righteousness. *Cindy*

Don't Be Deceived
Genesis 3:1–7

[The devil] is a liar and the father of lies.
—JOHN 8:44

The spotted lanternfly is a pretty insect with speckled outer wings and a splotch of bright red on its inner wings that flashes when it flies. But its beauty is a bit deceptive. This insect, first seen in the US in 2014, is considered invasive to North America, which means it has the potential to harm the environment and economy. The lanternfly will "eat the innards of practically any woody plant," which includes cherry and other fruit trees, and leaves a sticky goo that leads to mold—killing trees outright or leaving them with little energy to grow fruit.

In the story of Adam and Eve, we learn of a different kind of menace. The serpent, Satan, deceived the couple into disobeying God and eating the forbidden fruit so they would "be like God" (Genesis 3:4). But why listen to a serpent? Did his words alone entice Eve, or was there also something attractive about him? Scripture hints at Satan being created beautiful (Ezekiel 28:12). Yet Satan fell by the same temptation he used to entice Eve: "I will make myself like [God]" (Isaiah 14:14; Ezekiel 28:9).

Any beauty Satan now has is used to deceive (Genesis 3:1; John 8:44; 2 Corinthians 11:14). Just as he fell, he seeks to pull others down—or keep them from growing. But we have someone far more powerful on our side! We can run to Jesus, our beautiful Savior. *Alyson*

The Smiling Jesus
Hebrews 1:8–12

God, your God, has set you above your companions by
anointing you with the oil of joy. —HEBREWS 1:9

If you were to play the part of Jesus in a movie, how would you approach the role? That was the challenge faced by Bruce Marchiano, who played Jesus in the 1993 Visual Bible movie *Matthew*. Knowing that millions of viewers would draw conclusions about Jesus based on his work, the weight of getting Christ "right" felt overwhelming. He fell to his knees in prayer and begged Jesus for—well, for Jesus.

Bruce gained insight from the first chapter of Hebrews, where the writer tells us how God the Father set the Son apart by anointing Him "with the oil of joy" (1:9). This kind of joy is one of celebration—a gladness of connection to the Father expressed wholeheartedly. Such joy ruled in Jesus's heart throughout His life. As Hebrews 12:2 describes it, "For the joy set before him he endured the cross, scorning its shame, and sat down at the right hand of the throne of God."

Taking his cue from this Scriptural expression, Bruce offered a uniquely joy-filled portrayal of his Savior. As a result, he became known as "the smiling Jesus." We too can dare to fall to our knees and "beg Jesus for Jesus." May He so fill us with His character that people around us see the expression of His love in us! *Elisa*

Chirpy
1 Kings 17:2–6

*The ravens brought him bread and meat in the
morning and bread and meat in the evening, and he
drank from the brook.* —1 KINGS 17:6

For twelve years, Chirpy, a seagull, has made daily visits
to a man who'd helped him heal from a broken leg. John
wooed Chirpy to himself with dog biscuits and was then
able to nurse him back to health. Though Chirpy resides
in Instow Beach in Devon, England, only between September and March, he and John Sumner find each other
easily—Chirpy flies straight to him when he arrives at
the beach each day, though he doesn't approach any
other human. It's an uncommon relationship, to be sure.

John and Chirpy's bond reminds me of another uncommon relationship between man and bird. When
Elijah, one of God's prophets, was sent into the wilderness to "hide in the Kerith Ravine" during a time
of drought, God said he was to drink from the brook,
and He'd send ravens to supply him with food (1 Kings
17:3–4). Despite the difficult circumstances and surroundings, Elijah would have his needs for food and
water met. Ravens were unlikely caterers—naturally
feeding on unseemly meals themselves—yet they
brought Elijah wholesome food.

It may not surprise us that a man would help a bird,
but when birds provide for a man with "bread and meat
in the morning and bread and meat in the evening," it
can only be explained by God's power and care (v. 6).
Like Elijah, we too can trust in His provision for us.

 Kirsten

Turn and Run
1 Peter 5:8–10

Resist [the devil], standing firm in the faith.
—1 PETER 5:9

Ali was a beautiful, smart, and talented teenager with loving parents. But after high school something prompted her to try heroin. Her parents noticed changes in her and sent her to a rehabilitation facility after Ali eventually admitted the impact it was having on her. After treatment, they asked what she would tell her friends about trying drugs. Her advice: "Just turn and run." She urged that "just saying no" wasn't enough.

Tragically, Ali relapsed and died at age twenty-two of an overdose. In an attempt to keep others from the same fate, her heartbroken parents appeared on a local news program encouraging listeners to "run for Ali" by staying far from situations where they could be exposed to drugs and other dangers.

The apostle Paul urged his spiritual son Timothy (and us) to run from evil (2 Timothy 2:22), and the apostle Peter likewise warned, "Your enemy the devil prowls around like a roaring lion looking for someone to devour. Resist him, standing firm in the faith" (1 Peter 5:8–9).

None of us is immune to temptation. And often the best thing to do is to steer clear of situations where we'll be tempted—though they can't always be avoided. But we can be better prepared by having a strong faith in God based in the Bible and strengthened through prayer. When we "[stand] firm in the faith" we'll know when to turn and run to Him. ❧ *Alyson*

Trusting God in Times of Sorrow

2 Timothy 1:6–12

I know whom I have believed. —*2 TIMOTHY 1:12*

When a man known as "Papa John" learned he had terminal cancer, he and his wife, Carol, sensed God calling them to share their illness journey online. Believing that God would minister through their vulnerability, they posted their moments of joy and their sorrow and pain for two years.

When Carol wrote that her husband "went into the outstretched arms of Jesus," hundreds of people responded, with many thanking Carol for their openness. One person remarked that hearing about dying from a Christian point of view was healthy, for "we all have to die" someday. Another said that although she'd never met the couple personally, she couldn't express how much encouragement she'd received through their witness of trusting God.

Although Papa John sometimes felt excruciating pain, he and Carol shared their story so they could demonstrate how God upheld them. They knew their testimony would bear fruit for God, echoing what Paul wrote to Timothy when he suffered: "I know whom I have believed, and am convinced that he is able to guard what I have entrusted to him until that day" (2 Timothy 1:12).

God can use even the death of a loved one to strengthen our faith in Him (and the faith of others) through the grace we receive in Christ Jesus (v. 9). If you're experiencing anguish and difficulty, know that He can bring comfort and peace. *Amy*

Beautiful Fruit
Luke 8:4–8, 11–15

The seed is the word of God. —LUKE 8:11

"Kids should be able to throw a seed anywhere they want [in the garden] and see what pops up," suggests Rebecca Lemos-Otero, founder of City Blossoms. While this is not a model for careful gardening, it reflects the reality that each seed has the potential to burst forth with life. Since 2004, City Blossoms has created gardens for schools and neighborhoods in low-income areas. The kids are learning about nutrition and gaining job skills through gardening. Rebecca says, "Having a lively green space in an urban area . . . creates a way for kids to be outside doing something productive and beautiful."

Jesus told a story about the scattering of seed that had the potential of producing "a hundred times more than was sown" (Luke 8:8). That seed was God's good news planted on "good soil," which He explained is "honest, good-hearted people who hear God's word, cling to it, and patiently produce a huge harvest" (v. 15 NLT).

The only way we can be fruitful, Jesus said, is to stay connected to Him (John 15:4). As we're taught by Christ and cling to Him, the Spirit produces in us His fruit of "love, joy, peace, forbearance, kindness, goodness, faithfulness, gentleness and self-control" (Galatians 5:22–23). He uses the fruit He produces in us to touch the lives of others, who are then changed and grow fruit from their own lives. This makes for a beautiful life. ❦ *Anne*

Bring What You Have
John 6:4–14

"Bring them here to me," [Jesus] said.
—*MATTHEW 14:18*

"Stone Soup," an old tale with many versions, tells of a starving man who comes to a village, but no one there can spare a crumb of food for him. He puts a stone and water in a pot over a fire. Intrigued, the villagers watch him as he begins to stir his "soup." Eventually, one brings a couple of potatoes to add to the mix; another has a few carrots. One person adds an onion, another a handful of barley. A farmer donates some milk. Eventually, the "stone soup" becomes a tasty chowder.

That tale illustrates the value of sharing, but it also reminds us to bring what we have, even when it seems to be insignificant. In John 6:1–14 we read of a boy who appears to be the only person in a huge crowd who thought about bringing some food. Jesus's disciples had little use for the boy's sparse lunch of five loaves and two fishes. But when it was surrendered, Jesus increased it and fed thousands of hungry people!

I once heard someone say, "You don't have to feed the five thousand. You just have to bring your loaves and fishes." Just as Jesus took one person's meal and multiplied it far beyond anyone's expectations or imagination (v. 11), He'll accept our surrendered efforts, talents, and service. He just wants us to be willing to bring what we have to Him. *Cindy*

The Whispering Gallery

Psalm 18:1–6, 16–19

*In my distress I called to the LORD; I cried to
my God for help.* —PSALM 18:6

In the towering dome of London's St. Paul's Cathedral, visitors can climb 259 steps to access the Whispering Gallery. There you can whisper and be heard by another person anywhere along the circular walkway, even across the enormous abyss nearly one hundred feet away. Engineers explain this anomaly as a result of the spherical shape of the dome and the low intensity sound waves of a whisper.

How we long to be confident that God hears our agonized whispers! The Psalms are filled with testimonies that He hears us—our cries, prayers, and whispers. David writes, "In my distress I called to the Lord; I cried to my God for help" (Psalm 18:6). Over and over again, he and other psalmists plead, "Hear my prayer" (4:1), my voice (5:3), my groans (102:20). Sometimes the expression is more of a whispered, "Hear me" (77:1), where the "heart meditated and [the] spirit asked" (77:6).

In answer to these pleas, the psalmists—like David in Psalm 18:6—reveal that God is listening: "From his temple he heard my voice; my cry came before him, into his ears." Since the actual temple wasn't yet built, might David have been referring to God listening in His heavenly dwelling?

From His very own "whispering gallery" in the dome of the heavens above the earth, God bends to our deepest murmurs, even our whispers . . . and listens. *Elisa*

Homeless by Choice
Hebrews 2:9–18

Because he himself suffered when he was tempted,
he is able to help those who are being tempted.
—*HEBREWS 2:18*

Keith Wasserman has chosen to be homeless for a few days eleven different times in eleven different cities in order to grow in love and compassion. "I go to live on the streets to expand my perspective and understanding of people who have no homes to live in," says Keith, executive director of Good Works, Inc.

I'm wondering whether Keith's approach to become one with those he's serving might be a small picture of what Jesus did for us. God himself, the Creator of the universe, chose to confine himself to the vulnerable state of a baby, to live as a human, to experience what we all experience, and to ultimately die at the hand of humans so we can experience a relationship with God.

The writer of the book of Hebrews stated that Jesus "shared in [our] humanity so that by his death he might break the power of him who holds the power of death— that is, the devil" (2:14). Jesus was made lower than the angels, even though He's their Creator (v. 9). He became human and died, even though He's immortal. And He suffered for us, even though He's the all-powerful God. Why would He do this? So He could help bring reconciliation between us and God (vv. 17–18) and help us when we go through temptations.

May we experience His love today, knowing that He understands our humanity and has already provided the way for us to be cleansed from our sins. *Estera*

Qualified in God's Eyes
Genesis 6:9–18

[Noah] walked faithfully with God. —GENESIS 6:9

A technology-consulting firm hired me after college although I couldn't write a line of computer code and had very little business knowledge. During the interview process for my entry-level position, I learned that the company did not place high value on work experience. Instead, personal qualities such as the ability to solve problems creatively, exercise good judgment, and work well with a team were more important. The company assumed new workers could be taught the necessary skills as long as they were the kind of people the company was looking for.

Noah didn't have the right resume for the job of constructing the ark—he wasn't a boat builder or even a carpenter. Noah was a farmer, a man comfortable with dirt on his shirt and a plow in his hands. Yet as God decided how to deal with the evil in the world at that time, Noah stood out because "he walked faithfully with God" (Genesis 6:9). God valued the teachableness of Noah's heart—the strength to resist the corruption around him and to do what was right.

When opportunities to serve God come our way, we may not feel qualified for the work. Thankfully, God is not necessarily concerned with our skill set. He prizes our character, love for Him, and willingness to trust Him. When these qualities are being developed inside us by the Spirit, He can use us in big or small ways to accomplish His will on earth. *Jennifer*

The Maker of the Moon
Jeremiah 31:33–37

*[The Lord said,] "I will be their God and they will
be my people."* —*JEREMIAH 31:33*

In July 1969, after astronauts set the Eagle down in the
Sea of Tranquility, Neil Armstrong stepped onto the
moon's surface and said, "That's one small step for man,
one giant leap for mankind." He was the first human to
walk on the moon. Other space travelers followed, including the commander of the last Apollo mission, Gene
Cernan. "There I was, and there you are, the Earth—dy-
namic, overwhelming, and I felt . . . it was just too beautiful to happen by accident," Cernan said, "There has
to be somebody bigger than you and bigger than me."
Even from their unique view in deep space, these men
understood their smallness in comparison to the vastness
of the universe.

The prophet Jeremiah also considered the immensity
of God as Creator and Sustainer of the earth and beyond.
The Maker of all promised to reveal himself intimately as
He offered His people love, forgiveness, and hope (Jeremiah 31:33–34). Jeremiah affirms God's enormity as He
who "appoints the sun to shine by day, who decrees the
moon and stars to shine by night" (v. 35). Our Creator
and Lord Almighty will reign above all as He works to
redeem all of His people (vv. 36–37).

We'll never finish exploring the immeasurable vastness
of the heavens and depths of the earth's foundations. But
we can stand in awe at the complexity of the universe
and trust the maker of the moon—and the maker of everything else. *Xochitl*

The Sweetest Harvest

Isaiah 5:1–7

I am the vine; you are the branches. If you remain in me and I in you, you will bear much fruit. —*JOHN 15:5*

When we purchased our home, we inherited an established grapevine. As gardening novices, my family invested considerable time learning how to prune, water, and care for it. When our first harvest came, I popped a grape from the vine into my mouth—only to be disappointed with an unpleasant, sour taste.

The frustration I felt about painstakingly tending a grapevine, only to have a bitter harvest, echoes the tone of Isaiah 5. There we read an allegory of God's relationship to the nation of Israel. God, pictured as a farmer, had cleared the hillside of debris, planted good vines, built a watchtower for protection, and crafted a press to enjoy the results of His harvest (Isaiah 5:1–2). To the farmer's dismay, the vineyard, representing Israel, produced sour-tasting grapes of selfishness, injustice, and oppression (v. 7). Eventually, God reluctantly destroyed the vineyard while saving a remnant of vines that someday would produce a good harvest.

In the gospel of John, Jesus revisits the vineyard illustration, saying, "I am the vine; you are the branches. If you remain in me and I in you, you will bear much fruit" (John 15:5). In this parallel imagery, Jesus pictures believers in Him as grapevine branches connected to Him, the main vine. Now, as we remain connected to Jesus through prayerful reliance on His Spirit, we have direct access to the spiritual nourishment that will produce the sweetest fruit of all, love. *Lisa*

Rich Toward God
1 Timothy 6:1–11

Godliness with contentment is great gain.
—1 TIMOTHY 6:6

Growing up during the Great Depression, my parents knew deep hardship as children. As a result, they were thrifty adults—hard-working and grateful money stewards. At the same time, they were never greedy. They gave time, talent, and treasury to their church, charity groups, and the needy. Indeed, they handled their money wisely and gave cheerfully.

As believers in Jesus, my parents took to heart the apostle Paul's warning: "Those who want to get rich fall into temptation and a trap and into many foolish and harmful desires that plunge people into ruin and destruction" (1 Timothy 6:9). Paul gave this advice to Timothy, the young pastor in the city of Ephesus, a wealthy city where riches tempted rich and poor alike.

"The love of money is a root of all kinds of evil," Paul warned. "Some people, eager for money, have wandered from the faith and pierced themselves with many griefs" (v. 10). What, then, is the antidote to greed? Being "rich toward God," said Jesus (see Luke 12:13–21). By pursuing, appreciating, and loving our heavenly Father above all, He remains our chief delight. As the psalmist wrote, "Satisfy us in the morning with your unfailing love, that we may sing for joy and be glad all our days" (Psalm 90:14).

Rejoicing in Him daily relieves us of coveting, leaving us contented. May Jesus redeem our heart's desires, making us rich toward God! *Patricia*

Greedy Grasping
Ecclesiastes 4:4–8

*Better one handful with tranquility than two
handfuls with toil and chasing after the wind.*
—ECCLESIASTES 4:6

In the ancient fable *The Boy and the Filberts* (Nuts), a boy
sticks his hand into a jar of nuts and grabs a great fistful.
But his hand is so full that it gets stuck in the jar. Unwilling to lose even a little of his bounty, the boy begins
to weep. Eventually, he is counseled to let go of some of
the nuts so the jar will let go of his hand. Greed can be
a hard boss.

The wise teacher of Ecclesiastes illustrates this moral
with a lesson on hands and what they say about us. He
compared and contrasted the lazy with the greedy when
he wrote: "Fools fold their hands and ruin themselves.
Better one handful with tranquility than two handfuls
with toil and chasing after the wind" (4:5–6). While the
lazy procrastinate until they're ruined, those who pursue
wealth come to realize their efforts are "meaningless—a
miserable business!" (v. 8).

According to the teacher, the desired state is to relax
from the toil of greedy grasping in order to find contentment in what truly belongs to us. For that which is ours
will always remain. As Jesus said, "What good is it for
someone to gain the whole world, yet forfeit their soul"
(Mark 8:36). *Remi*

Healing Words
Proverbs 16:20–24

The hearts of the wise make their mouths prudent, and their lips promote instruction. —PROVERBS 16:23

A recent study has shown that encouraging words from a health-care provider can help patients recuperate faster from their ailments. A simple experiment exposed volunteer study participants to a skin allergen to make them itch and then compared the reactions between those who received assurance from their physician and those who didn't. Patients who received encouragement from their doctors had less discomfort and itching than their counterparts.

The writer of Proverbs knew how important encouraging words can be. "Gracious words" bring "healing to the bones," he wrote (Proverbs 16:24). The positive effect of words isn't limited to our health: when we heed the wisdom of instruction, we're also more likely to prosper in our efforts (v. 20). So too encouragement buoys us for the challenges we face now and may encounter in the future.

We may not yet fully understand how wisdom and encouragement bring strength and healing to our daily lives. Yet the cheers and guidance of our parents, coaches, and colleagues seem to help us endure difficulty and steer us toward success. Similarly, the inspired words of the Bible bring us encouragement when we face trials, equipping us to bear up under even the most unthinkable circumstances. *Help us, God, to be strengthened by your wisdom and to, in turn, offer the healing and hope of "gracious words" to those you've placed in our lives.*

Kirsten

Strong and Courageous

Joshua 1:1–9

As I was with Moses, so I will be with you; I will never leave you nor forsake you. —JOSHUA 1:5

Each night, as young Caleb closed his eyes, he felt the darkness envelop him. The silence of his room was regularly suspended by the creaking of the wooden house in Costa Rica. Then the bats in the attic became more active. His mother had put a nightlight in his room, but the young boy still feared the dark. One night Caleb's dad posted a Bible verse on the footboard of his bed. It read: "Be strong and courageous. Do not be afraid; . . . for the LORD your God will be with you" (Joshua 1:9). Caleb began to read those words each night—and he left that promise from God on his footboard until he went away to college.

In Joshua 1, we read of the transition of leadership to Joshua after Moses died. The command to "be strong and courageous" was repeated several times to Joshua and the Israelites to emphasize its importance (vv. 6–7, 9). Surely, they felt trepidation as they faced an uncertain future, but God reassuringly said, "As I was with Moses, so I will be with you; I will never leave you nor forsake you" (v. 5).

It's natural to have fears, but it's detrimental to our physical and spiritual health to live in a state of constant fear. Just as God encouraged His servants of old, we too can be strong and courageous because of the One who promises to always be with us. *Cindy*

A Divine Duet
John 15:1–11

*If you remain in me and I in you, you will
bear much fruit.* —JOHN 15:5

At a children's music recital, I watched a teacher and student seat themselves in front of a piano. Before their duet began, the teacher leaned over and whispered some last-minute instructions. As music flowed from the instrument, I noticed that the student played a simple melody while the teacher's accompaniment added depth and richness to the song. Near the end of the piece, the teacher nodded his approval.

Our life in Jesus is much more like a duet than a solo performance. Sometimes, though, I forget that He's "sitting next to me," and it's only by His power and guidance that I can "play" at all. I try to hit all the right notes on my own—to obey God in my own strength, but this usually ends up seeming fake and hollow. I try to handle problems with my limited ability, but the result is often discord with others.

My Teacher's presence makes all the difference. When I rely on Jesus to help me, I find my life is more honoring to God. I serve joyfully, love freely, and am amazed as God blesses my relationships. It's like Jesus told His first disciples, "If you remain in me and I in you, you will bear much fruit; apart from me you can do nothing" (John 15:5).

Each day we play a duet with our good Teacher—it's His grace and power that carry the melody of our spiritual lives. *Jennifer*

Removing the Intruder
Ephesians 5:25–33

Husbands, love your wives, just as Christ loved the church and gave himself up for her. —EPHESIANS 5:25

It wasn't quite dawn when my husband rose from bed and went into the kitchen. I saw the light flip on and off and wondered at his action. Then I recalled that the previous morning I'd yelped at the sight of an "intruder" on our kitchen counter. Translated: an undesirable creature of the six-legged variety. My husband knew my paranoia and immediately arrived to remove it. This morning he'd risen early to ensure our kitchen was bug-free so I could enter without concern. What a guy!

My husband awoke with me on his mind, putting my need before his own. To me, his action illustrates the love Paul describes in Ephesians 5:25, "Husbands, love your wives, just as Christ loved the church and gave himself up for her." Paul goes on, "Husbands ought to love their wives as their own bodies. He who loves his wife loves himself" (v. 28). Paul's comparison of a husband's love to the love of Christ pivots on how Jesus put our needs before His own. My husband knows I'm afraid of certain intruders, so he made my concern his priority.

That principle doesn't apply to husbands only. Following the example of Jesus, each of us can lovingly sacrifice to help remove an intruder of stress, fear, shame, or anxiety so someone else can move more freely in the world.

Elisa

The Kindness Man
Luke 7:11–17

When the Lord saw her, his heart went out to her.
—LUKE 7:13

Disillusioned and wanting a more meaningful life, Leon quit his job in finance. Then one day he saw a homeless man holding up this sign at a street corner: KINDNESS IS THE BEST MEDICINE. Leon says, "Those words rammed straight into me. It was an epiphany."

Leon decided to begin his new life by creating an international organization to promote kindness. He travels around the world, relying on strangers to provide him with food, gas, and a place to stay. Then he rewards them, through his organization, with good deeds such as feeding orphans or building on to a school for underprivileged children. He says, "It's sometimes seen as being soft. But kindness is a profound strength."

Christ's very essence as God is goodness, so kindness naturally flowed from Him. I love the story of what Jesus did when He came upon the funeral procession of a widow's only son (Luke 7:11–17). The grieving woman most likely was dependent on her son for financial support. We don't read in the story that anyone asked Jesus to intervene. Purely from the goodness of His nature (v. 13), He was concerned and brought her son back to life. The people said of Christ, "God has come to help his people" (v. 16). ❧ *Anne*

Strength for the Journey
1 Kings 19:1–9

*All at once an angel touched him and said,
"Get up and eat." —1 KINGS 19:5*

One summer, I faced what seemed an impossible task—a big writing project with a looming deadline. Having spent day after day on my own, endeavoring to get the words onto the page, I felt exhausted and discouraged, and I wanted to give up. A wise friend asked me, "When's the last time you felt refreshed? Maybe you need to allow yourself to rest and to enjoy a good meal."

I knew immediately that she was right. Her advice made me think of Elijah and the terrifying message he received from Jezebel (1 Kings 19:2)—although, of course, my writing project wasn't anywhere near the cosmic scale of the prophet's experience. After Elijah triumphed over the false prophets on Mount Carmel, Jezebel sent word that she would capture and kill him, and he despaired, longing to die. But then he enjoyed a good sleep and was twice visited by an angel who gave him food to eat. After God renewed his physical strength, he was able to continue with his journey.

When the "journey is too much" for us (v. 7), we might need to rest and enjoy a healthy and satisfying meal. For when we are exhausted or hungry, we can easily succumb to disappointment or fear. But when God meets our physical needs through His resources, as much as possible in this fallen world, we can take the next step in serving Him. *Amy*

Inside the Fire
Daniel 3:12–18

I see four men walking around in the fire, unbound and unharmed. —DANIEL 3:25

A wildfire in Andilla, Spain, scorched nearly 50,000 acres of woodland. However, in the middle of the devastation, a group of nearly 1,000 bright green cypress trees remained standing. The trees' ability to retain water had allowed them to safely endure the fire.

During King Nebuchadnezzar's reign in Babylon, a small cluster of friends survived the flames of the king's wrath. Shadrach, Meshach, and Abednego refused to worship a statue Nebuchadnezzar had created, and they told him, "If we are thrown into the blazing furnace, the God we serve is able to deliver us from it" (Daniel 3:17). Infuriated, the monarch cranked up the heat seven times hotter than normal (v. 19).

The soldiers who carried out the king's orders and tossed the friends into the blaze were burned up, yet onlookers watched Shadrach, Meshach, and Abednego walk around inside the flames "unbound and unharmed." Someone else was in the furnace as well—a fourth man who looked "like a son of the gods" (v. 25). Many scholars believe this was a preincarnate appearance of Jesus.

Jesus is with us when we face intimidation and trials. In the moments when we're urged to give in to pressure, we don't have to be afraid. We may not always know how or when God will help us, but we know He's with us. He'll give us the strength to stay faithful to Him through every "fire" we endure. *Jennifer*

Breath and Brevity
Psalm 139:7–16

*All the days ordained for me were written in your book
before one of them came to be.* —PSALM 139:16

Mom, my sisters, and I waited by Dad's bed as his breaths became shallower and less and less frequent—until they were no more. Dad was a few days shy of eighty-nine when he slipped quietly into the life beyond where God awaited him. His departure left us with a void where he once resided and only memories and mementos to remind us of him. Yet we have the hope that one day we'll be reunited.

We have that hope because we believe Dad is with God, who knows and loves him. When Dad breathed his first breath, God was there breathing breath into his lungs (Isaiah 42:5). Yet even before his first and with every breath in between, God was intimately involved in each detail of Dad's life, just as He is in yours and mine. It was God who wonderfully designed and "knit" him together in the womb (Psalm 139:13–14). And when Dad breathed his last breath, God's Spirit was there, holding him in love and carrying him to be with Him (vv. 7–10).

The same is true for all of God's children. Every moment of our brief life on Earth is known by Him (vv. 1–4). We're precious to Him. With each day remaining and in anticipation of the life beyond, let's join with "everything that has breath" to praise Him. "Praise the LORD"! (150:6). ❧ *Alyson*

Talking Tables
Acts 2:42–47

Every day they continued to meet together in the temple courts. —ACTS 2:46

Loneliness is one of the greatest threats to our sense of well-being, affecting our health through our behaviors on social media, food consumption, and the like. One study suggests that nearly two-thirds of all people—regardless of age or gender—feel lonely at least some of the time. One British supermarket has created "talking tables" in their store cafés as a way to foster connection between people. Those looking for human interaction simply seat themselves at a table designated for that purpose, joining others or indicating a desire to be joined. Conversation ensues, providing a sense of connection and community.

The people of the early church were committed to shared connection too. Without each other, they would likely have felt very alone in the practice of their faith, which was still new to the world. Not only did they "[devote] themselves to the apostles' teaching" to learn what following Jesus meant, they also "[met] together in the temple courts" and "broke bread in their homes" for mutual encouragement and fellowship (Acts 2:42, 46).

We need human connection; God designed us that way! Painful seasons of loneliness point to that need. Like the people of the early church, it's important for us to engage in the human companionship our well-being requires and to offer it to those around us who also need it. *Kirsten*

No Fishing Allowed
Psalm 130

[God will] hurl all our iniquities into the depths of the sea. —MICAH 7:19

Holocaust survivor Corrie ten Boom knew the importance of forgiveness. In her book *Tramp for the Lord*, she says her favorite mental picture was of forgiven sins thrown into the sea. "When we confess our sins, God casts them into the deepest ocean, gone forever. . . . I believe God then places a sign out there that says No Fishing Allowed."

She points to an important truth that believers in Jesus can sometimes fail to grasp—when God forgives our wrongdoing, we're forgiven fully! We don't have to keep dredging up our shameful deeds, wallowing in any mucky feelings. Rather we can accept His grace and forgiveness, following Him in freedom.

We see this idea of "no fishing allowed" in Psalm 130. The psalmist proclaims that although God is just, He forgives the sin of those who repent: "But with you there is forgiveness" (v. 4). As the psalmist waits for God, putting his trust in Him (v. 5), he states in faith that He "himself will redeem Israel from all their sins" (v. 8). Those who believe will find "full redemption" (v. 7).

When we're caught in feelings of shame and unworthiness, we can't serve God with our whole hearts. Instead, we're restricted by our past. If you feel stymied by the wrong you've done, ask God to help you fully believe in His gift of forgiveness and new life. He's cast your sins into the ocean! *Amy*

The Privilege of Prayer
1 Chronicles 29:11–19

Give my son Solomon the wholehearted devotion
to keep your commands, statutes and decrees.
—*1 CHRONICLES 29:19*

Country artist Chris Stapleton's deeply personal song, "Daddy Doesn't Pray Anymore," was inspired by his own father's prayers for him. The poignant lyrics reveal the reason his father's prayers ended: not disillusionment or weariness, but his own death. Stapleton imagines that now, instead of speaking with Jesus in prayer, his dad is walking and talking face-to-face with Jesus.

Stapleton's recollection of his father's prayers for him brings to mind a biblical father's prayer for his son. As King David's life ebbed away, he prepared for his son Solomon to take over as the next king of Israel.

After assembling the nation together to anoint Solomon, David led the people in prayer, as he'd done many times before. As David recounted God's faithfulness to Israel, he prayed for the people to remain loyal to Him. Then he included a personal prayer specifically for his son, asking God to "give my son Solomon the wholehearted devotion to keep your commands, statutes and decrees" (1 Chronicles 29:19).

We too have the remarkable privilege to faithfully pray for the people God has placed in our lives. Our example of faithfulness can make an indelible impact that will remain even after we're gone. Just as God continued to work out the answers to David's prayers for Solomon and Israel after he was gone, so too the impact of our prayers outlives us. *Lisa*

Sweeter than Honey
Proverbs 16:1–2, 21–24

*Gracious words are a honeycomb, sweet to the soul and
healing to the bones.* —PROVERBS 16:24

His topic was racial tension. Yet the speaker remained
calm and collected. Standing on stage before a large audience, he spoke boldly—but with grace, humility, kindness, and even humor. Soon the tense audience visibly
relaxed, laughing along with the speaker about the dilemma they all faced: how to resolve their hot issue, but
cool down their feelings and words. Yes, how to tackle a
sour topic with sweet grace.

King Solomon advised this same approach for all of
us: "Gracious words are a honeycomb, sweet to the soul
and healing to the bones" (Proverbs 16:24). In this way,
"The hearts of the wise make . . . their lips promote instruction" (v. 23).

Why would a powerful king like Solomon devote time
to addressing how we speak? Because words can destroy.
During Solomon's time, kings relied on messengers for
information about their nations, and calm and reliable
messengers were highly valued. They used prudent
words and reasoned tongues, not overreacting or speaking harshly, no matter the issue.

We all can benefit by gracing our opinions and thoughts
with godly and prudent sweetness. In Solomon's words,
"To humans belong the plans of the heart, but from the
LORD comes the proper answer of the tongue" (v. 1).

❦ *Patricia*

Perfectly Placed
Job 38:4–11

Where were you when I laid the earth's foundation?
—JOB 38:4

Scientists know our planet is precisely the right distance from the sun to benefit from its heat. A little closer and all the water would evaporate, as on Venus. Only a bit farther and everything would freeze like it does on Mars. Earth is also just the right size to generate the right amount of gravity. Less would make everything weightlessly sterile like our moon, while more gravity would trap poisonous gases that suffocate life as on Jupiter.

The intricate physical, chemical, and biological interactions that comprise our world bear the imprint of a sophisticated Designer. We catch a glimpse of this complex craftsmanship when God speaks to Job about things beyond our understanding. "Where were you when I laid the earth's foundation?" God asks. "Who marked off its dimensions? Surely you know! Who stretched a measuring line across it? On what were its footings set, or who laid its cornerstone?" (Job 38:4–6).

This glimpse of creation's magnitude causes us to wonder at Earth's mighty oceans bowing before the One who "shut up the sea behind doors when it burst forth from the womb, . . . [who said] 'This far you may come and no farther' " (vv. 8–11). In wonder may we sing with the morning stars and shout for joy with the angels (v. 7), for this elaborate world was made for us that we might know and trust God. *Remi*

Never Give Up Hope
Luke 8:40–48

*[Jesus] said to her, "Daughter, your faith has healed
you. Go in peace." —LUKE 8:48*

When my friend received a diagnosis of cancer, the doctor advised her to get her affairs in order. She called me, sobbing, worried about her husband and young children. I shared her urgent prayer request with our mutual friends. We rejoiced when a second doctor encouraged her to never give up hope and confirmed his team would do all they could to help. Though some days were harder than others, she focused on God instead of the odds stacked against her. She never gave up.

My friend's persevering faith reminds me of the desperate woman in Luke 8. Weary from twelve years of ongoing suffering, disappointment, and isolation, she approached Jesus from behind and stretched her hand toward the hem of His robe. Her immediate healing followed her act of faith: persistently hoping . . . believing Jesus was able to do what others couldn't . . . no matter how impossible her situation seemed (vv. 43–44).

We may experience pain that feels endless, situations that appear hopeless, or waiting that seems unbearable. We may endure moments when the odds against us are stacked high and wide. We may not experience the healing we long for as we continue trusting Christ. But even then, Jesus invites us to keep reaching for Him, to trust Him and never give up hope, and to believe He is always able, always trustworthy, and always within reach.

❧ *Xochitl*

Sending Out an SOS
Psalm 34:1–10

I sought the LORD, and he answered me.
—PSALM 34:4

When the hut of a settler in a mountainous region of Alaska caught fire, the settler was left without adequate shelter and with few provisions in the coldest state in the US—in the middle of a frigid winter. Three weeks later, the man was finally rescued when an aircraft flew over and spied the large SOS he had stamped out in the snow and darkened with soot.

The psalmist David was certainly in dire straits. He was being pursued by jealous King Saul, who sought to kill him. So he fled to the city of Gath, where he pretended to be insane in order to preserve his life (see 1 Samuel 21). Out of those events emerged Psalm 34, where David cried out in prayer to God and found peace (vv. 4, 6). God heard his pleas and delivered him.

Are you in a desperate situation and crying out for help? Be assured that God still hears and responds to our desperate prayers today. As with David, He's attentive to our distress calls and takes away our fears (v. 4)—and sometimes even saves us "out of [our] troubles" (v. 6). Scripture invites us to "cast [our] cares on the LORD and he will sustain [us]" (Psalm 55:22). When we turn our difficult circumstances over to God, we can trust that He'll provide the help we need. We're secure in His capable hands. *Alyson*

Strangers in Your Midst
Leviticus 19:33–37

*Love them as yourself, for you were foreigners
in Egypt.* —LEVITICUS 19:34

When I moved to a new country, one of my first experiences left me feeling unwelcome. After finding a seat in the little church where my husband was preaching that day, a gruff older gentleman startled me when he said, "Move along down." His wife apologized as she explained that I was sitting in the pew they always occupied. Years later I learned that congregations used to rent out pews, which raised money for the church and also ensured no one could take another person's seat. Apparently, some of that mentality carried on through the decades.

Later, I reflected on how God instructed the Israelites to welcome foreigners, in contrast to cultural practices such as I encountered. In setting out the laws that would allow His people to flourish, He reminded them to welcome foreigners because they themselves were once foreigners (Leviticus 19:34). Not only were they to treat strangers with kindness (v. 33) but they were also to "love them as [themselves]" (v. 34). God had rescued them from oppression in Egypt, giving them a home in a land "flowing with milk and honey" (Exodus 3:17). He expected His people to love others who also made their home there.

As you encounter strangers in your midst, ask God to reveal any cultural practices that might keep you from sharing His love with them. *Amy*

Wonderful Reward
Psalm 119:17–24

*Open my eyes that I may see wonderful things
in your law. —PSALM 119:18*

Donelan, a teacher, had always been a reader, but one day it literally paid off. She was planning a trip and reviewing her lengthy travel insurance policy when on page seven she discovered a wonderful reward. As part of their "It Pays to Read" contest, the company was giving $10,000 to the first person to read that far into the contract. They also donated thousands of dollars to schools in Donelan's area for children's literacy. She says, "I've always been that nerd who reads contracts. I was the most surprised of anyone!"

The psalmist wanted his eyes opened to "see wonderful things" about God (Psalm 119:18). He must have understood that God wants to be known, so he longed for a deeper closeness to Him. His desire was to see more of who God is, what He'd already given, and how to follow Him more closely (vv. 24, 98). He wrote, "Oh, how I love your law! I meditate on it all day long" (v. 97).

We too have the privilege of taking time to ponder God, His character, and His provisions—to learn about and grow closer to Him. God longs to instruct us, guide us, and open our hearts to who He is. When we search for Him, He rewards. *Anne*

Hand Made for You
Ephesians 2:4–10

We are God's handiwork, created in Christ Jesus to do good works, which God prepared in advance for us to do.
—EPHESIANS 2:10

My grandmother was a talented seamstress who won contests in her native Texas. Throughout my life, she celebrated hallmark occasions with a hand-sewn gift. A burgundy mohair sweater for my high school graduation. A turquoise quilt for my marriage. I'd fold over a corner of each custom-crafted item to discover her signature tag reading, "Handmade for you by Munna." With every embroidered word, I sensed my grandmother's love for me and received a powerful statement of her faith in my future.

Paul wrote to the Ephesians of their purpose in this world, describing them as "God's handiwork, created in Christ Jesus to do good works" (2:10). Here "handiwork" denotes a work of art or a masterpiece. Paul goes on to describe that God's handiwork in creating us would result in our handiwork of creating good works—or expressions of our restored relationship with Jesus—for His glory in our world. We can never be saved by our own good works, but when God hand makes us for His purposes, He can use us to bring others toward His great love.

With her head bowed over her needle, my Munna hand made items to communicate her love for me and her passion that I discover my purpose on this planet. And with His fingers shaping the details of our days, God stitches His love and purposes in our hearts that we might experience Him for ourselves and demonstrate His handiwork to others. *Elisa*

Loving Connection
Luke 10:38–42

Whoever heeds life-giving correction will be at home among the wise. —PROVERBS 15:31

For more than fifty years, my dad strove for excellence as an editor. His passion wasn't to just look for mistakes but also to make the copy better in terms of clarity, logic, flow, and grammar. Dad used a green pen for his corrections, rather than a red one. A green pen he felt was "friendlier," while slashes of red might be jarring to a novice or less confident writer. His objective was to gently point out a better way.

When Jesus corrected people, He did so in love. In some circumstances—such as when He was confronted with the hypocrisy of the Pharisees (Matthew 23)—He rebuked them harshly, yet still for their benefit. But in the case of his friend Martha, a gentle correction was all that was needed (Luke 10:38–42). While the Pharisees responded poorly to His rebuke, Martha remained one of His dearest friends (John 11:5).

Correction can be uncomfortable and few of us like it. Sometimes, because of our pride, it's hard to receive it graciously. The book of Proverbs talks much about wisdom and indicates that "heeding correction" is a sign of wisdom and understanding (15:31–32).

God's loving correction helps us to adjust our direction and to follow Him more closely. Those who refuse it are sternly warned (v. 10), but those who respond to it through the power of the Holy Spirit will gain wisdom and understanding (vv. 31–32). *Cindy*

Is There Hope?
Romans 8:31–39

If God is for us, who can be against us?
—ROMANS 8:31

Edward Payson (1783–1827) led an extremely difficult life. The death of his younger brother shook him to the core. He struggled with bipolar disorder, and he was affected by extreme migraine headaches for days. If this wasn't enough, a fall from a horse led to paralysis of his arm, and he almost died from tuberculosis! Surprisingly, his response wasn't one of despair and hopelessness. His friends said that before Edward passed away, his joy was intense. How could that be?

In his letter to the believers in Rome, the apostle Paul expressed his complete confidence in the reality of God's love regardless of circumstances. He asked with boldness, "If God is for us, who can be against us?" (Romans 8:31). If God gave His very own Son, Jesus, to save us, then He will provide everything we need to finish this life well. Paul listed seven seemingly unbearable situations that he himself faced: trouble, hardship, persecution, famine, nakedness, danger, and the sword (v. 35). He didn't imply that Christ's love would stop bad things from happening. But Paul said that "in all these things we are more than conquerors through him who loved us" (v. 37).

Through the uncertainty of this world, God can be trusted completely, knowing that nothing, absolutely nothing, "will be able to separate us from the love of God that is in Christ Jesus our Lord" (v. 39). *Estera*

A World of Provision
Psalm 104:10–18, 24–26

There is the sea, vast and spacious, teeming with
creatures beyond number. —PSALM 104:25

It's 2 a.m. when Nadia, a farmer of sea cucumbers, walks into a roped-off pen in the ocean shallows near her Madagascar village to harvest her "crop." The early hour doesn't bother her. "Life was very hard before I started farming," she says. "I didn't have any source of income." Now, as a member of a marine-protection program called Velondriake, meaning "to live with the sea," Nadia sees her income growing and stabilizing. "We thank God that this project appeared," she adds.

It appeared in large part because God's creation provided what their project needs—a natural supply of sea life. In praise of our providing God, the psalmist wrote, "He makes grass grow for the cattle, and plants for people to cultivate" (Psalm 104:14). As well, "there is the sea . . . teeming with creatures beyond number—living things both large and small" (v. 25).

It's a wonder, indeed, how God's wondrous creation also provides for us. The humble sea cucumber, for example, helps form a healthy marine food chain. Careful harvesting of sea cucumbers, in turn, grants Nadia and her neighbors a living wage.

Nothing is random in God's creation. He uses it all for His glory and our good. Thus, "I will sing to the LORD all my life," says the psalmist (v. 33). We too can praise Him today as we ponder all that He provides.

Patricia

Sounds of the Trumpets
Numbers 10:8–10

At your times of rejoicing—your appointed festivals and New Moon feasts—you are to sound the trumpets. —NUMBERS 10:10

"Taps" is a trumpet call played by the US military at the end of the day as well as at funerals. I was amazed when I read the unofficial lyrics and discovered that many of the verses end with the phrase "God is nigh" (God is near). Whether before the dark of each night settles in or while mourning the loss of a loved one, the lyrics offer soldiers the beautiful assurance that God is near.

In the Old Testament, trumpets were also a reminder to the Israelites that God was near. In the middle of celebrating the feasts and festivals that were part of the covenant agreement between God and the nation of Israel, the Jews were to "sound the trumpets" (Numbers 10:10). Blowing a trumpet was a reminder not only of God's presence but also that He was available when they needed Him most—and He longed to help them.

Today, we still need reminders that God is near. And in our own style of worship, we too can call out to God in prayer and song. Perhaps our prayers can be thought of as trumpets asking God to help us. And the beautiful encouragement is that God always hears those calls (1 Peter 3:12). To each of our pleas, He responds with the assurance of His presence that strengthens and comforts us in the difficulties and sorrows of life. 🌿 *Lisa*

You'll See Her Again

1 Corinthians 15:3–4, 12–22

For as in Adam all die, so in Christ all will be made alive. —1 CORINTHIANS 15:22

The room was dim and silent as I pulled a chair close to Jacquie's bed. Before a three-year battle with cancer, my friend had been a vibrant person. I could still picture her laughing—eyes full of life, her face lit with a smile. Now she was quiet and still, and I was visiting her in a special care facility.

Not knowing what to say, I decided to read some Scripture. I pulled my Bible out of my purse and turned to a reference in 1 Corinthians and began to read.

After the visit and an emotional time in the seclusion of my parked car, a thought came to mind that slowed my tears: You'll see her again. Caught up in sadness, I had forgotten that death is only temporary for believers (1 Corinthians 15:21–22). I knew I'd see Jacquie again because both of us had trusted in Jesus's death and resurrection for the forgiveness of our sin (vv. 3–4). When Jesus came back to life after His crucifixion, death lost its ultimate power to separate believers from each other and from God. After we die, we'll live again in heaven with God and all of our spiritual brothers and sisters—forever.

Because Jesus is alive today, believers in Him have hope in times of loss and sorrow. Death has been swallowed up in the victory of the cross (v. 54). *Jennifer*

Light in the Dark
Psalm 18:28–36, 46–49

*You, Lord, keep my lamp burning; my God turns
my darkness into light.* —PSALM 18:28

A severe thunderstorm passed through our new town, leaving high humidity and dark skies in its wake. I took our dog, Callie, for an evening stroll. The mounting challenges of my family's cross-country move grew heavier on my mind. Frustrated by the countless ways things had strayed so far from our high hopes and expectations, I slowed to let Callie sniff the grass. I listened to the creek that runs beside our house. Tiny lights flashed on and off while hovering over the patches of wildflowers climbing up the creek's bank. Fireflies.

The Lord wrapped me in peace as I watched the blinking lights cutting through the darkness. I thought of the psalmist David singing, "You, Lord, keep my lamp burning" (Psalm 18:28). Proclaiming that God turns his darkness into light, David demonstrated confident faith in the Lord's provision and protection (vv. 29–30). With God's strength, he could handle anything that came his way (vv. 32–35). Trusting the living Lord to be with him through all circumstances, David promised to praise Him among the nations and sing the praises of His name (vv. 36–49).

Whether we're enduring the unpredictable storms in life or enjoying the stillness after the rains have passed, the peace of God's constant presence lights our way through the darkness. Our living God will always be our strength, our refuge, our sustainer, and our deliverer.

Xochitl

Morning Mist
Isaiah 44:9–11, 21–23

*I have swept away your offenses . . . like the
morning mist.* —ISAIAH 44:22

One morning I visited a pond near my house. I sat on an overturned boat, thinking and watching as a gentle west wind chased a layer of mist across the water's surface. Wisps of fog circled and swirled. Mini "tornadoes" rose up and then exhausted themselves. Before long, the sunlight cut through the clouds and the mist disappeared.

This scene comforted me because I connected it with a verse I'd just read: "I have swept away your offenses like a cloud, your sins like the morning mist" (Isaiah 44:22). I visited the place hoping to distract myself from a series of sinful thoughts I'd been preoccupied with for days. Although I was confessing them, I began to wonder if God would forgive me when I repeated the same sin.

That morning, I knew the answer was yes. Through His prophet Isaiah, God showed grace to the Israelites when they struggled with the ongoing problem of idol worship. Although He told them to stop chasing false gods, God also invited them back to himself, saying, "I have made you, you are my servant; . . . I will not forget you" (v. 21).

I don't fully grasp forgiveness like that, but I do understand that God's grace is the only thing that can dissolve our sin completely and heal us from it. I'm thankful His grace is endless and divine like He is, and that it's available whenever we need it. *Jennifer*

Depths of Love
1 John 3:1–6

See what great love the Father has lavished on us, that we should be called children of God! And that is what we are! —1 JOHN 3:1

Three-year-old Dylan McCoy had just learned to swim when he fell through a rotted plywood covering into a forty-foot deep, stone-walled well in his grandfather's backyard. Dylan managed to stay afloat in ten feet of water until his father went down to rescue him. Although firefighters brought ropes to raise the boy, the father was so worried about his son that he climbed down the slippery rocks to make sure he was safe.

Oh, the love of a parent! Oh, the lengths (and depths) we will go for our children!

When the apostle John wrote to first-century believers who were struggling to find footing for their faith as they faced false teaching, he extended these words like a life-preserver: "See what great love the Father has lavished on us, that we should be called children of God! And that is what we are!" (1 John 3:1). Naming believers in Jesus as "children" of God is an intimate and legal labeling that brings validity to all who trust in Him.

Oh, the lengths and depths God will go for His children!

There are actions a parent will take only for their child—like Dylan's dad descending into a well to save his son. And like the ultimate act of our heavenly Father, who sent His only Son to gather us close to His heart and restore us to life with Him (vv. 5–6). *Elisa*

Listen and Learn
James 1:19–27

*Everyone should be quick to listen, slow to speak
and slow to become angry.* —JAMES 1:19

On one side of the street a homeowner displays in his yard a giant blow-up bald eagle draped in a US flag. A big truck sits in the driveway. Its side window features a painted flag and the back bumper is covered with patriotic stickers. Directly across the street in a neighbor's yard are signs that highlight the slogans for current social justice issues in the news.

We might wonder: Are the people in these homes feuding or friends? Is it possible that both families are believers in Jesus? God calls us to live out the words of James 1:19: "Everyone should be quick to listen, slow to speak and slow to become angry." Too often we stubbornly hold on to our opinions and aren't willing to consider what others are thinking. *Matthew Henry's Commentary* has this to say: "We should be swift to hear reason and truth on all sides, and be slow to speak . . . and, when we do speak, there should be nothing of wrath."

Someone has said, "Learning requires listening." The practical words from God in the book of James can only be accomplished if we're filled with God's loving Spirit and choose to respect others. He's willing to help us make changes in our hearts and attitudes. Are we open to listen and learn? *Anne*

When God Speaks
Isaiah 55:10–13

So is my word that goes out from my mouth:
It will not return to me empty. —ISAIAH 55:11

Lily, a Bible translator, was flying home to her country when she was detained at the airport. Her mobile phone was searched, and when the officials found an audio copy of the New Testament on it, they confiscated the phone and questioned her for two hours. At one point they asked her to play the Scripture app, which happened to be set at Matthew 7:1–2: "Do not judge, or you too will be judged. For in the same way you judge others, you will be judged, and with the measure you use, it will be measured to you." Hearing these words in his own language, one of the officers turned pale. Later, she was released and no further action was taken.

We don't know what happened in that official's heart at the airport, but we know that the "word that goes out from [God's] mouth" accomplishes what He desires (Isaiah 55:11). Isaiah prophesied these words of hope to God's people in exile, assuring them that even as the rain and snow make the earth bud and grow, so too what goes "out from [His] mouth" achieves His purposes (vv. 10–11).

We can read this passage to bolster our confidence in God. When we're facing unyielding circumstances, such as Lily with the airport officials, may we trust that God is working—even when we don't see the final outcome.

❧ *Amy*

In the Garden
John 20:11–18

*Mary Magdalene went to the disciples with the news:
"I have seen the Lord!" —JOHN 20:18*

My dad loved to sing the old hymns. One of his favorites was "In the Garden." A few years back, we sang it at his funeral. The chorus is simple: "And He walks with me, and He talks with me, and He tells me I am His own, and the joy we share as we tarry there none other has ever known." That song brought joy to my dad—as it does to me.

Hymn writer C. Austin Miles says he wrote this song in the spring of 1912 after reading John 20. "As I read it that day, I seemed to be part of the scene. I became a silent witness to that dramatic moment in Mary's life when she knelt before her Lord and cried, 'Rabboni [Aramaic for Teacher].'"

In John 20, we find Mary Magdalene weeping near Jesus's empty tomb. There she met a man who asked why she was crying. Thinking it was the gardener, she spoke with the risen Savior—Jesus! Her sorrow turned to joy, and she ran to tell the disciples, "I have seen the Lord!" (v. 18).

We too have the assurance that Jesus is risen! He's now in heaven with the Father, but He hasn't left us on our own. Believers in Christ have His Spirit inside us, and through Him we have the assurance and joy of knowing He's with us, and we are "His own." *Alyson*

Simply Ask
2 Kings 5:9–14

Before they call I will answer. —ISAIAH 65:24

Her doctor said her detached retinas couldn't be repaired. But after living without sight for fifteen years—learning Braille, and using a cane and service dog—a Montana woman's life changed when her husband asked another eye doctor a simple question: could she be helped? The answer was yes. As the doctor discovered, the woman had a common eye condition, cataracts, which the doctor removed from her right eye. When the eye patch came off the next day, her vision was 20/20. A second surgery for her left eye met with equal success.

A simple question also changed the life of Naaman, a powerful military man with leprosy. But Naaman raged arrogantly at the prophet Elisha's instructions to "wash yourself seven times in the Jordan, and your flesh will be restored" (2 Kings 5:10). Naaman's servants, however, asked the military leader a simple question: "If the prophet had told you to do some great thing, would you not have done it?" (v. 13). Persuaded, Naaman washed "and his flesh was restored and became clean" (v. 14).

In our lives, sometimes we struggle with a problem because we won't ask God. Will You help? Should I go? Will You lead? He doesn't require complicated questions from us to help. "Before they call I will answer," God promised His people (Isaiah 65:24). So today, simply ask Him. *Patricia*

Sacred Gathering
Leviticus 23:33–36

Rejoice before the LORD your God for seven days.
—*LEVITICUS 23:40*

Our group of friends reunited for a long weekend together on the shores of a beautiful lake. The days were spent playing in the water and sharing meals, but it was the evening conversations I treasured the most. As darkness fell, our hearts opened to one another with uncommon depth and vulnerability, sharing the pains of faltering marriages and the aftermath of trauma some of our children were enduring. Without glossing over the brokenness of our realities, we pointed one another to God and His faithfulness throughout such extreme difficulties. Those evenings are among the most sacred in my life.

I imagine those nights are similar to what God intended when He instructed His people to gather each year for the Festival of Tabernacles. This feast, like many others, required the Israelites to travel to Jerusalem. Once they arrived, God instructed His people to gather together in worship and to "do no regular work" for the duration of the feast—about a week! (Leviticus 23:35). The Festival of Tabernacles celebrated God's provision and commemorated their time in the wilderness after leaving Egypt (vv. 42–43).

This gathering cemented the Israelites' sense of identity as God's people and proclaimed His goodness despite their collective and individual hardships. When we gather with those we love to recall God's provision and presence in our lives, we too are strengthened in faith.

Kristen

It's Jesus
Colossians 1:27–29; 2:6–10

God has chosen to make known . . . the glorious riches of this mystery, which is Christ in you, the hope of glory.
—COLOSSIANS 1:27

During an episode of the popular US television talent competition America's Got Talent, a five-year-old girl sang with such exuberance that a judge compared her to a famous child singer and dancer from the 1930s. He remarked, "I think Shirley Temple is living somewhere inside of you." Her unexpected response: "Not Shirley Temple. Jesus!"

I marveled at the young girl's deep awareness that her joy came from Jesus living in her. Scripture assures us of the amazing reality that all who trust in Him not only receive the promise of eternal life with God but also Jesus's presence living in them through His Spirit—our hearts become Jesus's home (Colossians 1:27; Ephesians 3:17).

Jesus's presence in our hearts fills us with countless reasons for gratitude (Colossians 2:6–7). He brings the ability to live with purpose and energy (1:28–29). He cultivates joy in our hearts in the midst of all circumstances—in both times of celebration and times of struggle (Philippians 4:12–13). Christ's Spirit provides hope to our hearts that God is working all things together for good, even when we can't see it (Romans 8:28). And the Spirit gives a peace that persists regardless of the chaos swirling around us (Colossians 3:15).

With the confidence that comes from Jesus living in our hearts, we can allow His presence to shine through so that others can't help but notice. *Lisa*

Through Thick and Thin
Exodus 40:34–38

The cloud of the LORD was over the tabernacle by day, and fire was in the cloud by night, in the sight of all the Israelites during all their travels. —EXODUS 40:38

On January 28, 1986, the US Space Shuttle Challenger broke apart seventy-three seconds after takeoff. In a speech of comfort to the nation, President Ronald Reagan quoted from the poem "High Flight" in which John Gillespie Magee, a World War II pilot, had written of "the high untrespassed sanctity of space" and the sense of putting out his hand to touch "the face of God."

Although we can't literally touch God's face, we sometimes experience a stunning sunset or a place of meditation in nature that gives us an overwhelming sense that He's near. Some people call these moments "thin places." The barrier separating heaven and earth seems to grow a little thinner. God feels a little closer.

The Israelites may have experienced a "thin place" as they sensed the nearness of God in the desert wilderness. God provided a pillar of cloud by day and pillar of fire by night to lead them through the desert (Exodus 40:34–38). When they were staying in the camp, "the glory of the LORD filled the tabernacle" (v. 35). Throughout all their travels, they knew God was with them.

As we enjoy the incredible beauty of God's creation, we grow conscious that He's present everywhere. As we talk with Him in prayer, listen to Him, and read the Scriptures, we can enjoy fellowship with Him anytime and anywhere. *Cindy*

Instead of Revenge
Romans 12:17–21

If your enemy is hungry, feed him. —ROMANS 12:20

After Jim Elliot and four other missionaries were killed by Huaorani tribesmen in 1956, no one expected what happened next. Jim's wife, Elisabeth, their young daughter, and another missionary's sister willingly chose to make their home among the very people who killed their loved ones. They spent several years living in the Huaorani community, learning their language, and translating the Bible for them. These women's testimony of forgiveness and kindness convinced the Huaorani of God's love for them and many received Jesus as their Savior.

What Elisabeth and her friend did is an incredible example of not repaying evil with evil but with good (Romans 12:17). The apostle Paul encouraged the church in Rome to show through their actions the transformation that God had brought into their own lives. What did Paul have in mind? They were to go beyond the natural desire to take revenge; instead, they were to show love to their enemies by meeting their needs, such as providing food or water.

Why do this? Paul quotes a proverb from the Old Testament: "If your enemy is hungry, feed him; if he is thirsty, give him something to drink" (v. 20; Proverbs 25:21–22). The apostle was revealing that the kindness shown by believers to their enemies could win them over and light the fire of repentance in their hearts. 🌾 *Estera*

Anyone and Everyone
Romans 10:5–15

Everyone who calls on the name of the Lord
will be saved. —ROMANS 10:13

The country of El Salvador has honored Jesus by placing a sculpture of Him in the center of its capital city. Although the monument resides in the middle of a busy traffic circle, its height makes it easy to see, and its name—The Divine Savior of the World—communicates reverence for His supernatural status.

The monument's name affirms what the Bible says about Jesus (1 John 4:14). He's the one who offers salvation to everyone. Jesus crosses cultural boundaries and accepts any sincere person who wants to know Him, regardless of age, education, ethnicity, past sin, or social status.

The apostle Paul traveled the ancient world telling people about Jesus's life, death, and resurrection. He shared this good news with political and religious authorities, soldiers, Jews, Gentiles, men, women, and children. Paul explained that a person could begin a relationship with Christ by declaring "Jesus is Lord" and believing that God had indeed raised Him from the dead (Romans 10:9). He said, "Anyone who believes in him will never be put to shame. . . . Everyone who calls on the name of the Lord will be saved" (vv. 11, 13).

Jesus isn't a distant image to be honored; we must have a person-to-person connection with Him through faith. May we see the value of the salvation He offers and move forward into a spiritual relationship with Him today.

Jennifer

Thriving Together
Colossians 3:5–16

Let the peace of Christ rule in your hearts, since as members of one body you were called to peace. —COLOSSIANS 3:15

My husband, Alan, stood below the towering lights illuminating the athletic field, as a member of the opposing team hit a ball into the air. With his eyes fixed on the ball, Alan ran full speed toward the darkest corner of the field—and slammed into the chain link fence.

Later that night, I handed him an ice pack. "Are you feeling okay?" I asked. He rubbed his shoulder. "I'd feel better if my buddies had warned me that I was getting near the fence," he said.

Teams function best when they work together. Alan's injury could have been avoided, if only one of his teammates had yelled out a warning as he approached the fence.

Scripture reminds us that members of the church are designed to work together and watch out for each other like a team. The apostle Paul tells us that God cares about how we interact with each other, because the actions of one person can impact the whole community of believers (Colossians 3:13–14). When we all embrace opportunities to serve each other, fully devoted to unity and peace, the church flourishes (v. 15).

Paul instructed his readers to "let the message of Christ dwell among you richly as you teach and admonish one another with all wisdom through psalms, hymns, and songs from the Spirit" (v. 16). In this way we can inspire and protect one another through loving and honest relationships, obeying and praising God with grateful hearts—thriving together. *Xochitl*

When God Intervenes
Numbers 23:13–23

*Do not touch my anointed ones; do my prophets
no harm. —PSALM 105:15*

In a poem titled "This Child Is Beloved," Omawumi Efueye, known affectionately as Pastor O, writes about his parents' attempts to end the pregnancy that would result in his birth. After several unusual events that prevented them from aborting him, they decided to welcome their child instead. The knowledge of God's preservation of his life motivated Omawumi to give up a lucrative career in favor of full-time ministry. Today, he faithfully pastors a London church.

Like Pastor O, the Israelites experienced God's intervention at a vulnerable time in their history. While traveling through the wilderness, they came within sight of King Balak of Moab. Terrified of their conquests and their vast population, Balak engaged a seer named Balaam to place a curse on the unsuspecting travelers (Numbers 22:2–6).

But something amazing happened. Whenever Balaam opened his mouth to curse, a blessing issued instead. "I have received a command to bless; he has blessed, and I cannot change it," he declared. "No misfortune is seen in Jacob, no misery observed in Israel. The LORD their God is with them; . . . God brought them out of Egypt" (Numbers 23:20–22). God preserved the Israelites from a battle they didn't even know was raging!

Whether we see it or not, God still watches over His people today. May we worship in gratitude and awe the One who calls us blessed. *Remi*

A Joyful Celebration
Revelation 19:1–9

The wedding of the Lamb has come.
—REVELATION 19:7

My friend Sharon passed away one year prior to the death of my friend Dave's teenage daughter Melissa. They both had been tragically killed in car accidents. One night both Sharon and Melissa were in my dream. They giggled and talked as they hung streamers in a large banquet hall and ignored me when I stepped into the room. A long table with white tablecloths had been set with golden plates and goblets. I asked if I could help decorate, but they didn't seem to hear me and kept working.

But then Sharon said, "This party is Melissa's wedding reception."

"Who's the groom?" I asked.

Neither responded but smiled and looked at each other knowingly. Finally, it dawned on me—it's Jesus!

"Jesus is the groom," I whispered as I woke up.

My dream brings to mind the joyful celebration believers in Jesus will share together when He returns. It's portrayed in Revelation as a lavish feast called "the wedding supper of the Lamb" (19:9). John the Baptist, who prepared people for the first coming of Christ, had called Him "the Lamb of God, who takes away the sin of the world" (John 1:29). He also referred to Jesus as "the bridegroom" and to himself as the "friend" (like the best man) who waited for Him (3:29).

On that banquet day and for all eternity we will enjoy unbroken fellowship with Jesus, our groom, and with Sharon and Melissa and all of God's people. *Anne*

Our Father's Care
Matthew 10:16–20, 26–31

Are not two sparrows sold for a penny? Yet not one of
them will fall to the ground outside your Father's care.
—*MATTHEW 10:29*

Thwack! I looked up and craned my ear toward the sound. Spotting a smudge on the windowpane, I peered out onto the deck and discovered the still-beating body of a bird. My heart hurt. I longed to help the fragile feathered being.

In Matthew 10, Jesus described His Father's care for sparrows in order to comfort the disciples as He warned of upcoming dangers. He offered instructions to the twelve as He "gave them authority to drive out impure spirits and to heal every disease and sickness" (v. 1). While the power to do such deeds might have seemed grand to the disciples, many would oppose them, includ-ing governing authorities, their own families, and the ensnaring grip of the evil one (vv. 16–28).

Then in 10:29–31, Jesus told them not to fear what-ever they faced because they would never be out of their Father's care. "Are not two sparrows sold for a penny?" He asked. "Yet not one of them will fall to the ground outside your Father's care. . . . So don't be afraid; you are worth more than many sparrows."

I checked on the bird throughout the day, each time finding it alive but unmoved. Then, late into the eve-ning, it was gone. I prayed it had survived. Surely, if I cared this much about the bird, God cared even more. Imagine how much He cares for you and me! *Elisa*

Stopping Rumors
Exodus 23:1–3

Do not spread false reports. —*EXODUS 23:1*

After Charles Simeon (1759–1836) was named the minister of Holy Trinity Church in Cambridge, England, he faced years of opposition. As most in the congregation had wanted the associate minister to be appointed rather than Simeon, they spread rumors about him and rejected his ministry—even at times locking him out of the church. But Simeon, who desired to be filled by God's Spirit, sought to cope with the gossip by creating some principles to live by. One was never to believe rumors unless they were absolutely true and another was "always to believe, that if the other side were heard, a very different account would be given of the matter."

In this practice, Simeon followed God's instructions to His people to cease the gossip and malicious talk He knew would erode their love for each other. One of God's Ten Commandments reflects His desire for them to live truthfully: "You shall not give false testimony against your neighbor" (Exodus 20:16). Another instruction in Exodus reinforces this commandment: "Do not spread false reports" (23:1).

Think of how different the world would be if each of us never spread rumors and false reports and if we stopped them the moment we heard them. May we rely on the Holy Spirit to help us speak the truth in love as we use our words to bring glory to God. *Amy*

The Man in Seat 2D
1 Timothy 6:17–19

Be rich in good deeds, and [be] generous and
willing to share. —1 TIMOTHY 6:18

Kelsey navigated the narrow airplane aisle with her eleven-month-old daughter, Lucy, and Lucy's oxygen machine. They were traveling to seek treatment for her baby's chronic lung disease. Shortly after settling into their shared seat, a flight attendant approached Kelsey, saying a passenger in first class wanted to switch seats with her. With tears of gratitude streaming down her face, Kelsey made her way back up the aisle to the more spacious seat, while the benevolent stranger made his way toward hers.

Kelsey's benefactor embodied the kind of generosity Paul encourages in his letter to Timothy. Paul told Timothy to instruct those in his care with the command to "do good, to be rich in good deeds, and to be generous and willing to share" (1 Timothy 6:18). It's tempting, Paul says, to become arrogant and put our hope in the riches of this world. Instead, he suggests that we focus on living a life of generosity and service to others, becoming "rich" in good deeds, like the man from seat 2D on Kelsey's flight.

Whether we find ourselves with plenty or in want, we all can experience the richness of living generously by being willing to share what we have with others. When we do, Paul says we will "take hold of the life that is truly life" (v. 19). *Kirsten*

Look Up!

Psalm 8:3–4; Revelation 21:22–25

There will be no night there. —REVELATION 21:25

When filmmaker Wylie Overstreet showed strangers a live picture of the moon as seen through his powerful telescope, they were stunned at the up-close view, reacting with whispers and awe. To see such a glorious sight, Overstreet explained, "fills us with a sense of wonder that there's something much bigger than ourselves."

The psalmist David also marveled at God's heavenly light. "When I consider your heavens, the work of your fingers, the moon and the stars, which you have set in place, what is mankind that you are mindful of them, human beings that you care for them?" (Psalm 8:3–4).

David's humbling question puts our awe in perspective when we learn that, after God creates His new heaven and earth, we'll no longer need the moon or the sun. Instead, said John the apostle, God's shimmering glory will provide all necessary light. "The city does not need the sun or the moon to shine on it, for the glory of God gives it light, and the Lamb is its lamp. . . . There will be no night there" (Revelation 21:23–25).

What an amazing thought! Yet we can experience His heavenly light now—simply by seeking Christ, the Light of the world. In Overstreet's view, "We should look up more often." As we do, may we see God. *Patricia*

Anchored in Truth
Isaiah 22:15–20, 22–25

I will drive him like a peg into a firm place.
—ISAIAH 22:23

My family lives in a nearly century-old house with a lot of character, including wonderfully textured plaster walls. A builder cautioned me that with these walls, to hang a picture up I'd have to either drill the nail into a wood support or use a plaster anchor for support. Otherwise, I'd risk the picture crashing to the ground, leaving an ugly hole behind.

The prophet Isaiah used the imagery of a nail driven firmly into a wall to describe a minor biblical character named Eliakim. Unlike the corrupt official Shebna (Isaiah 22:15–19), as well as the people of Israel—who looked to themselves for strength (vv. 8–11)—Eliakim trusted in God. Prophesying Eliakim's promotion to palace administrator for King Hezekiah, Isaiah wrote that Eliakim would be driven like a "peg into a firm place" (v. 23). Being securely anchored in God's truth and grace would also allow Eliakim to be a support for his family and his people (vv. 22–24).

Yet Isaiah concluded this prophecy with a sobering reminder that no person can be the ultimate security for friends or family—we all fail (v. 25). The only completely trustworthy anchor for our lives is Jesus (Psalm 62:5–6; Matthew 7:24). As we care for others and share their burdens, may we also point them to Him, the anchor who will never fail. *Lisa*

Extending Grace to Others
Acts 4:32–35

God's grace was so powerfully at work in them all that there were no needy persons among them. —ACTS 4:33–34

Our son spent the early years of his life in a children's home prior to our adopting him. Before leaving the cinderblock building together to go home, we asked to collect his belongings. Sadly, he had none. We exchanged the clothes he was wearing for the new items we'd brought for him and also left some clothing for the other children. Even though I was grieved by how little he had, I rejoiced that we could now help meet his physical and emotional needs.

A few years later, we saw a person asking for donations for families in need. My son was eager to donate his stuffed animals and a few coins to help them. Given his background, he might have (understandably) been more inclined to hold tightly to his belongings.

I'd like to think the reason for his generous response was the same as that of the early church: "God's grace was so powerfully at work in them all" that nobody in their midst had need (Acts 4:33–34). The people willingly sold their own possessions to provide for one another's needs.

When we become aware of the needs of others, whether material or intangible, may God's grace be so powerfully at work in us that we respond as they did, willingly giving from our hearts to those in need. This makes us vessels of God's grace as fellow believers in Jesus, "one in heart and mind" (v. 32). *Kirsten*

The Reality of God
2 Kings 6:8–17

The LORD opened the servant's eyes, and he [saw] chariots of fire all around Elisha. —2 KINGS 6:17

In C. S. Lewis's *The Lion, the Witch and the Wardrobe*, all of Narnia is thrilled when the mighty lion Aslan reappears after a long absence. Their joy turns to sorrow, however, when Aslan concedes to a demand made by the evil White Witch. Faced with Aslan's apparent defeat, the Narnians experience his power when he emits an earsplitting roar that causes the witch to flee in terror. Although all seems to have been lost, Aslan ultimately proves to be greater than the villainous witch.

Like Aslan's followers in Lewis's allegory, Elisha's servant despaired when he got up one morning to see himself and Elisha surrounded by an enemy army. "Oh no, my lord! What shall we do?" he exclaimed (2 Kings 6:15). The prophet's response was calm: "Don't be afraid. . . . Those who are with us are more than those who are with them" (v. 16). Elisha then prayed, "Open his eyes, LORD, so that he may see" (v. 17). So, "the LORD opened the servant's eyes, and he looked and saw the hills full of horses and chariots of fire all around Elisha" (v. 17). Although things at first seemed bleak to the servant's eye, God's power ultimately proved greater than the enemy horde.

Our difficult circumstances may lead us to believe all is lost, but God desires to open our eyes and reveal that He is greater. *Remi*

Bright Spots in a Bleak Place
Psalm 86:1–13

*You, Lord, are forgiving and good, abounding in love
to all who call to you.* —PSALM 86:5

When my husband and I were exploring a small, rugged corner of the state of Wyoming, I spied a sunflower in a rocky, dry place where sagebrush, nettles, prickly cactus, and other scraggly plants grew. It wasn't as tall as the domestic sunflower, but it was just as bright—and I felt cheered.

This unexpected bright spot in rough terrain reminded me of how life, even for the believer in Jesus, can seem barren and cheerless. Troubles can seem insurmountable, and like the cries of the psalmist David, our prayers sometimes seem to go unheeded: "Hear me, Lord, and answer me, for I am poor and needy" (Psalm 86:1). Like him, we too long for joy (v. 4).

But David goes on to declare that we serve a faithful (v. 11), "compassionate and gracious God" (v. 15), who abounds in love for all who call on Him (v. 5). He does answer (v. 7).

Sometimes in bleak places, God sends a sunflower—an encouraging word or note from a friend; a comforting verse or Bible passage; a beautiful sunrise—that helps us to move forward with a lighter step, with hope. Even as we await the day we experience God's deliverance out of our difficulty, may we join the psalmist in proclaiming, "You are great and do marvelous deeds; you alone are God" (v. 10). *Alyson*

Irrational Fears
Isaiah 49:14–19

I will not forget you! —ISAIAH 49:15

It makes no logical sense, but when my parents died within a three-month period, I feared they would forget me. Of course they were no longer on earth, but that left me with a large uncertainty. I was a young, unmarried adult, and I wondered how to navigate life without them. Feeling really single and alone, I sought God.

One morning I told Him about my irrational fear and the sadness it brought (even though He knew it already). The Scripture passage that came for the devotional I read that day was Isaiah 49: "Can a mother forget the baby at her breast . . . ? Though she may forget, I will not forget you!" (v. 15). God reassured His people through Isaiah that He had not forgotten them and later promised to restore them to Himself through sending His Son Jesus. But the words ministered to my heart too. It's rare for a mother or a father to forget their child, yet it's possible. But God? No way. "I have engraved you on the palms of my hands," He said (v. 16).

God's answer to me could have brought more fear. But the peace He gave because of His own remembrance of me was exactly what I needed. It was the start of discovering that God is even closer than a parent or anyone else, and He knows the way to help us with everything—even our irrational fears. *Anne*

Rebuilding the Ruins
Jeremiah 33:6–11

*Then this city will bring me renown, joy,
praise and honor.* —*JEREMIAH 33:9*

At seventeen, Dowayne had to leave his family's home in Manenberg, a part of Cape Town, South Africa, because of his stealing and addiction to heroin. He didn't go far, building a shack of corrugated metal in his mother's backyard, which soon became known as the Casino, a place to use drugs. When he was nineteen, however, Dowayne came to saving faith in Jesus. His journey off drugs was long and exhausting, but he got clean with God's help and with the support of friends who are believers in Jesus. And ten years after Dowayne built the Casino, he and others turned the hut into a house church. What was once a dark and foreboding place now is a place of worship and prayer.

The leaders of this church look to Jeremiah 33 for how God can bring healing and restoration to people and places, as He's done with Dowayne and the former Casino. The prophet Jeremiah spoke to God's people in captivity, saying that although the city would not be spared, God would heal His people and would "rebuild them," cleansing them from their sin (Jeremiah 33:7–8). Then the city would bring Him joy, renown, and honor (v. 9).

When we're tempted to despair over the sin that brings heartbreak and brokenness, let's continue to pray that God will bring healing and hope, even as He's done in a backyard in Manenberg. *Amy*

Caring Letters
1 Peter 2:4–10

*You are a chosen people, a royal priesthood, a holy nation,
God's special possession.* —*1 PETER 2:9*

Decades ago, Dr. Jerry Motto discovered the power of a
"caring letter." His research found that simply sending a
letter expressing care to discharged patients who had previously attempted suicide reduced the rate of recurrence
by half. Recently, health care providers have rediscovered
this power when sending "caring" texts, postcards, and
even social media memes as follow-up treatment for the
severely depressed.

Twenty-one "books" in the Bible are actually letters—
epistles—caringly written to first-century believers who
struggled for a variety of reasons. Paul, James, and John
wrote letters to explain the basics of faith and worship,
and how to resolve conflict and build unity.

The apostle Peter, however, specifically wrote to believers who were being persecuted by the Roman em-
peror, Nero. Peter reminded them of their intrinsic value
to God, describing them this way in 1 Peter 2:9, "You are
a chosen people, a royal priesthood, a holy nation, God's
special possession." This lifted their gaze to God's great
purpose for them in their world: "that you may declare
the praises of him who called you out of darkness into
his wonderful light."

Our great God himself wrote a book filled with caring
letters to us—inspired Scripture—that we might always
have a record of the value He assigns us as His own. May
we read His letters daily and share them with others who
need the hope Jesus offers. *Elisa*

Day of Encouragement
1 Thessalonians 5:12–28

*We urge you, brothers and sisters, . . . encourage the
disheartened. —1 THESSALONIANS 5:14*

First responders show dedication and courage daily by
being on the front lines when disasters occur. In the attack on the World Trade Center in New York City in
2001 when thousands of people were killed or injured,
more than four hundred emergency workers also lost
their lives. In honor of first responders, the US Senate
designated September 12 as the National Day of Encouragement.

While it may seem unique that a government would
declare a national day of encouragement, the apostle
Paul certainly thought this was needed for the growth
of a church. He commended the young church in
Thessalonica, a city in Macedonia, to "encourage the
disheartened, help the weak, be patient with everyone" (1 Thessalonians 5:14). Although they were going
through persecution, Paul encouraged the believers to
"always strive to do what is good for each other and for
everyone else" (v. 15). He knew that as humans, they
would be prone to despair, selfishness, and conflict. But
he also knew they would not be able to uplift one another without God's help and strength.

Things are no different today. We all need to be up-
lifted, and we need to do the same for those around us.
Yet we can't do it in our own strength. That's why Paul's
encouragement that "the one who calls you [that is, Je-
sus] is faithful, and he will do it" is so reassuring (v. 24).
With His help, we can encourage one another every day.

❧ *Estera*

Something New
Isaiah 43:14–21

*See, I am doing a new thing! . . . I am making . . .
streams in the wasteland. —ISAIAH 43:19*

Farming is difficult in areas that lack fresh water. To help solve this problem, the Seawater Greenhouse company has created something new: "cooling houses" in Somaliland, Africa, and other countries with similar climates. Cooling houses use solar pumps to drizzle saltwater over walls made of corrugated cardboard. As the water moves down each panel, it leaves its salt behind. Much of the remaining fresh water evaporates inside the structure, which becomes a humid place where fruit and vegetable crops can flourish.

Through the prophet Isaiah, God promised to do a "new thing" as He provided "streams in the wasteland" for ancient Israel (Isaiah 43:19). This new thing contrasted with the old thing He had done to rescue His people from the Egyptian army. Remember the Red Sea account? God wanted His people to recall the past but not let it overshadow His current involvement in their lives (v. 18). He said, "See, I am doing a new thing! Now it springs up; do you not perceive it? I am making a way in the wilderness" (v. 19).

While looking to the past can bolster our faith in God's provision, living in the past can blind us to all the fresh work of God's Spirit today. We can ask God to show us how He's currently moving—helping, remaking, and sustaining His people. May this awareness prompt us to partner with Him to meet the needs of others, both near and far. *Jennifer*

Peace-filled Hearts
Proverbs 14:29–35

*A heart at peace gives life to the body, but envy
rots the bones. —PROVERBS 14:30*

For forty-five years after his career as a professional athlete ended, Jerry Kramer wasn't inducted into his sport's hall of fame (the highest recognition). He enjoyed many other honors and achievements, but this one eluded him. Although he'd been nominated for the honor ten times, it had never been bestowed. Despite having his hopes dashed so many times, Kramer was gracious, saying, "I felt like [the National Football League] had given me a hundred presents in my lifetime and to be upset or angry about one I didn't get was kind of stupid!"

Where others might have grown bitter after being denied so many times in favor of other players, Kramer wasn't. His attitude illustrates the way we can safeguard our hearts against the corrosive nature of envy, which "rots the bones" (Proverbs 14:30). When we become preoccupied with what we don't have—and fail to recognize the many things we do—the peace of God will elude us.

After an eleventh nomination, Jerry Kramer ultimately was inducted into the NFL Hall of Fame in February 2018. Our earthly desires may not be fulfilled as his finally were. Yet we can all have a "heart at peace" when we instead focus our attention on the many ways God has been generous toward us. No matter what we want but do not have, we can always enjoy the life-giving peace He brings to our lives. *Kirsten*

A Remarkable Life
1 Peter 2:9–12

Be careful to live properly among your unbelieving neighbors. —1 PETER 2:12 NLT

I came to learn about Catherine Hamlin, a remarkable Australian surgeon, through reading her obituary. In Ethiopia, Catherine and her husband established the world's only hospital dedicated to curing women from the devastating physical and emotional trauma of obstetric fistulas, a common injury in the developing world that can occur during childbirth. Catherine is credited with overseeing the treatment of more than 60,000 women.

Still operating at the hospital when she was ninety-two years old, and still beginning each day with a cup of tea and Bible study, Hamlin told curious questioners that she was an ordinary believer in Jesus who was simply doing the job God had given her to do.

I was grateful to learn about her remarkable life because she powerfully exemplified for me Scripture's encouragement to believers to live our lives in such a way that even people who actively reject God "may see your good deeds and glorify God" (1 Peter 2:12).

The power of God's Spirit that called us out of spiritual darkness into a relationship with Him (v. 9) can also transform our work or areas of service into testimonies of our faith. In whatever passion or skill God has gifted us, we can embrace added meaning and purpose in doing all of it in a manner that has the power to point people to Him. *Lisa*

Friendship Bench
Psalm 33:9–11

The LORD would speak to Moses face to face, as one speaks to a friend. —EXODUS 33:11

In the African country of Zimbabwe, war trauma and high unemployment can leave people in despair—until they find hope on a "friendship bench." Hopeless people can go there to talk with trained "grandmothers"—elderly women taught to listen to people struggling with depression, known in that nation's Shona language as kufungisisa, or "thinking too much."

The Friendship Bench Project is being launched in other places, including Zanzibar, London, and New York City. "We were thrilled to bits with the results," said one London researcher. A New York counselor agreed. "Before you know it, you're not on a bench, you're just inside a warm conversation with someone who cares."

The project evokes the warmth and wonder of talking with our Almighty God. Moses put up not a bench but a tent to commune with God, calling it the tent of meeting. There, "the LORD would speak to Moses face to face, as one speaks to a friend" (Exodus 33:11). Joshua, his assistant, wouldn't even leave the tent, perhaps because he so valued his time with God (v. 11).

Today we no longer need a tent of meeting. Jesus has brought the Father near. As He told His disciples, "I have called you friends, for everything that I learned from my Father I have made known to you" (John 15:15). Yes, our God awaits us. He's our heart's wisest helper, our understanding Friend. Talk with Him now. 🌿 *Patricia*

The God of All Comfort

2 Corinthians 1:3–7

[God] comforts us in all our troubles, so that we can comfort those in any trouble. —2 CORINTHIANS 1:4

Radamenes was just a kitten when his owner dropped him off at an animal shelter, thinking he was too ill to recover. The kitten was nursed back to health and adopted by the vet. He then became a fulltime resident at the shelter, spending his days "comforting" cats and dogs—just out of surgery or recovering from an illness—through his warm presence and gentle purr.

That story is a small picture of what our loving God does for us—and what we can do for others in return. He cares for us in our sickness and struggles, and He soothes us with His presence. The apostle Paul in 2 Corinthians calls our God, "the Father of compassion and the God of all comfort" (1:3). When we are discouraged, depressed, or mistreated, He's there for us. When we turn to Him in prayer, He "comforts us in all our troubles" (v. 4).

But verse 4 doesn't end there. Paul, who had experienced intense suffering, continues, "so that we can comfort those in any trouble with the comfort we ourselves receive from God." Our Father comforts us, and when we've experienced His comfort, we're enabled to comfort others.

Our compassionate Savior, who suffered for us, is more than able to comfort us in our suffering and distress (v. 5). He helps us through our pain and equips us to do the same for others. *Alyson*

People Forget
Deuteronomy 8:2, 10–18

Remember how the LORD your God led you
all the way. —DEUTERONOMY 8:2

A woman complained to her pastor that she'd noticed a lot of repetition in his sermons. "Why do you do that?" she queried. The preacher replied, "People forget."

There are lots of reasons we forget—the passage of time, growing older, or just being too busy. We forget passwords, names of people, or even where we parked our car. My husband says, "There's only so much I can fit in my brain. I have to delete something before I can remember something new."

The preacher was right. People forget. So we often need reminders to help us remember what God has done for us. The Israelites had a similar tendency. Even with the many miracles they'd seen, they still needed to be reminded of His care for them. In Deuteronomy 8, God reminded the Israelites that He'd allowed them to experience hunger in the wilderness, but then provided an amazing superfood for them every day—manna. He supplied clothing that never wore out. He led them through a wilderness of snakes and scorpions and provided water from a rock. They'd learned humility, as they realized how totally dependent they were on God's care and provision (vv. 2–4, 15–18).

God's faithfulness "continues through all generations" (Psalm 100:5). Whenever we find ourselves forgetting, we can think about the ways He's answered our prayers, and that reminds us of His goodness and faithful promises. *Cindy*

God's Protection
Psalm 63

I sing in the shadow of your wings. I cling to you; your right hand upholds me. —PSALM 63:7–8

Needles, milk, mushrooms, elevators, births, bees, and bees in blenders—these are just a fraction of the many phobias attributed to Mr. Adrian Monk, detective and title character of the TV show Monk. But when he and longtime rival Harold Krenshaw find themselves locked in a car trunk, Monk has a breakthrough that allows him to cross off at least one fear from his list—claustrophobia.

It's while Monk and Harold are both panicking that the epiphany comes, abruptly interrupting Monk's angst. "I think we've been looking at this the wrong way," he tells Harold. "This trunk, these walls . . . they're not closing in on us . . . they're protecting us, really. They're keeping the bad stuff out . . . germs, and snakes, and harmonicas." Eyes widening, Harold sees what he means and whispers in wonder, "This trunk is our friend."

In Psalm 63, it's almost as if David has a similar epiphany. Despite being in a "dry and parched land," when David remembers God's power, glory, and love (vv. 1–3), it's as if the desert transforms into a place of God's care and protection. Like a baby bird hiding in the shelter of a mother's wings, David finds that when he clings to God, even in that barren place, he can feast "as with the richest of foods" (v. 5), finding nourishment and strength in a love that "is better than life" (v. 3). *Monica*

The Frosting of Faith
2 Timothy 1:1–5

I am reminded of your sincere faith, which first lived in your grandmother Lois and in your mother Eunice and, I am persuaded, now lives in you also. —2 TIMOTHY 1:5

Hand in hand, my grandson and I skipped across the parking lot to find a special back-to-school outfit. A preschooler, he was excited about everything, and I was determined to ignite his happiness into joy. I'd just seen a coffee mug with the inscription, "Grandmas are moms with lots of frosting." Frosting equals fun, glitter, joy! That's my job description as his grandma, right? That . . . and more.

In his second letter to his spiritual son Timothy, Paul calls out his sincere faith—and then credits its lineage both to Timothy's grandmother, Lois, and his mother, Eunice (2 Timothy 1:5). These women lived out their faith in such a way that Timothy also came to believe in Jesus. Surely, Lois and Eunice loved Timothy and provided for his needs. But clearly, they did more. Paul points to the faith living in them as the source of the faith later living in Timothy.

My job as a grandmother includes the "frosting" moment of a back-to-school outfit. But even more, I'm called to the frosting moments when I share my faith: Bowing our heads over chicken nuggets. Noticing angelic cloud formations in the sky as God's works of art. Chirping along with a song about Jesus on the radio. Let's be wooed by the example of moms and grandmas like Eunice and Lois to let our faith become the frosting in life so others will want what we have. *Elisa*

"Feed My Sheep"
John 21:15–19

Jesus said, "Take care of my sheep." —JOHN 21:16

In a lecture in 1911, Oswald Chambers reflected on being a young shepherd in the highlands of Scotland: "When you have to carry across your shoulders a dirty old [goat] and bring it down the mountainside, you will soon know whether shepherding is poetry or not." He didn't want to romanticize this form of labor as "poetry" but rather called it "the most taxing, the most exhausting, and the most exasperating work." The hard work of shepherding people is what Jesus entrusted to Peter, for Peter would face criticism, misunderstanding, and other challenges in caring for His flock.

Chambers reflected, "To whom did He say, 'Feed My lambs'? To Peter. Who was Peter? A very wayward sheep." Even though Peter had denied knowing Jesus (see John 18:15–27), Jesus met him on the beach and lovingly restored him in front of the other disciples (21:15–19). Peter's bitter experience taught him how to be tender and watchful over the Lord's sheep. Having received the Holy Spirit, he was ready for the toil and joys of being a shepherd to people.

Like Peter, we may have failed Jesus through denials, wrongdoing, selfishness, or pride. But He seeks us out and forgives us, just as He did Peter. He restores us and gives us a new commission—helping us care for others. As we follow Jesus, we share our love for Him with those we meet. *Amy*

Got Plans?
Proverbs 16:3–9

In their hearts humans plan their course, but the LORD establishes their steps. —PROVERBS 16:9

Caden, a young man of almost eighteen, was anticipating attending his first choice of a college on an academic scholarship. He was involved in a campus ministry in high school and looked forward to participating in a similar ministry in the new environment. He'd saved money from his part-time job and also had an excellent lead on a new job. He'd established some great goals, and everything was coming together exactly on schedule.

And then in the spring of 2020 a global health crisis changed everything.

The school let Caden know that his first semester would probably be online. The campus ministry was on hiatus. The job prospect dried up when the business closed. As he despaired, his buddy glibly quoted words from a well-known professional boxer: "Yeah, everyone has a plan until they get punched in the mouth."

Proverbs 16 tells us that when we commit all we do to God, He'll establish our plans and work things out according to His will (vv. 3–4). True commitment, however, can be difficult. It involves an open heart to God's direction, along with a willingness to resist charting our course independently (v. 9; 19:21).

Dreams that don't come to fruition can bring disappointment, but our limited vision for the future can never compete with God's all-knowing ways. As we yield ourselves to Him, we can be certain that He's still lovingly directing our steps even when we don't see the path ahead (16:9). *Cindy*

The Picture of Despair
Psalm 107:4–9

Then they cried out to the LORD in their trouble, and he delivered them from their distress. —PSALM 107:6

During the Great Depression in the United States, photographer Dorothea Lange snapped a photo of Florence Owens Thompson and her children. This well-known photograph, "Migrant Mother," is the picture of a mother's despair in the aftermath of the failed pea harvest. Lange took it in Nipomo, California, while working for the Farm Security Administration, hoping to make people aware of the needs of the desperate seasonal farm laborers.

The book of Lamentations presents another snapshot of despair—that of Judah in the wake of the destruction of Jerusalem. Before the army of Nebuchadnezzar swept in to destroy the city, the people had suffered from starvation thanks to a siege (2 Kings 24:10–11). Though their turmoil was the result of years of disobedience to God, the writer of Lamentations cried out to God on behalf of his people (Lamentations 2:11–12).

While the author of Psalm 107 also describes a desperate time in Israel's history (during Israel's wanderings in the wilderness, vv. 4–5), the focus shifts to an action step to be taken in hard times: "Then they cried out to the LORD in their trouble" (v. 6). And what a wonderful result: "he delivered them from their distress."

In despair? Don't stay silent. Cry out to God. He hears and waits to restore your hope. Though He doesn't always take us out of hard situations, He promises to be with us always. *Linda*

Someone Who Leads
2 Kings 2:1–6

*As surely as the LORD lives and as you live,
I will not leave you. —2 KINGS 2:6*

Who do you think of when you hear the word mentor? For me, it's Pastor Rich. He saw my potential and believed in me when I didn't believe in myself. He modeled how to lead by serving in humility and love. As a result, I am now serving God by mentoring others.

The prophet Elijah played a critical role in Elisha's growth as a leader. Elijah found him plowing a field and invited him to be his protégé after God told him to anoint Elisha as his successor (1 Kings 19:16, 19). The young mentee watched his mentor perform incredible miracles and obey God no matter what. God used Elijah to prepare Elisha for a lifetime of ministry. Toward the end of Elijah's life, Elisha had the opportunity to leave. Instead, he chose to renew his commitment to his mentor. Three times Elijah offered to release Elisha from his duties, yet each time he refused, saying, "As surely as the LORD lives and as you live, I will not leave you" (2 Kings 2:2, 4, 6). As a result of Elisha's faithfulness, he too was used by God in extraordinary ways.

We all need someone who models what it means to follow Jesus. May God give us godly men and women who help us grow spiritually. And may we too, by the power of His Spirit, invest our lives in others. *Estera*

Fill In Your Name
Isaiah 40:25–31

He who brings out the starry host one by one and calls forth each of them by name. —ISAIAH 40:26

In *God's Love Letters*, Glenys Nellist invites children to interact with the Lord in a deeply personal way. These children's books include a note from God with a space for the child's name to be inserted after each Bible story. Personalizing scriptural truth helps her young readers understand that the Bible isn't just a storybook. They're being taught that the Lord wants a relationship with them and that He speaks to His greatly loved children through the Scriptures.

I bought the book for my nephew and filled in the blanks in the beginning of every note from God. Delighted when he recognized his name, my nephew said, "God loves me too!" What a comfort to know the deeply and completely personal love of our loving Creator.

When God spoke to the Israelites directly through the prophet Isaiah, He called their attention to the heavens. The Lord affirmed that He controls "the starry host" (Isaiah 40:26), determines the stars' individual value, and directs each one with love. He assured His people that He won't forget or lose one star . . . or one beloved child that He's sculpted with deliberate purpose and endless love.

As we celebrate our Almighty God's intimate promises and proclamations of love within Scripture, we can fill in our names. We can trust and declare with childlike delight, "God loves me too!" *Xochitl*

Navigating the Storms of Life

Psalm 43

Send me your light and your faithful care, let them lead me.
—PSALM 43:3

In the summer of 1999, the small plane piloted by John F. Kennedy Jr. crashed into the Atlantic Ocean. Investigators determined the cause of the accident to be a common error known as spatial disorientation. This phenomenon occurs when, due to poor visibility, pilots become disoriented and forget to rely on their instruments to help them successfully reach their destination.

As we navigate life, there are often times when life gets so overwhelming we feel disoriented. A cancer diagnosis, the death of a loved one, a job loss, a betrayal by a friend—life's unexpected tragedies can easily leave us feeling lost and confused.

When we find ourselves in these kinds of situations, we might try offering the prayer of Psalm 43. In this psalm, the psalmist is overwhelmed and feeling lost because he feels surrounded by evil and injustice. In despair, the psalmist pleads with God to provide His sure guidance to help him safely navigate through the situation to his desired destination, God's presence (vv. 3–4). In God's presence the psalmist knows he'll find renewed hope and joy.

What are the tools the psalmist requests for guidance? The light of truth and the assurance of God's presence by His Holy Spirit.

When you're feeling disoriented and lost, God's faithful guidance through His Spirit and loving presence can comfort you and light your way. *Lisa*

Imperfect Plans
Proverbs 19:20–23

Many are the plans in a person's heart, but it is the LORD's purpose that prevails. —PROVERBS 19:21

I was exploring a library on the bottom floor of a new community center when an overhead crash suddenly shook the room. A few minutes later it happened again, and then again. An agitated librarian finally explained that a weight-lifting area was positioned directly above the library, and the noise occurred every time someone dropped a weight. Architects and designers had carefully planned many aspects of this state-of-the-art facility, yet someone had forgotten to locate the library away from all the action.

In life as well, our plans are often flawed. We overlook important considerations. And it's tough to account for accidents or surprises as we make plans. Although planning helps us avoid financial shortfalls, time crunches, and health issues, even the most thorough strategies can't eliminate all problems from our lives. We live in a post-Eden, imperfect world.

With God's help, we can find the balance between prudently considering the future (Proverbs 6:6–8) and responding to difficulties. God often has a purpose for the trouble He allows into our lives. He may use it to develop patience in us, to increase our faith, or simply to bring us closer to Him. The Bible reminds us, "Many are the plans in a person's heart, but it is the LORD's purpose that prevails" (Proverbs 19:21). As we submit our goals and hopes for the future to Jesus, He'll show us what He wants to accomplish in us and through us—no matter what the circumstances. *Jennifer*

Borrowed Shoes
Galatians 5:13–26

Serve one another humbly in love. —GALATIANS 5:13

In the chaos of fleeing his home during the California wildfires of 2018, Gabe, a high school senior, missed the state-qualifying cross-country race for which he'd been training. Missing this meet meant he wouldn't have the chance to compete at the state meet—the culminating event of his four-year running career. In light of the circumstances, the state athletics board gave Gabe another chance: he'd have to run a qualifying time by himself on a rival high school's track. But all Gabe had were "street shoes," because his running shoes were in the charred rubble of his home. When he showed up to run, Gabe was surprised by his competitors, who showed up to help. They supplied him with running shoes, and then they ran alongside him to ensure he kept the pace necessary to be entered in the state meet.

Gabe's opponents had no obligation to help him. They could have given into their natural desires to look out for themselves (Galatians 5:13); doing so might have improved their own odds of winning. Their actions can serve to exemplify Paul teaching in that passage, in which he urges us to display the fruit of the Spirit in our lives—to "serve one another humbly in love" and to demonstrate "kindness" and "goodness" (vv. 13, 22). When we lean on the Spirit to help us not act on our natural instincts, we're better able to love those around us. *Kirsten*

God Our Rescuer
Ezekiel 34:5–12

I will rescue them from all the places where they were scattered. —EZEKIEL 34:12

Stationed the open water offshore, a rescuer positioned her kayak to assist triathlon competitors who panicked while competing in the swimming portion of a triathlon. "Don't grab the middle of the boat!" she called to struggling swimmers, knowing such a move would capsize her craft. Instead, she directed them to the bow, or front, of the kayak. There they could grab a loop, allowing the safety kayaker to help rescue them.

Whenever life or people threaten to pull us under, as believers in Jesus, we know we have a Rescuer. "For this is what the Sovereign LORD says: I myself will search for my sheep . . . I will rescue them from all the places where they were scattered" (Ezekiel 34:11–12).

This was the prophet Ezekiel's assurance to God's people when they were in exile. Their leaders had neglected and exploited them, plundering their lives and caring "for themselves rather than for [God's] flock" (v. 8). As a result, the people "were scattered over the whole earth, and no one searched or looked for them" (v. 6).

But "I will rescue my flock," declared the Lord (v. 10), and His promise still holds.

What do we need to do? Hold fast to almighty God and His promises. "I myself will search for my sheep and look after them," He says (v. 11). That's a saving promise worth holding tightly. *Patricia*

Our Reason for Joy
Psalm 149:1–5

Let Israel rejoice in their Maker; let the people of Zion be glad in their King. —PSALM 149:2

When the schoolyear began, fourteen-year-old C.J. would hop off the bus every afternoon and dance down his driveway. His mom recorded and shared videos of C.J.'s afterschool boogie time. He danced because he enjoyed life and "making people happy" with every move. One day, two garbage collectors took time out of their busy work schedule to stomp, spin, and sway with the young boy who inspires others to dance with him. This trio demonstrates the power of sincere and infectious joy.

The writer of Psalm 149 describes the original source of enduring and unconditional joy—God. The psalmist encourages God's people to join together and "sing to the LORD a new song" (v. 1). He invites Israel to "rejoice in their Maker" and "be glad in their King" (v. 2). He calls us to worship Him with dancing and music (vv. 1–3). Why? Because "the LORD takes delight in his people; he crowns the humble with victory" (v. 4).

Our adoring Father created us and sustains the universe. He delights in us just because we're His beloved children. He designed us, knows us, and invites us into a personal relationship with Him. What an honor! Our loving and living God is our reason for everlasting joy. We can rejoice in the gift of His constant presence and be grateful for every day our Maker has given us.

Xochitl

Is God Listening?
1 John 5:13–15

If we ask anything according to his will, he hears us.
—1 JOHN 5:14

When I served on my church's congregational care team, one of my duties was to pray over the requests penciled on pew cards during the services. For an aunt's health. For a couple's finances. For a grandson's discovery of God. Rarely did I hear the results of these prayers. Most were anonymous, and I had no way of knowing how God had responded. I confess that at times I wondered, Was He really listening? Was anything happening as a result of my prayers?

Over our lifetimes, most of us question, "Does God hear me?" I remember my own Hannah-like pleas for a child that went unanswered for years. And there were my pleas that my father find faith, yet he died without any apparent confession.

Etched across the millennia are myriad instances of God's ear bending to listen: to Israel's groans under slavery (Exodus 2:24); to Moses on Mount Sinai (Deuteronomy 9:19); to Joshua at Gilgal (Joshua 10:14); to Hannah's prayers for a child (1 Samuel 1:10–17); to David crying out for deliverance from Saul (2 Samuel 22:7).

First John 5:14 crescendos, "If we ask anything according to his will, he hears us." The word for "hears" means to pay attention and to respond on the basis of having heard.

As we go to God today, may we have the confidence of His listening ear spanning the history of His people. He hears our pleas. *Elisa*

Fueled by Fire
Daniel 3:13–18, 25–27

If we are thrown into the blazing furnace, the God we serve is able to deliver us. . . . But even if he does not . . . we will not serve your gods. —DANIEL 3:17–18

When two firefighters, weary and sooty, stopped at a restaurant for breakfast, the waitress recognized the men from news coverage and realized they'd spent the night battling a warehouse fire. To show her appreciation, she wrote a note on their bill, "Your breakfast is on me today. Thank you . . . for serving others and for running into the places everyone else runs away from. . . . Fueled by fire and driven by courage, what an example you are."

In the Old Testament, we see an example of courage in the actions of three young men: Shadrach, Meshach, and Abednego (Daniel 3). Instead of obeying the mandate to bow down to a statue of the Babylonian king, these young men courageously showed their love for God through their refusal. Their penalty was to be thrown into a blazing furnace. Yet the men didn't back down: "If we are thrown into the blazing furnace, the God we serve is able to deliver us from it, and he will deliver us from Your Majesty's hand. But even if he does not . . . we will not serve your gods or worship the image of gold" (vv. 17–18).

God did rescue them and even walked with them in the fire (vv. 25–27). In our fiery trials and troubles today, we too have the assurance that God is with us. He is able.

Alyson

Who You Are
Psalm 8

What is mankind that you are mindful of them?
—*PSALM 8:4*

His name is Dnyan, and he considers himself a student
of the world. And "this is a very big school," he says of
all the cities and towns he's passed through. He began
a four-year journey on his bicycle in 2016 to meet and
learn from people. When there's a language barrier, he
finds that sometimes people can understand just by
looking at each other. He also depends on a translation
app on his phone to communicate. He doesn't measure
his journey in the miles he's traveled or the sights he's
seen. Instead, he measures it in the people who've left an
imprint on his heart: "Maybe I do not know your language, but I would like to find out who you are."

It's a very big world, yet God knows everything about
it and the people in it—fully and completely. The psalmist David was in awe of God when he considered all the
works of His hands: the making of the heavens, the
moon, and the stars (Psalm 8:3). He wondered, "What
is mankind that you are mindful of them, human beings
that you care for them?" (v. 4).

God knows you more thoroughly than anyone else
possibly can and He cares for you. We can only respond,
"Lord, our Lord, how majestic is your name in all the
earth!" (vv. 1, 9). *Anne*

Being There
Job 2:11–13

*They sat on the ground with [Job] for seven days
and seven nights. —JOB 2:13*

When Jen, a theme park employee, saw Ralph collapse in tears on the ground, she rushed to help. Ralph, a young boy with autism, was sobbing because the ride he'd waited all day to enjoy had broken down. Instead of hurrying him to his feet or simply urging him to feel better, Jen got down onto the ground with Ralph, validating his feelings and allowing him the time to cry.

Jen's actions are a beautiful example of how we can come alongside those who are grieving or suffering. The Bible tells of Job's crippling grief after the loss of his home, his herds (his income), his health, and the simultaneous deaths of his ten children. When Job's friends learned of his pain, they "set out from their homes . . . to go . . . comfort him" (Job 2:11). Job sat on the ground in mourning. When they arrived, his friends sat down with him—for seven days—saying nothing because they saw the depth of his suffering.

In their humanness, Job's friends later offered Job insensitive advice. But for the first seven days, they gave him the wordless and tender gift of presence. We may not understand someone's grief, but we don't need to understand in order to love them well by simply being with them. *Kirsten*

A Ripening Process
Jeremiah 15:15–18

When your words came, I ate them; they were my joy and my heart's delight. —JEREMIAH 15:16

Early in his fifty-year ministry in Cambridge, England, Charles Simeon (1759–1836) met a neighboring pastor, Henry Venn, and his daughters. After the visit, the daughters remarked how harsh and self-assertive the young man seemed. In response, Venn asked his daughters to pick a peach from the trees. When they wondered why their father would want the unripe fruit, he responded, "Well, my dears, it is green now, and we must wait; but a little more sun, and a few more showers, and the peach will be ripe and sweet. So it is with Mr. Simeon."

Over the years Simeon did soften through God's transforming grace. One reason was his commitment to read the Bible and pray every day. A friend who stayed with him for a few months witnessed this practice and remarked, "Here was the secret of his great grace and spiritual strength."

Simeon in his daily time with God followed the practice of the prophet Jeremiah, who faithfully listened for God's words. Jeremiah depended on them so much that he said, "When your words came, I ate them." He mulled and chewed over God's words, which were his "joy" and "heart's delight" (Jeremiah 15:16).

If we too resemble sour green fruit, we can trust that God will help to soften us through His Spirit as we get to know Him through reading and obeying the Scriptures.

Amy

Crumbled from Within
Psalm 32:1–5, Matthew 7:1–5

I said, "I will confess my transgressions to the LORD."
And you forgave the guilt of my sin. —PSALM 32:5

When I was a teenager, my mom painted a mural on our living room wall. The painting depicted an ancient Greek scene of a ruined temple with white columns lying on their sides, a crumbling fountain, and a broken statue. As I looked at the Hellenistic architecture that had once held great beauty, I tried to imagine what had destroyed it. I was curious, especially when I began studying about the tragedy of once great and thriving civilizations that had decayed and crumbled from within.

The sinful depravity and wanton destruction we see around us today can be troubling. It's natural for us to try to explain it by pointing to people and nations that have rejected God. But shouldn't we be casting our gaze inwardly as well? Scripture warns us about being hypocrites when we call out others to turn from their sinful ways without also taking a deeper look inside our own hearts (Matthew 7:1–5).

Psalm 32 challenges us to see and confess our own sin. It's only when we recognize and confess our personal sin that we can experience freedom from guilt and the joy of true repentance (vv. 1–5). And as we rejoice in knowing that God offers us complete forgiveness, we can share that hope with others who are also struggling with sin. *Cindy*

Prays on *La Playa*
Psalm 148

Let them praise the name of the LORD, for his name
alone is exalted. —PSALM 148:13

During a trip to celebrate our twenty-fifth anniversary, my husband and I read our Bibles on the beach. As vendors passed and called out the prices of their wares, we thanked each one but didn't buy anything. One vendor, Fernando, smiled wide at my rejection and insisted we consider buying gifts for friends. After I declined his invitation, Fernando packed up and began walking away . . . still grinning. "I pray God will bless your day," I said.

Fernando turned toward me and said, "He has! Jesus changed my life." Fernando knelt between our chairs. "I feel His presence here." He then shared how God had delivered him from drug and alcohol abuse more than fourteen years earlier.

My tears flowed as he recited entire poems from the book of Psalms and prayed for us. Together, we praised God and rejoiced in His presence . . . on *la playa*.

Psalm 148 is a prayer of praise. The psalmist encourages all of creation to "praise the name of the LORD, for at his command [everything was] created" (v. 5), "for his name alone is exalted; his splendor is above the earth and the heavens" (v. 13).

Though God invites us to bring our needs before Him and then trust that He hears and cares for us, He also delights in prayers of grateful praise wherever we are. Even on the beach. *Xochitl*

Flourish Again
Exodus 1:6–14

The more they were oppressed, the more they multiplied and spread. —*EXODUS 1:12*

Given enough sunlight and water, vibrant wildflowers carpet areas of California, such as Antelope Valley and Figueroa Mountain. But what happens when drought strikes? Scientists have discovered that certain wildflowers store large quantities of their seeds underground instead of allowing them to push through the soil and bloom. After the drought, the seeds below the ground push through the surface and flourish.

The ancient Israelites thrived in the land of Egypt, despite harsh conditions. Slave masters forced them to work in fields and make bricks. Ruthless overseers required them to build entire cities for Pharaoh. The king of Egypt even tried to use infanticide to reduce their numbers. However, because God sustained them, "the more they were oppressed, the more they multiplied and spread" (Exodus 1:12). Many Bible scholars estimate that the population of Israelite men, women, and children grew to two million or more during their time in Egypt.

God, who preserved His people then, is upholding us today as well. He can help us in any environment. We may worry about enduring through another tough season of life. But the Bible assures us that God, who "cares so wonderfully for wildflowers that are here today and [are gone] tomorrow," can provide for our needs (Matthew 6:30 NLT). You can flourish again. ❦ *Jennifer*

Recovering What's Lost
1 Samuel 30:1–6, 18–19

But David found strength in the LORD his God.
—1 SAMUEL 30:6

At the phone store, the young pastor steeled himself for bad news. His smart phone, accidentally dropped during our Bible class, was a total loss, right? Actually, no. The store clerk recovered all of the pastor's data, including his Bible videos and photos. She also recovered "every photo I'd ever deleted," he said. The store also "replaced my broken phone with a brand-new phone." As he said, "I recovered all I had lost and more."

David once led his own recovery mission after an attack by the vicious Amalekites. Spurned by Philistine rulers, David and his army discovered that the Amalekites had raided and burned down their town of Ziklag—taking captive "the women and everyone else in it," including all their wives and children (1 Samuel 30:2–3). "So David and his men wept aloud until they had no strength left to weep" (v. 4). The soldiers were so bitter with their leader David that they talked of "stoning him" (v. 6).

"But David found strength in the LORD his God" (v. 6). As God promised, David pursued the Amalekites and "recovered everything the Amalekites had taken. . . . Nothing was missing: young or old, boy or girl, plunder or anything else they had taken. David brought everything back" (vv. 18–19). As we face spiritual attacks that "rob" us even of hope, may we find renewed strength in God. He will be with us in every challenge of life.

Patricia

Light for the Path
Psalm 119:97–105

*How sweet are your words to my taste, sweeter than
honey to my mouth!* —PSALM 119:103

On Chicago Day on October 9, 1893, the city's theaters shut down because the owners figured everyone would be attending the World's Fair. Over seven hundred thousand people went, but Dwight Moody (1837–1899) wanted to fill a music hall at the other end of Chicago with preaching and teaching. His friend R. A. Torrey (1856–1928) was skeptical that Moody could draw a crowd on Chicago Day at the Fair. But by God's grace, he did. As Torrey later concluded, the crowds came because Moody knew "the one Book that this old world most longs to know—the Bible." Torrey longed for others to love the Bible as Moody did, reading it regularly with dedication and passion.

God through His Spirit brought people back to himself at the end of the nineteenth century in Chicago, and He continues to speak today. We can echo the psalmist's love for God and His Scriptures as he exclaims, "How sweet are your words to my taste, sweeter than honey to my mouth!" (Psalm 119:103). For the psalmist, God's messages of grace and truth acted as a light for his path, a lamp for his feet (v. 105).

How can we grow more in love with the Savior and His message? As we immerse ourselves in Scripture, God will increase our devotion to Him and guide us, shining His light along the paths we walk. ❦ *Amy*

Carried Through the Storm
Psalm 107:1–3, 23–32

*He stilled the storm to a whisper; the waves of the sea
were hushed. —PSALM 107:29*

During Scottish missionary Alexander Duff's first voyage to India in 1830, he was shipwrecked in a storm off the coast of South Africa. He and his fellow passengers made it to a small, desolate island; and a short time later, one of the crew found a copy of a Bible belonging to Duff that had washed ashore on the beach. When the book dried, Duff read Psalm 107 to his fellow survivors, and they took courage. Finally, after a rescue and yet another shipwreck, Duff arrived in India.

Psalm 107 lists some of the ways God delivered the Israelites. Perhaps Duff and his shipmates identified with and took comfort in the words: "He stilled the storm to a whisper; the waves of the sea were hushed. They were glad when it grew calm, and he guided them to their desired haven" (vv. 29–30). And, like the Israelites, they "[gave] thanks to the LORD for his unfailing love and his wonderful deeds for mankind" (v. 31).

We see a parallel to Psalm 107:28–30 in the New Testament (Matthew 8:23–27; Mark 4:35–41). Jesus and His disciples were in a boat at sea when a violent storm began. His disciples cried out in fear, and Jesus—God in flesh—calmed the sea. We too can take courage! Our powerful God and Savior hears and responds to our cries and comforts us in the midst of our storms. *Alyson*

God's Restoring Ways
Hosea 14

People will dwell again in his shade; they will flourish like the grain, they will blossom like the vine. —HOSEA 14:7

One of the most moving songs in the musical *The Greatest Showman* is "From Now On." Sung after the main character comes to some painful self-realizations about the ways he's wounded family and friends, the song celebrates the joy of coming back home and finding that what we already have is more than enough.

The book of Hosea concludes with a similar tone—one of breathless joy and gratitude at the restoration God makes possible for those who return to Him. Much of the book, which compares the relationship between God and His people to a relationship with an unfaithful spouse, grieves Israel's failures to love Him and live for Him.

But in chapter 14, Hosea lifts up the promise of God's boundless love, grace, and restoration—freely available to those who return to Him heartbroken over the ways they've abandoned Him (vv. 1–3). "I will heal their waywardness," God promises, "and love them freely" (v. 4). And what had seemed broken beyond repair will once more find wholeness and abundance, as God's grace, like dew, causes His people to "blossom like a lily" and "flourish like the grain" (vv. 5–7).

When we've hurt others or taken for granted God's goodness in our life, it's easy to assume we've forever marred the good gifts we've been given. But when we humbly turn to Him, we find His love is always reaching to embrace and restore. *Monica*

Our Father Sings
Zephaniah 3:14–20

He . . . will rejoice over you with singing.
—ZEPHANIAH 3:17

Dandy loves encouraging people by singing to them. One day he was having lunch at his favorite restaurant, and he noticed that the waitress was having a hard day. He asked her a few questions and then started quietly singing a catchy, upbeat song to cheer her up. "Well, kind sir, you just made my day. Thank you so much," she said with a big smile, as she wrote down his food order.

When we open the book of Zephaniah, we find that God loves to sing. The prophet masterfully drew a picture with his words in which he described God as a musician who loves to sing for and with His children. He wrote that God "will take great delight in you; in his love he will no longer rebuke you, but will rejoice over you with singing" (3:17). God promised to be present forever with those who have been transformed by His mercy. But it doesn't stop there! He invites and joins in with His people to "be glad and rejoice with all your heart" (v. 14).

We can only imagine the day when we'll be together with God and with all those who've put their trust in Jesus as their Savior. How amazing it will be to hear our heavenly Father sing songs for and with us and experience His love, approval, and acceptance. *Estera*

Surrendering All
Mark 10:26–31

Then Peter spoke up, "We have left everything to follow you!"
—MARK 10:28

Two men who left a legacy of serving others in Jesus's name began their careers in the arts. But they set those professions aside to following a different calling from God. James O. Fraser (1886–1938) decided not to pursue being a concert pianist in England so he could serve the Lisu people in China, while the American Judson Van DeVenter (1855–1939) chose to become an evangelist instead of pursuing a career in art. He later wrote the hymn "I Surrender All."

While having a vocation in the arts is the perfect calling for many, these men believed God called them to relinquish one career for another. They did what the rich, young ruler could not do when Jesus challenged him to give up his possessions and follow Him (Mark 10:17–25). Witnessing the exchange between Jesus and the reluctant young man, Peter exclaimed, "We have left everything to follow you!" (v. 28). Jesus assured him that God would give those who follow Him "a hundred times as much in this present age" and eternal life (v. 30). But He would give according to His wisdom: "Many who are first will be last, and the last first" (v. 31).

No matter where God has placed us, we're called to daily surrender our lives to Christ, obeying His gentle call to follow Him and serve Him with our talents and resources—whether in the home, office, community, or far from home. As we submit to His call, He'll also inspire us to love others. ❦ *Amy*

Printed on our Hearts
Proverbs 7:1–5

*Bind them on your fingers; write them on the tablet of
your heart.* —PROVERBS 7:3

When Johannes Gutenberg combined the printing press
with moveable type in 1450, he ushered in the era of
mass communications in the West, spreading learning
into new social realms. Literacy increased across the
globe and new ideas produced rapid transformations in
social and religious contexts. Gutenberg produced the
first-ever printed version of the Bible. Prior to this, Bibles were painstakingly hand-copied, taking scribes up
to a year to produce a single copy.

For centuries since, the printing press has provided
people like you and me the privilege of direct access to
Scripture. While we also have electronic versions available to us, many of us often hold a physical Bible in our
hands because of his invention. What was once inaccessible given the sheer cost and time to have a Bible copied
is readily at our fingertips today.

Having access to God's truth is an amazing privilege.
The writer of Proverbs indicates that we should treat His
instructions to us in the Scriptures as something to be
cherished, as "the apple of [our] eye" (Proverbs 7:2), and
we should write His words of wisdom on "the tablet of
[our] heart" (v. 3). As we seek to understand the Bible
and live according to its wisdom, we, like scribes, are
drawing God's truth from our "fingers" down into our
hearts, to be taken with us wherever we go. *Kirsten*

Jesus's Promise to You
John 14:15–21, 25–27

He will give you another advocate to help you and
be with you forever. — JOHN 14:16

Jason wailed as his parents handed him over to Amy. It was the two-year-old's first time in the church nursery while Mom and Dad attended the worship service—and he was not happy. Amy assured them he'd be fine. She tried to soothe him with toys and books, by rocking in a chair, walking around, standing still, and talking about what fun he could have. But everything was met with bigger tears and louder cries. Then she whispered five simple words in his ear: "I will stay with you." Peace and comfort quickly came.

Jesus offered His friends similar words of comfort during the week of His crucifixion: "The Father . . . will give you another advocate to help you and be with you forever—the Spirit of truth" (John 14:16–17). After His resurrection He gave them this promise: "Surely I am with you always, to the very end of the age" (Matthew 28:20). Jesus was soon to ascend to heaven, but He would send the Spirit to "stay" and live within His people.

We experience the Spirit's comfort and peace when our tears flow. We receive His guidance when we're wondering what to do (John 14:26). He opens our eyes to understand more of God (Ephesians 1:17–20), and He helps us in our weakness and prays for us (Romans 8:26–27).

We are never alone. He stays with us forever. *Anne*

Rest Well
Matthew 11:25–30

Come to me, all you who are weary and burdened, and I will give you rest. —MATTHEW 11:28

The clock blinked 1:55 a.m. Burdened by a late-night text conversation, sleep wasn't coming. I unwound the mummy-like clutch of my tangled sheets and padded quietly to the couch. I Googled what to do to fall asleep but instead found what not to do: don't take a nap or drink caffeine or work out late in the day. Check. Reading further on my tablet, I was advised not to use "screen time" late either. Oops. Texting hadn't been a good idea. When it comes to resting well, there are lists of what not to do.

In the Old Testament, God handed down rules regarding what not to do on the Sabbath in order to embrace rest. In the New Testament, Jesus offered a new way. Rather than stressing regulations, Jesus called the disciples into relationship. "Come to me, all you who are weary and burdened, and I will give you rest" (Matthew 11:28). In the preceding verse, Jesus pointed to His own ongoing relationship of oneness with His Father—the One He's revealed to us. The provision of ongoing help Jesus enjoyed from the Father is one we can experience as well.

While we're wise to avoid certain pastimes that can interrupt our sleep, resting well in Christ has more to do with relationship than regulation. I clicked my reader off and laid my burdened heart down on the pillow of Jesus's invitation: "Come to me . . ." *Elisa*

All Kinds of Prayers
Matthew 6:9–13

Pray continually, give thanks in all circumstances;
for this is God's will for you in Christ Jesus.
—*1 THESSALONIANS 5:17–18*

My family remembers my Grandpa Dierking as a man of strong faith and prayer. But it wasn't always so. My aunt recalls the first time her father announced to the family, "We're going to start giving thanks to God before we eat." His first prayer was far from eloquent, but Grandpa continued the practice of prayer for the next fifty years, praying often throughout each day. When he died, my husband gave my grandmother a "praying hands" plant, saying, "Grandpa was a man of prayer." His decision to follow God and talk to Him each day changed him into a faithful servant of Christ.

The Bible has a lot to say about prayer. In Matthew 6:9–13, Jesus gave a pattern for prayer to His followers, teaching them to approach God with sincere praise for who He is. As we bring our requests to God, we trust Him to provide "our daily bread" (v. 11). As we confess our sins, we ask Him for forgiveness and for help to avoid temptation (vv. 12–13).

But we aren't limited to praying the "Lord's Prayer." God wants us to pray "all kinds of prayers" on "all occasions" (Ephesians 6:18). Praying is vital for our spiritual growth, and it gives us the opportunity to be in continual conversation with Him every day (1 Thessalonians 5:17–18).

As we approach God with humble hearts that yearn to talk with Him, may He help us know and love Him better. *Cindy*

Laundry Day
Matthew 28:16–20

Go, then, to all peoples everywhere and make them my disciples. — MATTHEW 28:19 GNT

Driving through a low-income area near his church, Colorado pastor Chad Graham started praying for his "neighbors." When he noticed a small laundromat, he stopped to take a look inside and found it filled with customers. One asked Graham for a spare coin to operate the clothes dryer. That small request inspired a weekly "Laundry Day" sponsored by Graham's church. Members donate coins and soap to the laundromat, pray with customers, and support the owner of the laundry facility.

Their neighborhood outreach, which dares to include a laundromat, reflects Jesus's Great Commission to His disciples. As He said, "I have been given all authority in heaven and on earth. Go, then, to all peoples everywhere and make them my disciples: baptize them in the name of the Father, the Son, and the Holy Spirit" (Matthew 28:18–19 GNT).

His Holy Spirit's powerful presence enables "everywhere" outreach, including even a laundromat. Indeed, we don't go alone. As Jesus promised, "I will be with you always, to the end of the age" (v. 20 GNT).

Pastor Chad experienced that truth after praying at the laundromat for a customer named Jeff, who was battling cancer. As Chad reported, "When we opened our eyes, every customer in the room was praying with us, hands stretched out toward Jeff. It was one of the most sacred moments I have experienced as a pastor."

The lesson? Let's go everywhere to proclaim Christ.

Patricia

Unbreakable Faith
Isaiah 26:3–13

You will keep in perfect peace those whose minds are steadfast, because they trust in you. —ISAIAH 26:3

After doctors diagnosed their first-born son with autism, Diane Dokko Kim and her husband grieved facing a lifetime of caring for a cognitively disabled child. In her book *Unbroken Faith*, she admits to struggling with adjusting their dreams and expectations for their beloved son's future. Yet through this painful process, they learned that God can handle their anger, doubts, and fears. Now, with their son reaching adulthood, Diane uses her experiences to encourage parents of children with special needs. She tells others about God's unbreakable promises, limitless power, and loving faithfulness. She assures people that He gives us permission to grieve when we experience the death of a dream, an expectation, a way, or a season of life.

In Isaiah 26, the prophet declares that God's people can trust in the Lord forever, "for the LORD . . . is the Rock eternal" (v. 4). He's able to sustain us with supernatural peace in every situation (v. 12). Focusing on His unchanging character and crying out to Him during troublesome times revitalizes our hope (v. 15).

When we face any loss, disappointment, or difficult circumstance, God invites us to be honest with Him. He can handle our ever-changing emotions and our questions. He remains with us and refreshes our spirits with enduring hope. Even when we feel like our lives are falling apart, God can make our faith unbreakable.

🌿 *Xochitl*

Hotel Corona

2 Corinthians 5:14–20

Christ's love compels us, because we are convinced that one died for all . . . . From now on we regard no one from a worldly point of view. —2 CORINTHIANS 5:14, 16

The Dan Hotel in Jerusalem became known by a different name in 2020—"Hotel Corona." The government dedicated the hotel to patients recovering from COVID-19, and the hotel became known as a rare site of joy and unity during a difficult time. Since the residents already had the virus, they were free to sing, dance, and laugh together. And they did! In a country where tensions between different political and religious groups run high, the shared crisis created a space where people could learn to see each other as human beings first—and even become friends.

It's natural, normal even, for us to be drawn toward those we see as similar to us—people we suspect share similar experiences and values to our own. But as the apostle Paul often emphasized, the gospel is a challenge to any barriers between human beings that we see as "normal" (2 Corinthians 5:15). Through the lens of the gospel, we see a bigger picture than our differences—a shared brokenness and a shared longing and the need to experience healing in God's love.

If we believe that "one died for all," then we can also no longer be content with surface-level assumptions about others. Instead, "Christ's love compels us" (v. 14) to share His love and mission with those God loves more than we can imagine—all of us. ❦ *Monica*

Growing in God's Grace
2 Peter 1:3–11

Make every effort to add to your faith goodness; and to goodness, knowledge. —*2 PETER 1:5*

The English preacher Charles H. Spurgeon (1834–1892) lived life "full throttle." He became a pastor at age nineteen—and soon was preaching to large crowds. He personally edited all of his sermons, which eventually filled sixty-three volumes, and he wrote many commentaries, books on prayer, and other works. Plus he typically read six books a week! In one of his sermons, Spurgeon said, "The sin of doing nothing is about the biggest of all sins, for it involves most of the others. . . . Horrible idleness! God save us from it!"

Charles Spurgeon lived with diligence, which meant he "[made] every effort" (2 Peter 1:5) to grow in God's grace and to live for Him. If we're Christ's followers, God can instill in us that same desire and capacity to grow more like Jesus, to "make every effort to add to [our] faith goodness; and to goodness, knowledge . . . self-control, perseverance . . . godliness" (vv. 5–7)

We each have different motivations, abilities, and energy levels—not all of us can, or should, live at Charles Spurgeon's pace! But when we understand all Jesus has done for us, we have the greatest motivation for diligent, faithful living. And we find our strength through the resources God has given us to live for and serve Him. God through His Spirit can empower us in our efforts—big and small—to do so. *Alyson*

Shining Stars
Philippians 2:12–18

You will shine among them like stars in the sky as you hold firmly to the word of life. —PHILIPPIANS 2:15–16

I can close my eyes and go back in time to the house where I grew up. I remember stargazing with my father. We took turns squinting through his telescope, trying to focus on glowing dots that shimmered and winked. These pinpricks of light, born of heat and fire, stood out in sharp contrast to the smooth, ink-black sky.

Do you consider yourself to be a shining star? I'm not talking about reaching the heights of human achievement, but standing out against a dark background of brokenness and evil. The apostle Paul told the Philippian believers that God would shine in and through them as they held "firmly to the word of life" and avoided grumbling and arguing (Philippians 2:14–16).

Our unity with other believers and our faithfulness to God can set us apart from the world. The problem is that these things don't come naturally. We constantly strive to overcome temptation so we can maintain a close relationship with God. We wrestle against selfishness to have harmony with our spiritual brothers and sisters.

But still, there's hope. Alive in each believer, God's Spirit empowers us to be self-controlled, kind, and faithful (Galatians 5:22–23). Just as we are called to live beyond our natural capacity, God's supernatural help makes this possible (Philippians 2:13). If every believer became a "shining star" through the power of the Spirit, just imagine how the light of God would repel the darkness around us! *Jennifer*

Pursued by Love
Jonah 2:1–9

I will say, "Salvation comes from the LORD."
—JONAH 2:9

"I fled Him, down the nights and down the days," opens the famous poem "The Hound of Heaven" by English poet Francis Thompson. Thompson describes Jesus's unceasing pursuit—despite his efforts to hide, or even run away, from God. The poet imagines God speaking to him and saying, "I am He whom thou seekest!"

The pursuing love of God is a central theme of the book of Jonah. The prophet received an assignment to tell the people of Nineveh (notorious enemies of Israel) about their need to turn to God, but instead "Jonah ran away from the LORD" (Jonah 1:3). He secured passage on a ship sailing in the opposite direction of Nineveh, but the vessel was soon overcome by a violent storm. To save the ship's crew, Jonah was thrown overboard before being swallowed by a large fish (1:15–17).

In his own beautiful poem, Jonah recounted that despite his best efforts to run away from God, God pursued him. When Jonah was overcome by his situation and needed to be saved, he cried out to God in prayer and turned toward His love (2:2, 8). God answered and provided rescue not only for Jonah but for his Assyrian enemies as well (3:10).

As described in both poems, there may be seasons of our lives when we try to run from God. Even then Jesus loves us and is at work guiding us back into restored relationship with Him (1 John 1:9). ❧ *Lisa*

Rivals or Allies?

1 Corinthians 1:10–17

Be perfectly united in mind and thought.
—1 CORINTHIANS 1:10

The city of Texarkana sits squarely on the state border between Texas and Arkansas. The city of 70,000 inhabitants has two mayors, two city councils, and two police and fire departments. The crosstown sporting rivalry between high schools draws an uncommonly high attendance, reflecting the deep allegiance each town has to its own school. More significant challenges arise as well, such as disputes over the shared water system, governed by two sets of state laws. Yet the town is known for its unity despite the line that divides it. Residents gather annually for a dinner held on State Line Avenue to share a meal in celebration of their oneness as a community.

The believers in Corinth may not have drawn a line down their main thoroughfare, but they were divided. They'd been quarreling as a result of their allegiances to those who taught them about Jesus: Paul, Apollos, or Cephas (Peter). Paul called them all to oneness "in mind and thought" (1 Corinthians 1:10), reminding them it was Christ who was crucified for them, not their spiritual leaders.

We behave similarly today, don't we? We sometimes oppose even those who share our singularly important belief—Jesus's sacrifice for our wrongdoings—making them rivals instead of allies. Just as Christ himself is not divided, we, as His earthly representation—His body—mustn't allow differences over nonessentials to divide us. Instead, may we celebrate our oneness in Him.

Kirsten

It's Okay to Lament
Lamentations 3:19–26

The LORD is good to those whose hope is in him.
—LAMENTATIONS 3:25

I dropped to my knees and let my tears fall to the floor. "God, why aren't you taking care of me?" I cried. It was during the COVID-19 pandemic in 2020. I'd been laid off for almost a month, and something had gone wrong with my unemployment application. I hadn't received any money yet, and the stimulus check the US government had promised hadn't arrived. Deep down, I trusted that God would work out everything. I believed He truly loved me and would take care of me, but in that moment, I felt abandoned.

The book of Lamentations reminds us it's okay to lament. The book was likely written during or soon after the Babylonians destroyed Jerusalem in 587 BC. It describes the affliction (3:1, 19), oppression (1:18), and starvation (2:20; 4:10) the people faced. Yet, in the middle of the book the author remembers why he could hope: "Because of the LORD's great love we are not consumed, for his compassions never fail. They are new every morning; great is your faithfulness" (3:22–23). Despite the devastation, the author remembered that God remains faithful.

Sometimes it feels impossible to believe that "the LORD is good to those whose hope is in him, to the one who seeks him" (v. 25), especially when we don't see an end to our suffering. But we can cry out to Him, trusting that He hears us and will be faithful to see us through.

Julie

Everyone Needs a Mentor

Titus 2:1–8

To Titus, my true son in our common faith. —TITUS 1:4

Several years ago, while working for a previous employer, I walked into my new supervisor's office feeling wary and emotionally raw. My old supervisor had run our department with harshness and condescension, often leaving me (and others) in tears. Now I wondered, What would my new boss be like? Soon after I stepped into my new boss's office, I felt my fears dissipate as he welcomed me warmly and asked me to share about myself and my frustrations. He listened intently, and I knew by his kind expression and gentle words that he truly cared. A believer in Jesus, he became my work mentor, encourager, and friend.

The apostle Paul was a spiritual mentor to Titus, his "true son in our common faith" (Titus 1:4). In his letter to Titus, Paul offered him helpful instructions and guidelines for his role in the church. He not only taught but modeled how to "teach what is appropriate to sound doctrine" (2:1), set "an example by doing what is good," and "show integrity, seriousness and soundness of speech" (vv. 7–8). As a result, Titus became his partner, brother, and coworker (2 Corinthians 2:13; 8:23)—and a mentor of others.

Many of us have benefited from a mentor—a teacher, coach, grandparent, youth leader, or pastor—who guided us with their knowledge, wisdom, encouragement, and faith in God. Who could benefit from the spiritual lessons you've learned in your journey with Jesus?

Alyson

Missing: Wisdom
1 Kings 3:5–12

Give your servant a discerning heart . . . to distinguish
between right and wrong. —1 KINGS 3:9

Two-year-old Kenneth went missing. Yet within three minutes of his mom's 9-1-1 Call, an emergency worker found him just two blocks from home at the county fair. His mom had promised he could go later that day with his grandpa. But he'd driven his toy tractor there and parked it at his favorite ride. When the boy was safely home, his dad wisely removed the toy's battery.

Kenneth was actually rather smart to get where he wanted to go, but two-year-olds are missing another key quality: wisdom. And as adults we sometimes lack it too. Solomon, who'd been appointed king by his father David (1 Kings 2), admitted he felt like a child. God appeared to him in a dream and said, "Ask for whatever you want me to give you" (3:5). He replied, "I am only a little child and do not know how to carry out my duties. . . . So give your servant a discerning heart to govern your people and to distinguish between right and wrong" (vv. 7–9). God gave Solomon "a breadth of understanding as measureless as the sand on the seashore" (4:29).

Where can we get the wisdom we need? Solomon said the beginning of wisdom is a "fear" or awe of God (Proverbs 9:10). So we can start by asking Him to teach us about himself and to give us wisdom beyond our own.

❦ *Anne*

She Did What She Could
Mark 14:3–9

*She did what she could. She poured perfume on
my body beforehand to prepare for my burial.*
—*MARK 14:8*

She loaded the plastic container of cupcakes onto the conveyor belt, sending it toward the cashier. Next came the birthday card and various bags of chips. Hair escaped from her ponytail, crowning her fatigued forehead. Her toddler clamored for attention. The clerk announced the total and the mom's face fell. "Oh, I guess I'll have to put something back. But these are for her party," she sighed, glancing regretfully at her child.

Standing behind her in line, another customer recognized such pain. Jesus's words to Mary of Bethany echoed in her mind: "She did what she could" (Mark 14:8). After anointing Him with a bottle of expensive nard before His death and burial, Mary was ridiculed by the disciples. Jesus corrected His followers by celebrating what she had done. He didn't say, "She did all she could," but rather, "She did what she could." The lavish cost of the perfume wasn't His point. It was Mary's investment of her love in action that mattered. A relationship with Jesus results in a response.

In that moment, before the mom could object, the second customer leaned forward and inserted her credit card into the reader, paying for the purchase. It wasn't a large expense, and she had extra funds that month. But to that mom, it was everything. A gesture of pure love poured out in her moment of need. *Elisa*

We're Not God
Ezekiel 28:1–10

In the pride of your heart you say, "I am a god."
—*EZEKIEL 28:2*

In *Mere Christianity*, C. S. Lewis recommended asking ourselves some questions to find out if we're proud: "How much do I dislike it when other people snub me, or refuse to take any notice of me, . . . or patronize me, or show off?" Lewis saw pride as a vice of the "utmost evil" and the chief cause of misery in homes and nations. He called it a "spiritual cancer" that eats up the very possibility of love, contentment, and even common sense.

Pride has been a problem throughout the ages. Through the prophet Ezekiel, God warned the leader of the powerful coastal city of Tyre against his pride. He said the king's pride would result in his downfall: "Because you think you are . . . as wise as a god, I am going to bring foreigners against you" (Ezekiel 28:6–7). Then he would know he wasn't a god, but a mortal (v. 9).

In contrast to pride is humility, which Lewis named as a virtue we receive through knowing God. Lewis said that as we get in touch with Him, we become "delightedly humble," feeling relieved to be rid of the silly nonsense about our own dignity that previously made us restless and unhappy.

The more we worship God, the more we'll know Him and the more we can humble ourselves before Him. May we be those who love and serve with joy and humility.

❦ *Amy*

A Good Man
Romans 3:10–18

*By grace you have been saved, through faith—and that
is not from yourselves, it is the gift of God.*
—EPHESIANS 2:8

"Jerry was a good man," the pastor said at Jerald Stevens's
memorial service. "He loved his family. He was faithful
to his wife. He served his country in the armed services.
He was an excellent dad and grandfather. He was a great
friend."

But then the pastor went on to tell the friends and
family gathered that Jerry's good life and good deeds
were not enough to assure him a place in heaven. And
that Jerry himself would have been the first to tell them
that!

Jerry believed these words from the Bible: "All have
sinned and fall short of the glory of God" (Romans
3:23) and "the wages of sin is death" (6:23). Jerry's final
and eternal destination in life's journey was not determined by whether he lived a really good life but entirely
by Jesus—the perfect Son of God—dying in his place
to pay sin's penalty. He believed that each of us must
personally accept the free gift of God, which is "eternal
life in Christ Jesus our Lord" (v. 23).

Jerry was a good man, but he could never be "good
enough." He, like us, had to learn that salvation and
righteousness aren't the results of human effort. They're
gifts by God's grace (Ephesians 2:8).

"Thanks be to God for his indescribable gift!" (2 Corinthians 9:15). *Cindy*

Working with God
1 Corinthians 3:1–9

We are co-workers in God's service; you are God's field,
God's building. —1 CORINTHIANS 3:9

During his 1962 visit to Mexico, Bill Ashe helped fix windmill hand pumps at an orphanage. Fifteen years later, inspired by a deep desire to serve God by helping provide clean water to villages in need, Bill founded a nonprofit organization. He said, "God awoke me to 'make the most of the time' by finding others with a desire to bring safe drinking water to the rural poor." Later, having learned about the global need for safe water through the requests of thousands of pastors and evangelists from more than one hundred countries, Bill invited others to join the ministry's efforts.

God welcomes us to team up to serve with Him and others in various ways. When the people of Corinth argued over which teachers they preferred, the apostle Paul affirmed his role as a servant of Jesus and a teammate of Apollos, fully dependent on God for spiritual growth (1 Corinthians 3:1–7). He reminds us that all work has God-given value (v. 8). Acknowledging the privilege of working with others while serving Him, Paul encourages us to build each other up as He transforms us in love (v. 9).

Though our mighty Father doesn't need our help to accomplish His great works, He equips us and invites us to partner with Him. *Xochitl*

Rise Again
Proverbs 24:15–18

Though the righteous fall seven times, they rise again.
—PROVERBS 24:16

Olympic runner Ryan Hall is the US record holder for the half marathon. He completed the event distance of 13.1 miles (21 kilometers) in a remarkable time of fifty-nine minutes and forty-three seconds, making him the first US athlete to run the race in under one hour. While Hall has celebrated record-setting victories, he has also known the disappointment of not being able to finish a race.

Having tasted both success and failure, Hall credits his faith in Jesus for sustaining him. One of his favorite Bible verses is an encouraging reminder from the book of Proverbs that "though the righteous fall seven times, they rise again" (24:16). This proverb reminds us that the righteous, those who trust in and have a right relationship with God, will still experience difficulties and hardships. However, as they continue to seek Him even in the midst of difficulty, God is faithful to give them the strength to rise again.

Have you recently experienced a devastating disappointment or failure and feel like you will never recover? Scripture encourages us not to rely on our strength but to continue to put our confidence in God and His promises. As we trust Him, God's Spirit gives us strength for every difficulty we encounter in this life, from seemingly mundane to significant struggles (2 Corinthians 12:9).

Lisa

Slowing Time Down
Psalm 90:4, 12–15

Teach us to number our days, that we may gain a heart of wisdom. —PSALM 90:12

A lot has changed since the electric clock was invented in the 1840s. We now keep time on smart watches, smart phones, and laptops. The entire pace of life seems faster—with even our "leisurely" walking speeding up. This is especially true in cities and can have a negative effect on health, scholars say. "We're just moving faster and faster and getting back to people as quickly as we can," Professor Richard Wiseman observed. "That's driving us to think everything has to happen now."

Moses, the writer of one of the oldest of the Bible's psalms, reflected on time. He reminds us that God controls life's pace. "A thousand years in your sight are like a day that has just gone by, or like a watch in the night," he wrote (Psalm 90:4).

The secret to time management, therefore, isn't to go faster or slower. It's to abide in God, spending more time with Him. Then we get in step with each other, but first with Him—the One who formed us (139:13) and knows our purpose and plans (v. 16).

Our time on earth won't last forever. Yet we can manage it wisely, not by watching the clock, but by giving each day to God. As Moses said, "Teach us to number our days, that we may gain a heart of wisdom" (90:12). Then, with God we'll always be on time, now and forever. *Patricia*

God's Plan for You

Psalm 37:3–7

Take delight in the LORD, and he will give you the
desires of your heart. —PSALM 37:4

For six years, Agnes tried to make herself the "perfect minister's wife," modeling herself after her adored mother-in-law (also a pastor's wife). She thought that in this role she couldn't also be a writer and painter, but in burying her creativity she became depressed and contemplated suicide. Only the help of a neighboring pastor moved her out of the darkness as he prayed with her and assigned her two hours of writing each morning. This awakened her to what she called her "sealed orders"—the calling God had given her. She wrote, "For me to be really myself—my complete self—every . . . flow of creativity that God had given me had to find its channel."

Later, she pointed to one of David's songs that expressed how she found her calling: "Take delight in the LORD, and he will give you the desires of your heart" (Psalm 37:4). As she committed her way to God, trusting Him to lead and guide her (v. 5), He made a way for her not only to write and paint but to help others to better communicate with Him.

God has a set of "sealed orders" for each of us, not only that we'll know we're His beloved children but understand the unique ways we can serve Him through our gifts and passions. He'll lead us as we trust and delight in Him. *Amy*

Jesus's Unpopular Ideas
Matthew 5:38–48

Give to the one who asks you. —MATTHEW 5:42

For fifteen years, Mike Burden held hate-filled meetings in the memorabilia shop he ran in his small town. But when his wife began to question his involvement, his heart softened. He realized how wrong his racist views were and didn't want to be that person any longer. The militant group retaliated by kicking his family out of the apartment they'd been renting from one of the members.

Where did he turn for help? Surprisingly, he went to a local black pastor with whom he'd clashed. The pastor and his church provided housing and groceries for Mike's family for some time. When asked why he agreed to help, Pastor Kennedy explained, "Jesus Christ did some very unpopular things. When it's time to help, you do what God wants you to do." Later Mike spoke at Kennedy's church and apologized to the black community for his part in spreading hatred.

Jesus taught some unpopular ideas in the Sermon on the Mount: "Give to the one who asks you. . . . Love your enemies and pray for those who persecute you" (Matthew 5:42, 44). That's the upside-down way of thinking God calls us to follow. Though it looks like weakness, it's actually acting out of God's strength.

The One who teaches us is the One who gives the power to live out this upside-down life in whatever way He asks of us. 🌿 *Anne*

Infinite Dimensions
Ephesians 3:16–21

I pray that you . . . [will] grasp how wide and long and high and deep is the love of Christ. —EPHESIANS 3:17–18

I lay still on the vinyl-covered mat and held my breath on command as the machine whirred and clicked. I knew lots of folks had endured MRIs, but for claustrophobic me, the experience required focused concentration on something—Someone—much bigger than myself.

In my mind, a phrase from Scripture: "how wide and long and high and deep is the love of Christ" (Ephesians 3:18) moved in rhythm with the machine's hum. In Paul's prayer for the Ephesian church, he described four dimensions to God's love in order to stress the unending parameters of His love and presence.

My position while lying down for the MRI provided a new image for my understanding. Wide: the six inches on either side of where my arms were tightly pinned to my body within the tube. Long: the distance between the cylinder's two openings, extending out from my head and feet. High: the six inches from my nose up to the "ceiling" of the tube. Deep: the support of the tube anchored to the floor beneath me, holding me up. Four dimensions illustrating God's presence surrounding and holding me in the MRI tube-and in every circumstance of life.

God's love is ALL around us. Wide: He extends His arms to reach all people everywhere. Long: His love never ends. High: He lifts us up. Deep: He dips down, holding us in all situations. Nothing can separate us from Him! (Romans 8:38–39). *Elisa*

Choosing to Honor God
Psalm 18:20–27

To the faithful you show yourself faithful.
—*PSALM 18:25*

In the novella *Family Happiness* by Leo Tolstoy, main characters Sergey and Masha meet when Masha is young and impressionable. Sergey is an older, well-traveled businessman who understands the world beyond the rural setting where Masha lives. Over time, the two fall in love and marry.

They settle in the countryside, but Masha becomes bored with her surroundings. Sergey, who adores her, arranges a trip to St. Petersburg. There, Masha's beauty and charm bring her instant popularity. Just as the couple is about to return home, a prince arrives in town, wanting to meet her. Sergey knows he can force Masha to leave with him, but he lets her make the decision. She chooses to stay, and her betrayal breaks his heart.

Like Sergey, God will never force us to be faithful to Him. Because He loves us, he lets us choose for or against Him. Our first choice for Him happens when we receive His Son, Jesus Christ, as the sacrifice for our sin (1 John 4:9–10). After that, we have a lifetime of decisions to make.

Will we choose faithfulness to God as His Spirit guides us, or let the world entice us? David's life wasn't perfect, but he often wrote about keeping "the ways of the LORD" and the good outcomes that came from doing so (Psalm 18:21–24). When our choices honor God, we can experience the blessing David described: to the faithful, God shows himself faithful. *Jennifer*

Surviving Drought
Jeremiah 17:5–8

*The one who trusts in the LORD . . . will be like a tree
planted by the water.* —JEREMIAH 17:7–8

During one recent spring, a suburban neighborhood in
Victorville, California, became buried in tumbleweeds.
High winds pushed the rolling thistles into the development from the adjacent Mojave Desert where the plant
grows. At maturity, the pesky weed can grow to up to six
feet in height—a formidable size when it releases itself
from its roots to "tumble" with the wind to scatter its
seeds.

Tumbleweeds are what I picture when I read Jeremiah's description of a person "whose heart turns away
from the LORD" (Jeremiah 17:5). He says that those
who draw their strength from "mere flesh" will be like
"a bush in the wastelands" and be unable to "see prosperity when it comes" (vv. 5–6). In sharp contrast are
those who put their trust in God instead of people. Like
trees, their strong, deep roots draw strength from Him,
enabling them to remain full of life, even in the midst of
drought-like circumstances.

Tumbleweeds and trees both have roots. Tumbleweeds, however, don't stay connected to their life-source,
causing them to dry out and die. Trees, on the other
hand, remain connected to their roots, enabling them to
flourish and thrive, anchored to that which will sustain
them in times of difficulty. When we hold fast to God,
drawing strength and encouragement from the wisdom
found in the Bible and talking to Him in prayer, we too
can experience the life-giving, life-sustaining nourishment He provides. *Kirsten*

New Every Morning
Lamentations 3:19–26

[God's] compassions never fail. They are new every morning.
—LAMENTATIONS 3:22–23

My brother Paul grew up battling severe epilepsy, and when he entered his teenage years it became even worse. Nighttime became excruciating for him and my parents, as he'd experience continuous seizures for often more than six hours at a time. Doctors couldn't find a treatment that would alleviate the symptoms while also keeping him conscious for at least part of the day. My parents cried out in prayer: "God, oh God, help us!"

Although their emotions were battered and their bodies exhausted, Paul and my parents received enough strength from God for each new day. In addition, my parents found comfort in the words of the Bible, including the book of Lamentations. Here Jeremiah voiced his grief over the destruction of Jerusalem by the Babylonians, remembering "the bitterness and the gall" (3:19). Yet Jeremiah didn't lose hope. He called to mind the mercies of God, that His compassions "are new every morning" (v. 23). So too did my parents.

Whatever you're facing, know that God is faithful every morning. He renews our strength day by day and gives us hope. And sometimes, as with my family, He brings relief. After several years, a new medication became available that stopped Paul's continuous nighttime seizures, giving my family restorative sleep and hope for the future.

When our souls are downcast within us (v. 20), may we call to mind the promises of God that His mercies are new every morning. *Amy*

Dig It Up
Ruth 1:3–5, 20–21

Get rid of all bitterness. —EPHESIANS 4:31

When Rebecca's brother and sister-in-law started having marriage problems, Rebecca prayed earnestly for their reconciliation. But they divorced. Then her sister-in-law took the children out of state, and their dad didn't protest. Rebecca never again saw the nieces she dearly loved. Years later she said, "Because of trying to handle this sadness on my own, I let a root of bitterness start in my heart, and it began to spread to my family and friends."

The book of Ruth tells about a woman named Naomi who struggled with a heart of grief that grew into bitterness. Her husband died in a foreign land, and ten years later both her sons died. She was left destitute with her daughters-in-law, Ruth and Orpah (1:3–5). When Naomi and Ruth returned to Naomi's home country, the whole town was excited to see them. But Naomi told her friends: "The Almighty has made my life very bitter. . . . The LORD has afflicted me" (vv. 20–21). She even asked them to call her "Mara," meaning bitter.

Who hasn't faced disappointment and been tempted toward bitterness? Someone says something hurtful, an expectation isn't met, or demands from others make us resentful. When we acknowledge to ourselves and God what's happening deep in our hearts, our tender Gardener can help us dig up any roots of bitterness—whether they're still small or have been growing for years—and can replace them with a sweet, joyful spirit. *Anne*

The Wisdom We Need
Proverbs 1:1–9

Fear of the LORD is the foundation of true knowledge.
—PROVERBS 1:7 NLT

Ellen opened her mailbox and discovered a bulky envelope with her dear friend's return address. Just a few days prior, she'd shared a relational struggle with that friend. Curious, she unwrapped the package and found a colorful beaded necklace on a simple jute string. Attached was a card with a company's slogan, "Say It in Morse Code," and words translating the necklace's hidden and wise message, "Seek God's Ways." Ellen smiled as she fastened it around her neck.

The book of Proverbs is a compilation of wise sayings—many penned by Solomon, who was acclaimed as the wisest man of his era (1 Kings 10:23). Its thirty-one chapters call the reader to listen to wisdom and avoid folly, starting with the core message of Proverbs 1:7, "Fear of the LORD is the foundation of true knowledge" (NLT). Wisdom—knowing what to do when—comes from honoring God by seeking His ways. In the introductory verses, we read, "Listen when your father corrects you. Don't neglect your mother's instruction. What you learn from them will crown you with grace and be a chain of honor around your neck" (vv. 8–9 NLT).

Ellen's friend had directed her to the Source of the wisdom she needed: Seek God's ways. Her gift focused Ellen's attention on where to discover the help she needed.

When we honor God and seek His ways, we'll receive the wisdom we need for all the matters we face in life. Each and every one. ~ *Elisa*

The Gift of Peace
Luke 2:25–35

My eyes have seen your salvation. —LUKE 2:30

"I believe in Jesus, and He is my Savior, and I have no fear of death," said Barbara Bush, the wife of former US President George H. W. Bush, to her son before she died. This incredible and confident statement suggests a strong and deep-rooted faith. She experienced God's gift of peace that comes from knowing Jesus, even when faced with death.

Simeon, a resident of Jerusalem during the first century, also experienced profound peace because of Jesus. Moved by the Holy Spirit, Simeon went to the temple where Mary and Joseph brought baby Jesus "to present him to the Lord" (Luke 2:22). Although not much is known about Simeon, from Luke's description one can tell he was a special man of God, just and devout, waiting faithfully for the coming Messiah, and "the Holy Spirit was on him" (v. 25). Yet Simeon did not experience shalom (peace), a deep sense of completeness, until he saw Jesus.

While holding Jesus in his arms, Simeon broke into a song of praise, expressing full satisfaction in God: "You may now dismiss your servant in peace. For my eyes have seen your salvation, which you have prepared in the sight of all nations" (vv. 29–31). He had peace because he foresaw the future hope of the whole world.

Each time we think of and celebrate the life, death, and resurrection of Jesus, the promised Savior, may we rejoice in God's gift of peace. *Estera*

Know His Voice
John 10:1–10

*I am the good shepherd; I know my sheep and my sheep
know me. —JOHN 10:14*

One year for vacation Bible school, Ken's church decided
to bring in live animals to illustrate the Scripture. When
he arrived to help, Ken was asked to take a sheep inside.
He had to practically drag the wooly animal by a rope
into the church gymnasium. But as the week went on,
it became less reluctant to follow him. By the end of the
week, Ken didn't have to hold the rope anymore; he just
called the sheep and it followed, knowing it could trust
him.

In the New Testament, Jesus compares himself to a
shepherd, stating that His people, the sheep, will follow
Him because they know His voice (John 10:4). But those
same sheep will run from a stranger or thief (v. 5). Like
sheep, we (believers in Jesus) get to know the voice of our
Shepherd through our relationship with Him. And as we
do, we see His character and learn to trust Him.

As we grow to know and love God, we'll be discerning
of His voice and better able to run from the "the thief
[who] comes only to steal and kill and destroy" (v. 10)—
from those who try to deceive and draw us away from
Him. Unlike those false teachers, we can trust the voice
of our Shepherd to lead us to safety. *Julie*

Love Locks
Song of Songs 8:5–7

Place me like a seal over your heart, like a seal on your arm.
—SONG OF SONGS 8:6

I stood amazed at the hundreds of thousands of padlocks, many engraved with the initials of sweethearts, attached to every imaginable part of the Pont des Arts bridge in Paris. The pedestrian bridge across the Seine River was inundated with these symbols of love, a couple's declaration of "forever" commitment. In 2014, the love locks were estimated to weigh a staggering fifty tons and had even caused a portion of the bridge to collapse, necessitating the locks' removal.

The presence of so many love locks points to the deep longing we have as human beings for assurance that love is secure. In Song of Songs, an Old Testament book that depicts a dialogue between two lovers, the woman expresses her desire for secure love by asking her beloved to "place me like a seal over your heart, like a seal on your arm" (Song of Songs 8:6). Her longing was to be as safe and secure in his love as a seal impressed on his heart or a ring on his finger.

The longing for enduring romantic love expressed in Song of Songs points us to the New Testament truth in Ephesians that we are marked with the "seal" of God's Spirit (1:13). While human love can be fickle, and locks can be removed from a bridge, Christ's Spirit living in us is a permanent seal demonstrating God's never-ending, committed love for each of His children. *Lisa*

Useful Temptation
James 1:2–5, 12–21

*Humbly accept the word planted in you,
which can save you.* —*JAMES 1:21*

Fifteenth-century monk Thomas à Kempis, in the beloved classic *The Imitation of Christ*, offers a perspective on temptation that might be a bit surprising. Instead of focusing on the pain and difficulties temptation can lead to, he writes, "[temptations] are useful because they can make us humble, they can cleanse us, and they can teach us." Kempis explains, "The key to victory is true humility and patience; in them we overcome the enemy."

Humility and patience. How different my walk with Christ would be if that were how I naturally responded to temptation! More often, I react with shame, frustration, and impatient attempts to get rid of the struggle.

But as we learn from James 1, the temptations and trials we face don't have to be without purpose or merely a threat we endure. Although giving in to temptation can bring heartbreak and devastation (vv. 13–15), when we turn to God with humble hearts seeking His wisdom and grace, we find He "gives generously to all without finding fault" (v. 5). Through His power in us, our trials and struggles to resist sin build perseverance, "so that [we] may be mature and complete, not lacking anything" (v. 4).

As we trust in Jesus, there's no reason to live in fear. As God's dearly loved children, we can find peace as we rest in His loving arms even as we face temptation.

Monica

Making His Music

2 Corinthians 3:17–18

We all . . . are being transformed into his image.
—2 CORINTHIANS 3:18

Choir director Arianne Abela spent her childhood sitting on her hands—to hide them. Born with fingers missing or fused together on both hands, she also had no left leg and was missing toes on her right foot. A music lover and lyric soprano, she'd planned to major in government at Smith College. But one day her choir teacher asked her to conduct the choir, which made her hands quite visible. From that moment, she found her career, going on to conduct church choirs and serving now as director of choirs at another university. "My teachers saw something in me," Abela explains.

Her inspiring story invites believers to ask, *What does God, our holy Teacher, see in us, regardless of our "limits"?* More than anything, He sees himself. "So God created human beings in his own image. In the image of God he created them; male and female he created them" (Genesis 1:27 NLT).

As His glorious "image bearers," when others see us, we should reflect Him. For Abela, that means Jesus, not her hands—or her lack of fingers—matters most. The same is true for all believers. "And we all, who with unveiled faces contemplate the Lord's glory, are being transformed into his image," says 2 Corinthians 3:18.

Similar to Abela, we can conduct our lives by Christ's transforming power (v. 18), offering a life song that rings out to the honor of God. *Patricia*

An Unexpected Guest
Luke 19:1–10

[Jesus said], "Zacchaeus, come down immediately.
I must stay at your house today." —LUKE 19:5

Zach was a lonely guy. When he walked down the city streets, he could feel the hostile glares. But then his life took a turn. Clement of Alexandria, one of the church fathers, says that Zach became a very prominent Christian leader and a pastor of the church in Caesarea. Yes, we're talking about Zacchaeus, the chief tax collector who climbed a sycamore tree to see Jesus (Luke 19:1–10).

What prompted him to climb the tree? Tax collectors were perceived as traitors because they heavily taxed their own people to serve the Roman Empire. Yet Jesus had a reputation for accepting them. Zacchaeus might have wondered if Jesus would accept him too. Being short in stature, however, he couldn't see over the crowd (v. 3). Perhaps he climbed a tree to seek Him out.

And Jesus was seeking Zacchaeus too. When Christ reached the tree where he was perched, He looked up and said, "Zacchaeus, come down immediately. I must stay at your house today" (v. 5). Jesus considered it absolutely necessary that He be a guest in this outcast's home. Imagine that! The Savior of the world wanting to spend time with a social reject.

Whether it's our hearts, relationships, or lives that need mending, like Zacchaeus we can have hope. Jesus will never reject us when we turn to Him. He can restore what's been lost and broken and give our lives new meaning and purpose. *Poh Fang*

Good Measure
Luke 6:32–38

Give, and it will be given to you. —LUKE 6:38

At a gas station one day, Staci encountered a woman who had left home without her bank card. Stranded with her baby, she was asking passersby for help. Although unemployed at the time, Staci spent $15 to put gas in the stranger's tank. Days later, Staci came home to find a gift basket of children's toys and other presents waiting on her porch. Friends of the stranger had reciprocated Staci's kindness and converted her $15 blessing into a memorable Christmas for her family.

This heartwarming story illustrates the point Jesus made when he said, "Give, and it will be given to you. A good measure, pressed down, shaken together and running over, will be poured into your lap. For with the measure you use, it will be measured to you" (Luke 6:38).

It can be tempting to hear this and focus on what we get out of giving, but doing so would miss the point. Jesus preceded that statement with this one: "Love your enemies, do good to them, and lend to them without expecting to get anything back. Then your reward will be great, and you will be children of the Most High, because he is kind to the ungrateful and wicked" (v. 35).

We don't give to get things; we give because God delights in our generosity. Our love for others reflects His loving heart toward us. *Remi*

On the Same Team
1 Thessalonians 5:1–11, 16–18

Encourage one another and build each other up.
—1 THESSALONIANS 5:11

When quarterback Carson Wentz returned to the field after healing from a severe injury, his backup quarterback for the Philadelphia Eagles at the time, Nick Foles, returned to the bench without complaint. Although competing for the same position, the two men chose to support each other and remained confident in their roles. One reporter observed that the two athletes have a "unique relationship rooted in their faith in Christ" shown through their ongoing prayers for each other. As others watched, they brought honor to God by remembering they were on the same team—not just as Eagles quarterbacks, but as believers in Jesus representing Him.

The apostle Paul reminds believers to live as "children of the light" awaiting Jesus's return (1 Thessalonians 5:5–6). With our hope secure in the salvation Christ has provided, we can shrug off any temptations to compete out of jealousy, insecurity, fear, or envy. Instead, we can "encourage one another and build each other up" (v. 11). We can respect spiritual leaders who honor God and "live in peace" as we serve together to accomplish our shared goal—telling people about the gospel and encouraging others to live for Jesus (vv. 12–15).

As we serve on the same team, we can heed Paul's command: "Rejoice always, pray continually, give thanks in all circumstances; for this is God's will for you in Christ Jesus" (vv. 16–18). 🌿 *Xochitl*

A New Calling
2 Timothy 1:6–14

He has saved us and called us to a holy life.
—*2 TIMOTHY 1:9*

Teenage gang leader Casey and his followers broke into homes and cars, robbed convenience stores, and fought other gangs. Eventually, Casey was arrested and sentenced. In prison, he became a "shot caller," someone who handed out homemade knives during riots.

Sometime later, he was placed in solitary confinement. While daydreaming in his cell, Casey experienced a "movie" of sorts replaying key events of his life—and of Jesus, being led to and nailed to the cross and telling him, "I'm doing this for you." Casey fell to the floor weeping and confessed his sins. Later, he shared his experience with a chaplain, who explained more about Jesus and gave him a Bible. "That was the start of my journey of faith," Casey said. Eventually, he was released into the mainline prison population, where he was mistreated for his faith. But he felt at peace, because "[he] had found a new calling: telling other inmates about Jesus."

In his letter to Timothy, the apostle Paul talks about the power of Christ to change lives: God calls us from lives of wrongdoing to follow and serve Jesus (2 Timothy 1:9). When we receive Him by faith, we desire to be a living witness of Christ's love. The Holy Spirit enables us to do so, even when suffering, in our quest to share the good news (v. 8). Like Casey, let's live out our new calling. 🕊 *Alyson*

The Reason to Rest
Ecclesiastes 2:17–26

What do people get for all the toil and anxious striving with which they labor under the sun? —ECCLESIASTES 2:22

If you want to live longer, take a vacation! Forty years after a study of middle-aged, male executives who each had a risk of heart disease, researchers in Helsinki, Finland, followed up with their study participants. The scientists discovered something they hadn't been looking for in their original findings: the death rate was lower among those who had taken time off for vacations.

Work is a necessary part of life—a part God appointed to us even before our relationship with Him was fractured in Genesis 3. Solomon wrote of the seeming meaninglessness of work experienced by those not working for God's honor—recognizing its "anxious striving" and "grief and pain" (Ecclesiastes 2:22–23). Even when they're not actively working, he says their "minds do not rest" because they're thinking about what still needs to be done (v. 23).

We too might at times feel like we're "chasing after the wind" (v. 17) and grow frustrated by our inability to "finish" our work. But when we remember that God is part of our labor—our purpose—we can both work hard and take time to rest. We can trust Him to be our Provider, for He's the giver of all things. Solomon acknowledges that "without him, who can eat or find enjoyment?" (v. 25). Perhaps by reminding ourselves of that truth, we can work diligently for Him (Colossians 3:23) and also allow ourselves times of rest. 🌿 *Kirsten*

Giving Thanks Always
Isaiah 12:1–6

Give praise to the Lord, proclaim his name; make known among the nations what he has done. —ISAIAH 12:4

In the seventeenth century, Martin Rinkart served as a clergyman in Saxony, Germany, for more than thirty years during times of war and plague. One year he conducted more than 4,000 funerals, including his wife's, and at times food was so scarce that his family went hungry. Although he could have despaired, his faith in God remained strong and he gave thanks continually. In fact, he poured his gratitude into "Nun danket alle Gott," the song that became the well-loved English hymn, "Now Thank We All Our God."

Rinkart followed the example of the prophet Isaiah, who instructed God's people to give thanks at all times, including when they'd disappointed God (Isaiah 12:1) or when enemies oppressed them. Even then they were to exalt God's name, making "known among the nations what he has done" (v. 4).

We might give thanks easily during harvest celebrations such as Thanksgiving, when we're enjoying an abundant feast with friends and family. But can we express our gratitude to God in difficult times, such as when we're missing someone from our table or when we're struggling with our finances or when we're locked in conflict with one close to us?

Let's echo Pastor Rinkart, joining hearts and voices as we give praise and thanks to "the eternal God, whom earth and Heaven adore." We can "sing to the Lord, for he has done glorious things" (v. 5). *Amy*

If Only We Could . . .
Psalm 28

The LORD is the strength of his people. —PSALM 28:8

The weeping Alaskan cedar tree whipped from side to side in the storm's strong winds. Regie loved the tree, which had not only provided shelter from the summer sun but had also given her family privacy. Now the fierce storm was tearing the roots from the ground. Quickly, Regie, with her fifteen-year-old son in tow, ran to try to rescue the tree. With her hands and ninety-pound frame firmly planted against it, she and her son tried to keep it from falling over. But they weren't strong enough.

God was King David's strength when he called out to Him in another kind of storm (Psalm 28:8). Some commentators say he wrote this during a time when his world was falling apart. His own son rose in rebellion against him and tried to take the throne (2 Samuel 15). He felt so vulnerable and weak that he feared God might remain silent, and he would die (Psalm 28:1). "Hear my cry for mercy as I call to you for help," he said to God (v. 2). God gave David strength to go on, even though his relationship with his son never mended.

How we long to prevent bad things from happening! If only we could. But in our weakness, God promises we can always call to Him to be our Rock (vv. 1–2). When we don't have the strength, He's our shepherd, and He will carry us forever (vv. 8–9). *Anne*

A Call to Leave
Matthew 4:18–22

At once they left their nets and followed him.
—MATTHEW 4:20

As a young woman, I imagined myself married to my high school sweetheart—until we broke up. My future yawned emptily before me and I struggled with what to do with my life. At last I sensed God leading me to serve Him by serving others, so I enrolled in seminary. Then the reality crashed through that I'd be moving away from my roots, friends, and family. In order to respond to God's call, I had to leave everything that was familiar.

Jesus was walking beside the Sea of Galilee when He saw Peter and his brother Andrew casting nets into the sea, fishing for a living. He invited them to "Come, follow me . . . and I will send you out to fish for people" (Matthew 4:19). Then Jesus saw two other fishermen, James and his brother John, and offered them a similar invitation (v. 21).

When these disciples came to Jesus, they also left something. Peter and Andrew "left their nets" (v. 20). James and John "left the boat and their father and followed him" (v. 22). Luke puts it this way: "So they pulled their boats up on shore, left everything and followed him" (Luke 5:11).

Every call to Jesus also includes a call from something else. Net. Boat. Father. Friends. Home. God calls all of us to a relationship with himself. Then He calls each of us to serve. *Elisa*

Touch the Needy
Luke 13:10–17

He put his hands on her, and immediately she straightened up and praised God. —LUKE 13:13

It wasn't surprising when Mother Teresa received the Nobel Peace Prize. True to form, she received the award "in the name of the hungry, of the naked, of the homeless, of the blind, of the lepers, of all those who feel unwanted, unloved, uncared for throughout society." Those were the people she ministered to for most of her life.

Jesus modeled how to care for and love the marginalized, regardless of circumstances. Unlike the synagogue leaders who respected the Sabbath law more than the sick (Luke 13:14), when Jesus saw an ill woman at the temple, He was moved with compassion. He looked beyond the physical impairment and saw God's beautiful creation in bondage. He called her to Him and said she was healed. Then He "put his hands on her, and immediately she straightened up and praised God" (v. 13). By touching her, He upset the leader of the synagogue because it was the Sabbath. Jesus, the Lord of the Sabbath (Luke 6:5), compassionately chose to heal the woman—a person who had faced discomfort and humiliation for nearly two decades.

I wonder how often we see someone as underserving of our compassion. Or maybe we've experienced rejection because we didn't meet somebody else's standard. May we not be like the religious elite who cared more about rules than fellow humans. Instead, let's follow Jesus's example and treat others with compassion, love, and dignity.

Estera

Small Fish
Matthew 19:16–26

Come, follow me. —*MATTHEW 19:21*

Over several years, a British couple living in West Africa developed a strong friendship with a man in their town and many times shared the love of Jesus and the story of salvation with him. Their friend, however, was reluctant to relinquish the lifetime of allegiance he had to another religion, even though he came to recognize that faith in Christ was "the greater truth." His concern was partly financial, since he was a leader in his faith and depended on the compensation he received. He also feared losing his reputation among the people in his community.

With sadness, he explained, "I'm like a man fishing with my hands in a stream. I have caught a small fish in one, but a bigger fish is swimming by. To catch the bigger fish, I have to let go of the smaller one!"

The rich young ruler Matthew wrote about in chapter nineteen of his gospel had a similar problem. When he approached Jesus, he asked, "What good thing must I do to get eternal life?" (v. 16). He seemed sincere, but he didn't want to fully surrender his life to Jesus. He was rich, not only in money, but also in his pride of being a rule-follower. Although he desired eternal life, he loved something else more and rejected Christ's words.

When we humbly surrender our life to Jesus and accept His free gift of salvation, He invites us, "Come, follow me" (v. 21). *Cindy*

Something Much Bigger
1 Corinthians 3:5–9

We are co-workers in God's service.
—1 CORINTHIANS 3:9

More than two hundred volunteers assisted October Books, a bookstore in Southampton, England, move its inventory to an address down the street. Helpers lined the sidewalk and passed books down a "human conveyor belt." Having witnessed the volunteers in action, a store employee said, "It was . . . a really moving experience to see people [helping]. . . . They wanted to be part of something bigger."

We can also be part of something much bigger than ourselves. God uses us to reach the world with the message of His love. Because someone shared the message with us, we can turn to another person and pass it on. Paul compared this—the building of God's kingdom—to growing a garden. Some of us plant seeds while some of us water the seeds. We are, as Paul said, "co-workers in God's service" (1 Corinthians 3:9).

Each job is important, yet all are done in the power of God's Spirit. By His Spirit, God enables people to thrive spiritually when they hear that He loves them and sent His Son to die in their place so that they can be free from their sin (John 3:16).

God does much of His work on earth through "volunteers" like you and me. Although we are a part of a community that's much bigger than any contribution we may make, we can help it grow by working together to share His love with the world. *Jennifer*

The Baggage Activity
Leviticus 19:32–34

Love them as yourself, for you were foreigners
in Egypt. —LEVITICUS 19:34

Karen, a middle school teacher, created an activity to teach her students how to better understand one another. In "The Baggage Activity" students wrote down some of the emotional weights they were carrying. The notes were shared anonymously, giving the students insight into each other's hardships, often with a tearful response from their peers. The classroom has since been filled with a deeper sense of mutual respect among the young teens, who now have a greater sense of empathy for one another.

Throughout the Bible, God has nudged His people to treat one another with dignity and show empathy in their interaction with others (Romans 12:15). As early in the history of Israel as the book of Leviticus, God pointed the Israelites toward empathy—especially in their dealings with foreigners. He said to "love them as [themselves]" because they too had been foreigners in Egypt and knew that hardship intimately (Leviticus 19:34).

Sometimes the burdens we carry make us feel like foreigners—alone and misunderstood—even among our peers. We don't always have a similar experience to draw on as the Israelites did with the foreigners among them. Yet we can always treat those God puts in our paths with the respect and understanding that we, ourselves, desire. Whether a modern-day middle schooler, an Israelite, or anything in between, we honor God when we do.

Kirsten

Frolicking in Freedom
Malachi 4:1–3

You will go out and frolic like well-fed calves.
—MALACHI 4:2

A third-generation farmer, Jim was so moved when he read "You who revere my name . . . will go out and frolic like well-fed calves" (Malachi 4:2) that he prayed to receive Jesus's offer of eternal life. Vividly recalling his own calves' leaps of excitement after exiting their confined stalls at high speed, Jim finally understood God's promise of true freedom.

Jim's daughter told me this story because we'd been discussing the imagery in Malachi 4, where the prophet made a distinction between those who revered God's name, or remained faithful to Him, and those who only trusted in themselves (4:1–2). The prophet was encouraging the Israelites to follow God at a time when so many, including the religious leaders, disregarded God and His standards for faithful living (1:12–14; 3:5–9). Malachi called the people to live faithfully because of a coming time when God would make the final distinction between these two groups. In this context, Malachi used the unexpected imagery of a frolicking calf to describe the unspeakable joy that the faithful group will experience when "the sun of righteousness will rise with healing in its rays" (4:2).

Jesus is the ultimate fulfillment of this promise, bringing the good news that true freedom is available to all people (Luke 4:16–21). And one day, in God's renewed and restored creation, we'll experience this freedom fully. What indescribable joy it will be to frolic there! *Lisa*

Fearless Love
1 John 3:11–14

We know that we have passed from death to life, because we love each other. Anyone who does not love remains in death.
—*1 JOHN 3:14*

There are some images so powerful they can never be forgotten. That was my experience when I viewed a famous photograph of the late Princess Diana of Wales. At first glance, the captured scene looks mundane: smiling warmly, the princess is shaking the hand of an unidentified man. But it's the photograph's story that makes it remarkable.

In the late 1980s, when Princess Diana visited London Middlesex Hospital, the United Kingdom was engulfed in a wave of panic as it confronted the AIDS epidemic. Not knowing how the disease—which often killed with terrifying speed—was spread, the public at times treated AIDS victims like social pariahs.

So it was a stunning moment when Diana, with ungloved hands and a genuine smile, calmly shook an AIDS patient's hand that day. That image of respect and kindness would move the world to treat victims of the disease with similar mercy and compassion.

The picture reminds me of something I often forget: freely and generously offering the love of Jesus to others is worth it. John reminded early believers in Christ that to let love wither or hide in the face of our fear is really to live "in death" (1 John 3:14). And to love freely and unafraid, filled and empowered with the Spirit's self-giving love, is to experience resurrection life in all its fullness (vv. 14, 16). *Monica*

Gentle Speech
2 Timothy 2:22–26

The Lord's servant must not be quarrelsome.
—2 TIMOTHY 2:24

I was on Facebook, arguing. Bad move. What made me think I was obligated to "correct" a stranger on a hot topic—especially a divisive one? The results were heated words, hurt feelings (on my part anyway), and a broken opportunity to witness well for Jesus. That's the sum outcome of "internet anger." It's the term for the harsh words flung daily across the blogosphere. As one ethics expert explained, people wrongly conclude that rage "is how public ideas are talked about."

Paul's wise advice to Timothy gave the same caution. "Don't have anything to do with foolish and stupid arguments, because you know they produce quarrels. And the Lord's servant must not be quarrelsome but must be kind to everyone" (2 Timothy 2:23–24).

Paul's good counsel, written to Timothy from a Roman prison, was sent to prepare the young pastor for teaching God's truth. The apostle's advice is just as timely for us today, especially when the conversation turns to our faith. "Opponents must be gently instructed, in the hope that God will grant them repentance leading them to a knowledge of the truth" (v. 25).

Speaking kindly to others is part of this challenge, but not just for pastors. For all who love God and seek to tell others about Him, may we speak His truth in love. With every word, the Holy Spirit will help us. *Patricia*

Riding the Waves
Psalm 89:5–17

*Who is like you, LORD God Almighty? You, LORD,
are mighty and your faithfulness surrounds you.*
—*PSALM 89:8*

As my husband strolled down the rocky beach taking photos of the Hawaiian horizon, I sat on a large rock fretting over another medical setback. Though my problems would be waiting for me when I returned home, I needed peace in that moment. I stared at the incoming waves crashing against the black, jagged rocks. A dark shadow in the curve of the wave caught my eye. Using the zoom option on my camera, I identified the shape as a sea turtle riding the waves peacefully. Its flippers spread wide and still. Turning my face into the salty breeze, I smiled.

The "heavens praise [God's] wonders" (Psalm 89:5). Our incomparable God rules "over the surging sea; when its waves mount up, [God] stills them" (v. 9). He "founded the world and all that is in it" (v. 11). He made it all, owns it all, manages it all, and purposes it all for His glory and our enjoyment.

Standing on the foundation of our faith—the love of our unchanging Father—we can "walk in the light of [His] presence" (v. 15). God remains mighty in power and merciful in His dealings with us. We can rejoice in His name all day long (v. 16). No matter what obstacles we face or how many setbacks we have to endure, God holds us as the waves rise and fall. *Xochitl*

No Misunderstanding
Romans 8:26–30

We know that in all things God works for the good of those who love him. —ROMANS 8:28

Alexa, Siri, and other voice assistants embedded in smart devices in our homes occasionally misunderstand what we're saying. A six-year-old talked to her family's new device about cookies and a dollhouse. Later her mom received an email saying that an order of seven pounds of cookies and a $170 dollhouse were on their way to her home. Even a talking parrot in London, whose owner had never bought anything online, somehow ordered a package of golden gift boxes without her knowledge. One person asked their device to "turn on the living room lights," and it replied, "There is no pudding room."

There's no such misunderstanding on God's part when we talk with Him. He's never confused, because He knows our hearts better than we do. The Spirit not only searches our hearts but also understands God's will. The apostle Paul told the churches in Rome that God promises He'll accomplish His good purpose of maturing us and making us more like His Son (Romans 8:28). Even when because of "our weakness" we don't know what we need in order to grow, the Spirit prays according to God's will for us (vv. 26–27).

Troubled about how to express yourself to God? Not understanding what or how to pray? Say what you can from the heart. The Spirit will understand and accomplish God's purpose. *Anne*

Looking Up
Colossians 3:1–4

Set your minds on things above, not on earthly things.
—COLOSSIANS 3:2

The cockeyed squid lives in the ocean's "twilight zone" where sunlight barely filters through the deep waters. The squid's nickname is a reference to its two extremely different eyes: the left eye develops during its lifetime to become considerably larger than the right—almost twice as big. Scientists studying the mollusk have deduced that the squid uses its right, the smaller one, to look down into the darker depths. The larger, left eye, gazes upward, toward the sunlight.

The squid is an unlikely depiction of what it means to live in our present world and also in the future certainty we await as people who "have been raised with Christ" (Colossians 3:1). In Paul's letter to the Colossians, he insists we ought to "set [our] minds on things above" because our lives are "hidden with Christ in God" (vv. 2–3).

As earth-dwellers awaiting our lives in heaven, we keep an eye trained on what's happening around us in our present reality. But just as the squid's left eye develops over time into one that's larger and more sensitive to what's happening overhead, we, too, can grow in our awareness of the ways God works in the spiritual realm. We may not have yet fully grasped what it means to be alive in Jesus, but as we look "up," our eyes will begin to see it more and more. *Kirsten*

Life to the Full
John 10:7–11

I have come that they may have life, and have it to the full. I am the good shepherd. —JOHN 10:10–11

Seventeenth-century philosopher Thomas Hobbes famously wrote that human life in its natural state is "solitary, poor, nasty, brutish, and short." Hobbes argued that our instincts tend toward war in a bid to attain dominance over others; thus the establishment of government would be necessary to maintain law and order.

The bleak view of humanity sounds like the state of affairs that Jesus described when He said, "All who have come before me are thieves and robbers" (John 10:8). But Jesus offers hope in the midst of despair. "The thief comes only to steal and kill and destroy," but then the good news: "I have come that they may have life, and have it to the full" (v. 10).

Psalm 23 paints a refreshing portrait of the life our Shepherd gives us. In Him, we "lack nothing" (v. 1) and are refreshed (v. 3). He leads us down the right paths of His perfect will, so that even when we face dark times, we need not be afraid; for He is present to comfort us (vv. 3–4). He causes us to triumph in the face of adversity and overwhelms us with blessings (v. 5). His goodness and love follow us every day, and we have the privilege of His presence forever (v. 6).

May we answer the Shepherd's call and experience the full, abundant life He came to give us. *Remi*

Dwelling in Our Hearts
Ephesians 3:14–21

I pray that . . . he may strengthen you with power through his Spirit in your inner being, so that Christ may dwell in your hearts through faith. —EPHESIANS 3:16–17

Sometimes the words of children can jolt us into a deeper understanding of God's truth. One evening when my daughter was young, I told her about one of the great mysteries of the Christian faith—that God through His Son and Spirit dwells in His children. As I tucked her into bed, I said that Jesus was with her and in her. "He's in my tummy?" she asked. "Well, you haven't swallowed Him," I replied. "But He's right there with you."

My daughter's literal translation of Jesus being "in her tummy" made me stop and consider how when I asked Jesus to be my Savior, He came and took residence within me.

The apostle Paul referred to this mystery when he prayed that the Holy Spirit would strengthen the believers in Ephesus so that Christ would "dwell in [their] hearts through faith" (Ephesians 3:17). With Jesus living within, they could grasp how deeply He loved them. Fueled by this love, they would mature in their faith and love others with humility and gentleness while speaking the truth in love (4:2, 25).

Jesus dwelling inside His followers means that His love never leaves those who've welcomed Him into their lives. His love that surpasses knowledge (3:19) roots us to Him, helping us to understand how deeply He loves us.

Words written for children can say it best: "Yes, Jesus loves me!" *Amy*

In-Service Training
Matthew 16:21–28

On this rock I will build my church. —MATTHEW 16:18

A manager at a company in Brazil requested a written report from the custodians in her building. Each day she wanted to know who cleaned each room, which rooms were left untouched, and how much time employees spent in each room. The first "daily" report arrived a week later, partially completed.

When the manager looked into the matter, she discovered most of the cleaning employees couldn't read. She could have fired them, but instead she arranged for them to have literacy lessons. Within five months, everyone was reading at a basic level and continued in their jobs.

God often uses our struggles as opportunities to equip us to continue working for Him. Peter's life was marked by inexperience and mistakes. His faith faltered as he tried to walk on water. He wasn't sure if Jesus should pay the temple tax (Matthew 17:24–27). He even rejected Christ's prophecy about the crucifixion and resurrection (16:21–23). Through each issue Jesus taught Peter more about who He was—the promised Messiah (v. 16). Peter listened and learned what he needed to know to help found the early church (v. 18).

If you're discouraged by some failure today, remember that Jesus may use it to teach you and lead you forward in your service for Him. He continued to work with Peter despite his shortcomings, and He can use us to continue to build His kingdom until He returns. *Jennifer*

Rainbow Halo
Genesis 9:12–17

My rainbow . . . will be the sign of the covenant between me and the earth. —GENESIS 9:13

On a hike in the mountains, Adrian found himself above some low-lying clouds. With the sun behind him, Adrian looked down and saw not only his shadow but also a brilliant display known as a Brocken spectre. This phenomenon resembles a rainbow halo, encircling the shadow of the person. It occurs when the sunlight reflects back off the clouds below. Adrian described it as a "magical" moment, one that delighted him immensely.

We can imagine how similarly stunning seeing the first rainbow must have been for Noah. More than just a delight to his eyes, the refracted light and resulting colors came with a promise from God. After a devastating flood, God assured Noah, and all the "living creatures" who've lived since, that "never again [would] the waters become a flood to destroy all life" (Genesis 9:15).

Our earth still experiences floods and other frightening weather that results in tragic loss, but the rainbow is a promise that God will never judge the earth again with a worldwide flood. This promise of His faithfulness can remind us that though we individually will experience personal losses and physical death on this earth—whether by disease, natural disaster, wrongdoing, or advancing age—God bolsters us with His love and presence throughout the difficulties we face. Sunlight reflecting colors through water is a reminder of His faithfulness to fill the earth with those who bear His image and reflect His glory to others. *Kirsten*

Hosting Royalty
Galatians 3:26–29

So in Christ Jesus you are all children of God through faith. —GALATIANS 3:26

After meeting the Queen of England at a ball in Scotland, Sylvia and her husband received a message that the royal family would like to visit them for tea. Sylvia started cleaning and prepping, nervous about hosting the royal guests. Before they were due to arrive, she went outside to pick some flowers for the table, her heart racing. Then she sensed God reminding her that He's the King of kings and that He's with her every day. Immediately she felt peaceful and thought, "After all, it's only the Queen!"

Sylvia is right. As the apostle Paul noted, God is the "King of kings and Lord of lords" (1 Timothy 6:15) and those who follow Him are "children of God" (Galatians 3:26). When we belong to Christ, we're heirs of Abraham (v. 29). We are no longer bound by division—such as that of race, social class, or gender—for we're "all one in Christ Jesus" (v. 28). We're children of the King.

Although Sylvia and her husband had a marvelous meal with the Queen, I don't anticipate receiving an invitation from the monarch anytime soon. But I love the reminder that the highest King of all is with me every moment—and that those who believe in Jesus wholeheartedly (v. 27) can live in unity, knowing they're God's children.

How could holding onto this truth shape the way we live today? *Amy*

Finding Joy in Praise
Habakkuk 3:6, 16–19

I will be joyful in God my Savior. —HABAKKUK 3:18

When the famous British writer C. S. Lewis first gave his life to Jesus, he initially resisted praising God. In fact, he called it "a stumbling block." His struggle was "in the suggestion that God himself demanded it." Yet Lewis finally realized "it is in the process of being worshipped that God communicates His presence" to His people. Then we, "in perfect love with God," find joy in Him no more separable "than the brightness a mirror receives" from the "brightness it sheds."

The prophet Habakkuk arrived at this conclusion centuries earlier. After complaining to God about evils aimed at the people of Judah, Habakkuk came to see that praising Him leads to joy—not in what God does, but in who He is. Thus, even in a national or world crisis, God is still great. As the prophet declared:

"Though the fig tree does not bud and there are no grapes on the vines, though the olive crop fails and the fields produce no food, though there are no sheep in the pen and no cattle in the stalls, yet I will rejoice in the LORD" (Habakkuk 3:17–18). "I will be joyful in God my Savior," he added.

As C. S. Lewis realized, "The whole world rings with praise." Habakkuk, likewise, surrendered to praising God always, finding rich joy in the One who "Marches on forever" (v. 6). *Patricia*

Helping Each Other
1 Thessalonians 5:11–25

Live in peace with each other.
—*1 THESSALONIANS 5:13*

When playing basketball with her girlfriends, Amber realized her community could benefit from an all-female league. So she started a nonprofit organization to foster teamwork and impact the next generation. The leaders of Ladies Who Hoop strive to build confidence and character in the women and girls and encourage them to become meaningful contributors to their local communities. One of the original players, who now mentors other girls, said, "There is so much camaraderie among us. This is something I'd been missing. We support each other in so many different ways. I love seeing the girls succeed and grow."

God intends His people to team up to help each other as well. The apostle Paul urged the Thessalonians to "encourage one another and build each other up" (1 Thessalonians 5:11). God has put us into the family of His people for support in our lives. We need each other to keep walking the path of life in Christ. Sometimes that may mean listening to someone who's struggling, providing for a practical need, or speaking a few words of encouragement. We can celebrate successes, offer a prayer for strength in a difficulty, or challenge each other to grow in faith. And in everything, we can "always strive to do what is good for each other" (v. 15).

What camaraderie we can enjoy as we team up with other believers in Jesus to keep trusting God together!

Anne

A Royal Role
John 1:9–14

To all who did receive him, to those who believed in his name, he gave the right to become children of God.
—*JOHN 1:12*

The closer someone in a royal family is to the throne, the more the public hears about him or her. Others are almost forgotten. The British royal family has a line of succession that includes nearly sixty people. One of them is Lord Frederick Windsor, who's fifty-first in line for the throne. Instead of being in the limelight, he quietly goes about his life. Though he works as a financial analyst, he's not considered a "working royal"—one of the family members who are paid for representing the family.

David's son Nathan (2 Samuel 5:14) is another royal who lived outside the limelight. Very little is known about him. But while the genealogy of Jesus in Matthew mentions his son Solomon (tracing Joseph's line, Matthew 1:6), Luke's genealogy, which many scholars believe is Mary's family line, mentions Nathan (Luke 3:31). Though Nathan didn't hold a scepter, he still had a role in God's forever kingdom.

As believers in Christ, we're also royalty. The apostle John wrote that God gave us "the right to become children of God" (John 1:12). Though we may not be in the spotlight, we're children of the King! God considers each of us important enough to represent Him here on earth and to one day reign with Him (2 Timothy 2:11–13). Like Nathan, we may not wear an earthly crown, but we still have a part to play in God's kingdom. *Linda*

Choosing Hope
Micah 7:2–7

*But as for me, I watch in hope for the L*ORD*.*
—*MICAH 7:7*

I am one of millions of people worldwide who suffer from SAD (seasonal affective disorder), a type of depression common in places with limited sunlight due to short winter days. When I begin to fear winter's frozen curse will never end, I'm eager for any evidence that longer days and warmer temperatures are coming.

The first signs of spring—flowers successfully braving their way through the lingering snow—also powerfully remind me of the way God's hope can break through even our darkest seasons. The prophet Micah confessed this even while enduring a heart-rending "winter" as the Israelites turned away from God. As Micah assessed the bleak situation, he lamented that "not one upright person" seemed to remain (Micah 7:2).

Yet, even though the situation appeared dire, the prophet refused to give up hope. He trusted that God was at work (v. 7)—even if, amid the devastation, he couldn't yet see the evidence.

In our dark and sometimes seemingly endless "winters," when spring doesn't appear to be breaking through, we face the same struggle as Micah. Will we give into despair? Or will we "watch in hope for the LORD"? (v. 7).

Our hope in God is never wasted (Romans 5:5). He's bringing a time with no more "winter": a time with no more mourning or pain (Revelation 21:4). Until then, may we rest in our Lord, confessing, "My hope is in you" (Psalm 39:7). *Lisa*

A Critical Reaction
Proverbs 15:1–2, 31–33

The one who is patient calms a quarrel.
—PROVERBS 15:18

Tough words hurt. So my friend—an award-winning author—struggled with how to respond to the criticism he received. His new book had earned five-star reviews plus a major award. Then a respected magazine reviewer gave him a backhanded compliment, describing his book as well-written yet still criticizing it harshly. Turning to friends, the author asked, "How should I reply?"

One friend advised, "Let it go." I shared advice from writing magazines, including tips to ignore such criticism or learn from it even while continuing to work and write.

Finally, however, I decided to see what Scripture—which has the best wisdom of all—has to say about how to react to strong criticism. The book of James advises, "Everyone should be quick to listen, slow to speak and slow to become angry" (1:19). The apostle Paul counsels us to "live in harmony with one another" (Romans 12:16).

An entire chapter of Proverbs, however, offers extended wisdom on reacting to disputes. "A gentle answer turns away wrath," says Proverbs 15:1. "The one who is patient calms a quarrel" (v. 18). Also, "The one who heeds correction gains understanding" (v. 32). Considering such wisdom, may God help us hold our tongues, as my friend did. More than all, however, wisdom instructs us to "fear the LORD" because "humility comes before honor" (v. 33). 🕊 *Patricia*

A Lifestyle of Worship
Psalm 100

Worship the LORD with gladness; come before him with joyful songs. —PSALM 100:2

As I waited in the breakfast buffet line at a Christian conference center, a group of women entered the dining hall. I smiled, saying hello to a woman who stepped into the line behind me. Returning my greeting, she said, "I know you." We scooped scrambled eggs onto our plates and tried to figure out where we'd met. But I was pretty sure she'd mistaken me for someone else.

When we returned for lunch, the woman approached me. "Do you drive a white car?"

I shrugged. "I used to. A few years ago."

She laughed. "We stopped at the same traffic light by the elementary school almost every morning," she said. "You'd always be lifting your hands, singing joyfully. I thought you were worshiping God. That made me want to join in, even on tough days."

Praising God, we prayed together, hugged, and enjoyed lunch.

My new friend affirmed that people notice how Jesus's followers behave, even when we think no one is watching. As we embrace a lifestyle of joyful worship, we can come before our Creator anytime and anywhere. Acknowledging His enduring love and faithfulness, we can enjoy intimate communion with Him and thank Him for His ongoing care (Psalm 100). Whether we're singing praises in our cars, praying in public, or spreading God's love through kind acts, we can inspire others to "praise his name" (v. 4). Worshiping God is more than a Sunday morning event. *Xochitl*

Gifts from Above
Matthew 1:18–25

The virgin will conceive and give birth to a son, and they will call him Immanuel. —MATTHEW 1:23

According to an old story, a man named Nicholas (born in AD 270) heard about a father who was so poor he couldn't feed his three daughters, much less provide for their future marriages. Wanting to assist the father, but hoping to keep his help a secret, Nicholas threw a bag of gold through an open window, which landed in a sock or shoe drying on the hearth. That man was known as St. Nicholas, who later became the inspiration for Santa Claus.

When I heard that story of a gift coming down from above, I thought of God the Father, who out of love and compassion sent to earth the greatest gift, His Son, through a miraculous birth. According to Matthew's gospel, Jesus fulfilled the Old Testament prophecy that a virgin would conceive and give birth to a son whom they would call Immanuel, meaning "God with us" (1:23).

As lovely as Nicholas's gift was, how much more amazing is the gift of Jesus. He left heaven to become a man, died and rose again, and is God living with us. He brings us comfort when we're hurting and sad; He encourages us when we feel downhearted; He reveals the truth to us when we might be deceived. ❦ *Amy*

Bigger than Our Problems
Job 40:15–24

Look at Behemoth, which I made along with you.
—JOB 40:15

What do you imagine dinosaurs looked like when they were alive? Big teeth? Scaly skin? Long tails? Artist Karen Carr recreates these extinct creatures in large murals.

One of her panoramas is over twenty feet tall and sixty feet long. Because of its size, it required a crew of experts to install it in sections where it resides in the Sam Noble Oklahoma Museum of Natural History.

It would be hard to stand in front of this mural without feeling dwarfed by the dinosaurs. I get a similar sensation when I read God's description of the powerful animal called "Behemoth" (Job 40:15). This big guy munched grass like an ox and had a tail the size of a tree trunk. His bones were like iron pipes. He lumbered through the hills grazing, stopping occasionally to relax at the local swamp. When floodwaters surged, Behemoth never raised an eyebrow.

No one could tame this incredible creature—except its Maker (v. 19). God reminded Job of this truth during a time when Job's problems had cast ominous shadows over his life. Grief, bewilderment, and frustration filled his field of vision until he began to question God. But God's response helped Job see the real size of things. God was bigger than all his issues and powerful enough to handle problems that Job couldn't resolve on his own. In the end, Job conceded, "I know that you can do all things" (42:2). *Jennifer*

Joy to the World
John 3:1–8, 13–16

God so loved the world. —JOHN 3:16

Every Christmas we decorate our home with nativity scenes from around the world. We have a German nativity pyramid, a manger scene fashioned out of olive wood from Bethlehem, and a brightly colored Mexican folk version. Our family favorite is a whimsical entry from Africa. Instead of the more traditional sheep and camels, a hippopotamus gazes contently at the baby Jesus.

The unique cultural perspective brought to life in these nativity scenes warms my heart as I ponder each beautiful reminder that Jesus's birth was not just for one nation or culture. It's good news for the whole earth, a reason for people from every country and ethnicity to rejoice.

The little baby depicted in each of our nativity scenes revealed this truth of God's heart for the entire world. As John wrote in relation to Christ's conversation with an inquisitive Pharisee named Nicodemus, "For God so loved the world that he gave his one and only Son, that whoever believes in him shall not perish but have eternal life" (John 3:16).

The gift of Jesus is good news for everyone. No matter where on earth you call home, Jesus's birth is God's offer of love and peace to you. And all who find new life in Christ, "from every tribe and language and people and nation" will one day celebrate God's glory forever and ever (Revelation 5:9). *Lisa*

Sharing Your Faith
2 Corinthians 12:5–10

My grace is sufficient for you, for my power is made perfect in weakness. —2 CORINTHIANS 12:9

When author and evangelist Becky Pippert lived in Ireland, she longed to share the good news of Jesus with Heather, who'd done her nails for two years. But Heather hadn't seemed remotely interested. Feeling unable to start a conversation, Becky prayed before her appointment.

While Heather worked on her nails, Becky flipped through an old magazine and paused at a picture of one of the models. When Heather asked why she was so riveted, Becky told her the photograph was of a close friend who'd years before been a *Vogue* cover model. Becky shared some of her friend's story of coming to faith in God, which Heather listened to with rapt attention.

Becky left for a trip, and later when she returned to Ireland, she learned that Heather had moved to a new location. Becky reflected, "I had asked God to provide an opportunity to share the gospel, and He did!"

Becky looked to God for help in her weakness, inspired by the apostle Paul. When Paul was weak and pleaded with God to remove the thorn in his flesh, the Lord said, "My grace is sufficient for you, for my power is made perfect in weakness" (2 Corinthians 12:9). Paul had learned to rely on God in all things—the big and the small.

When we depend on God to help us love those around us, we too will find opportunities to share our faith authentically. *Amy*

The Giver's Delight
Luke 2:4–14

Today in the town of David a Savior has been born to you; he is the Messiah, the Lord. —LUKE 2:11

Remember Tickle Me Elmo? Cabbage Patch Kids? The Furby? What do they have in common? Each rank among the twenty most popular Christmas gifts of all time. Also included on the list are familiar favorites such as Monopoly, the Nintendo Game Boy, and Wii.

We all delight in giving gifts at Christmas, but that's nothing compared to God's delight in giving the first Christmas gift. This gift came in the form of a baby, born in a Bethlehem manger (Luke 2:7).

Despite Jesus's humble birth, His arrival was proclaimed by an angel who declared, "I bring you good news that will cause great joy for all the people. Today in the town of David a Savior has been born to you; he is the Messiah, the Lord" (vv. 10–11). Following this magnificent news, a "heavenly host" appeared, "praising God and saying, 'Glory to God in the highest heaven, and on earth peace to those on whom his favor rests'" (vv. 13–14).

This Christmas, enjoy giving gifts to your loved ones, but never lose sight of the reason for the giving—the spectacular favor of God on His creation crystallized in the gift of His own Son to save us from our sin. We give because He gave. Let's worship Him in gratitude!

Remi

No Glitz, Just Glory
Isaiah 53:1–9

Because your love is better than life, my lips will glorify you.
—PSALM 63:3

Looking at the handmade Christmas ornaments my son, Xavier, crafted over the years and the annual mismatched baubles Grandma had sent him, I couldn't figure out why I was not content with our decorations. I'd always valued the creativity and memories each ornament represented. So, why did the allure of the retail stores' holiday displays tempt me to desire a tree adorned with perfectly matched bulbs, shimmering orbs, and satin ribbons?

As I began to turn away from our humble decor, I glimpsed a red, heart-shaped ornament with a simple phrase scripted on it—"Jesus, My Savior." How could I have forgotten that my family and my hope in Christ are the reasons I love celebrating Christmas? Our simple tree looked nothing like the trees in the storefronts, but the love behind every decoration made it beautiful.

Like our modest tree, the Messiah didn't meet the world's expectations in any way (Isaiah 53:2). Jesus "was despised and rejected" (v. 3). Yet, in an amazing display of love, He still chose to be "pierced for our transgressions" (v. 5). He endured punishment, so we could enjoy peace (v. 5). Nothing is more beautiful than that.

With renewed gratitude for our imperfect decorations and our perfect Savior, I stopped longing for glitz and praised God for His glorious love. Sparkling adornments could never match the beauty of His sacrificial gift—Jesus. 🕊 *Xochitl*

Remember to Sing
Psalm 147:1–7

How good it is to sing praises to our God.
—PSALM 147:1

Nancy Gustafson, a retired opera singer, was devastated when she visited her mother and observed her decline from dementia. Her mom no longer recognized her and barely spoke. After several monthly visits, Nancy had an idea. She started singing to her. Her mother's eyes lit up at the musical sounds, and she began singing too—for twenty minutes! Then Nancy's mom laughed, joking they were "The Gustafson Family Singers!" The dramatic turnaround suggested the power of music, as some therapists conclude, to evoke lost memories. Singing "old favorites" has also been shown to boost mood, reduce falls, lessen visits to the emergency room, and decrease the need for sedative drugs.

More research is underway on a music-memory link. Yet, as the Bible reveals, the joy that comes from singing is a gift from God—and it's real. "How good it is to sing praises to our God, how pleasant and fitting to praise him!" (Psalm 147:1).

Throughout the Scriptures, in fact, God's people are urged to lift their voices in songs of praise to Him. "Sing to the LORD, for he has done glorious things" (Isaiah 12:5). "He put a new song in my mouth, a hymn of praise to our God. Many will see and fear the Lord and put their trust in him" (Psalm 40:3). Our singing inspires not just us but also those who hear it. Our God is great and worthy of praise. *Patricia*

The Yard-Sale Christmas

1 Timothy 6:6–10, 17–19

If we have food and clothing, we will be content
with that. —1 TIMOTHY 6:8

A mom felt she'd been overspending on family Christmas gifts, so one year she decided to try something different. For a few months before the holiday, she scrounged through yard sales for inexpensive, used items. She bought more than usual but for far less money. On Christmas Eve, her children excitedly opened gift after gift after gift. The next day there were more! Mom had felt guilty about not getting new gifts, so she had additional gifts for Christmas morning. The kids began opening them but quickly complained, "We're too tired to open any more! You've given us so much!" That's not a typical response from children on a Christmas morning!

God has blessed us with so much, but it seems we're always looking for more: a bigger house, a better car, a larger bank account, or [fill in the blank]. Paul encouraged Timothy to remind people in his congregation that "we brought nothing into this world, and we can take nothing out of it. But if we have food and clothing, we will be content with that" (1 Timothy 6:7–8).

God has given us our very breath and life—and providing for our needs. How refreshing it might be to enjoy and be content with His gifts and to say, You've given us so much! We don't need more. "Godliness with contentment is great gain" (v. 6). *Anne*

Curling Up with a Good Book

2 Timothy 3:14–17

All Scripture is God-breathed. —2 TIMOTHY 3:16

The small country of Iceland is a nation of readers. In fact, it's reported that each year this nation publishes and reads more books per person than any other country. On Christmas Eve, it's a tradition for Icelanders to give books to family and friends and then read long into the night. This tradition dates back to World War II, when imports were restricted but paper was cheap. Icelandic publishers began flooding the market with new titles in late fall. Now a catalog of the country's new releases is sent to every Icelandic home in mid-November. This tradition is known as the Christmas Book Flood.

We can be thankful God blessed so many with the ability to craft a good story and to educate, inspire, or motivate others through their words. There's nothing like a good book! The best-selling book of all, the Bible, was composed by many authors who wrote in poetry and prose—some great stories, some not so—but all of it inspired. As the apostle Paul reminded Timothy, "All Scripture is God-breathed and is useful for teaching, rebuking, correcting and training in righteousness" and equipping God's people "for every good work" (2 Timothy 3:16–17). Reading the Bible convicts, inspires, and helps us to live for Him—and guides us into the truth (2:15).

In our reading, let's not forget to find time to curl up with the greatest book of all, the Bible. *Alyson*

A Christmas Visitor
Luke 2:25–33

Sovereign Lord, . . . you may now dismiss your servant in peace. —LUKE 2:29

On Christmas Eve 1944, a man known as "Old Brinker" lay dying in a prison hospital, waiting for the makeshift Christmas service led by fellow prisoners. "When does the music start?" he asked William McDougall, who was imprisoned with him in Muntok Prison in Sumatra. "Soon," replied McDougall. "Good," replied the dying man. "Then I'll be able to compare them with the angels."

Although decades earlier Brinker had moved away from his faith in God, in his dying days he confessed his sins and found peace with Him. Instead of greeting others with a sour look, he would smile, which "was quite a transformation," said McDougall.

Brinker died peacefully after the choir of eleven emaciated prisoners sang his request, "Silent Night." Knowing that Brinker once again followed Jesus and would be united with God in heaven, McDougall observed, "Perhaps Death had been a welcome Christmas visitor to old Brinker."

How Brinker anticipated his death reminds me of Simeon, a holy man to whom the Holy Spirit revealed that "he would not die before he had seen the Lord's Messiah" (v. 26). When Simeon saw Jesus in the temple, he exclaimed, "You may now dismiss your servant in peace. For my eyes have seen your salvation" (vv. 29–30).

As with Brinker, the greatest Christmas gift we can receive or share is that of saving faith in Jesus. *Amy*

Faith Investments
Deuteronomy 11:18–20

Teach [these words of mine] to your children.
—*DEUTERONOMY 11:19*

On his twelfth Christmas, the boy eagerly awaited the opening of the gifts under the tree. He was yearning for a new bike, but his hopes were dashed—the last present he received was a dictionary. On the first page, he read: "To Charles from Mother and Daddy, 1958. With love and high hopes for your best work in school."

In the next decade, Chuck did do well in school. He graduated from college and later, aviation training. He became a pilot working overseas, fulfilling his passion to help people in need and to share Jesus with them. Now some sixty years after receiving this gift, he shared the well-worn dictionary with his grandchildren. It had become for him a symbol of his parents' loving investment in his future, and Chuck still treasures it. But he's even more grateful for the daily investment his parents made in building his faith by teaching him about God and the Scriptures.

Deuteronomy 11 talks about the importance of taking every opportunity to share the words of Scripture with children: "Teach them to your children, talking about them when you sit at home and when you walk along the road, when you lie down and when you get up" (v. 19).

For Chuck, the eternal values planted when he was a boy bloomed into a lifetime of service for his Savior. With God's enablement, who knows how much our investment in someone's spiritual growth will yield.

Cindy

A String of Yeses
Luke 2:15–19

Mary treasured up all these things and pondered them in her heart. —LUKE 2:19

One Christmas, my grandmother gave me a beautiful pearl necklace. The beautiful beads glowed about my neck until one day the string broke. Balls bounced in all directions off our home's hardwood flooring. Crawling over the planks, I recovered each tiny orb. On their own, they were small. But oh, when strung together, those pearls made such an impression!

Sometimes my yeses to God seem so insignificant—like those individual pearls. I compare myself to Mary, the mother of Jesus who was so fantastically obedient. She said yes when she embraced God's call for her to carry the Messiah. "'I am the Lord's servant,' Mary answered. 'May your word to me be fulfilled'" (Luke 1:38). Did she understand all that would be required of her? That an even bigger yes to relinquishing her Son on the cross loomed ahead?

After the visits of the angels and shepherds, Luke 2:19 tells us that Mary "treasured up all these things and pondered them in her heart." *Treasure* means to "store up." *Ponder* means to "thread together." The phrase is repeated of Mary in Luke 2:51. She would respond with many yeses over her lifetime.

As with Mary, the key to our obedience might be a threading together of various yeses to our Father's invitations, one at a time, until they string into the treasure of a surrendered life. *Elisa*

Our Compassionate God
Psalm 138

You stretch out your hand against the anger of
my foes. —PSALM 138:7

The winter night was cold when someone threw a large stone through a Jewish child's bedroom window. A star of David had been displayed in the window, along with a menorah to celebrate Hanukkah, the Jewish Festival of Lights. In the child's town of Billings, Montana, thousands of people—many of them believers in Jesus—responded to the hateful act with compassion. Choosing to identify with the hurt and fear of their Jewish neighbors, they pasted pictures of menorahs in their own windows.

As believers in Jesus, we too receive great compassion. Our Savior humbled himself to live among us (John 1:14), identifying with us. On our behalf, He, "being in very nature God . . . made himself nothing by taking the very nature of a servant" (Philippians 2:6–7). Then, feeling as we feel and weeping as we weep, He died on a cross, sacrificing His life to save ours.

Nothing we struggle with is beyond our Savior's concern. If someone "throws rocks" at our lives, He comforts us. If life brings disappointments, He walks with us through despair. "Though the LORD is exalted, he looks kindly on the lowly; though lofty, he sees them from afar" (Psalm 138:6). In our troubles, He preserves us, stretching out His hand against both "the anger of [our] foes" (v. 7) and our own deepest fears. *Thank you, God, for your compassionate love.* ❧ *Patricia*

Waiting in Hope
Romans 12:9–13

Be joyful in hope, patient in affliction, faithful in prayer.
—ROMANS 12:12

Rogelio served as our waiter during our weeklong vacation. In one conversation, he credited Jesus for blessing him with Kaly, a compassionate wife with strong faith. After they had their first baby, God gave them the opportunity to help care for their niece who had Down syndrome. Soon after, Rogelio's mother-in-law needed live-in care.

Rogelio works with joy, often taking on double shifts to ensure his wife can stay home to care for the people God entrusted to them. When I shared how the couple inspired me to love better because of the way they opened their hearts and home to serve their family members, he said, "It is my pleasure to serve them . . . and you."

Rogelio's life affirms the power of living with generosity and trusting God to provide as we serve one another selflessly. The apostle Paul urged God's people to be "devoted to one another in love . . . joyful in hope, patient in affliction, [and] faithful in prayer" as we "share with the Lord's people who are in need. Practice hospitality" (Romans 12:10–13).

Our life can change in an instant, leaving us or those we love in circumstances that feel impossible to bear. But when we're willing to share all God has given us while we wait on Him, we can cling to His enduring love . . . together. *Xochitl*

Living Well
Ecclesiastes 7:1–4

Death is the destiny of everyone; the living should take this to heart. —ECCLESIASTES 7:2

Free funerals for the living. That's the service offered by an establishment in South Korea. Since it opened in 2012, more than 25,000 people—from teenagers to retirees—have participated in mass "living funeral" services, hoping to improve their lives by considering their deaths. Officials say "the simulated death ceremonies are meant to give the participant a truthful sense of their lives, inspire gratitude, and aid in forgiveness and reconnection among family and friends."

These words echo the wisdom given by the teacher who wrote Ecclesiastes. "Death is the destiny of everyone; the living should take this to heart" (Ecclesiastes 7:2). Death reminds us of the brevity of life and that we only have a certain amount of time to live and love well. It loosens our grip on some of God's good gifts—such as money, relationships, and pleasure—and frees us to enjoy them in the here and now as we store up "treasures in heaven, where moths and vermin do not destroy, and where thieves do not break in and steal" (Matthew 6:20).

As we remember that death may come knocking anytime, perhaps it'll compel us to not postpone that visit with our parents, delay our decision to serve God in a particular way, or compromise our time with our children for our work. With God's help, we can learn to live wisely. *Poh Fang*

Eternal Eyes
2 Corinthians 4:7–18

We fix our eyes not on what is seen, but on what is unseen.
—2 CORINTHIANS 4:18

Eternal eyes, that's what my friend Madeline prays her children and grandchildren would have. Her family has gone through a tumultuous season that ended with the death of her daughter. As the family grieves from this horrific loss, Madeline longs for them to be less and less nearsighted—consumed by the pain of this world. She desires to be more and more farsighted—filled with hope in our loving God.

The apostle Paul and his coworkers experienced great suffering at the hands of persecutors and even from believers who tried to discredit them. Yet they had their eyes fixed on eternity. Paul boldly acknowledged that "we fix our eyes not on what is seen, but on what is unseen, since what is seen is temporary, but what is unseen is eternal" (2 Corinthians 4:18).

Although they were doing God's work, they lived with the reality of being "hard pressed on every side," "perplexed," "persecuted," and "struck down" (vv. 8–9). Shouldn't God have delivered them from these troubles? But instead of being disappointed, Paul built his hope on the "eternal glory" that supersedes momentary troubles (v. 17). He knew God's power was at work in him and had complete assurance that "the one who raised the Lord Jesus from the dead will also raise us with Jesus" (v. 14).

When our world around us feels shaky, may we turn our eyes to God—the eternal Rock that will never be destroyed. 🌿 *Estera*

Fireworks of Life
Ephesians 2:22–26

He himself is our peace. —*EPHESIANS 2:14*

On New Year's Eve, when high-powered fireworks detonate across cities and towns worldwide, the noise is loud on purpose. By their nature, say manufacturers, flashy fireworks are meant to split the atmosphere, literally. "Repeater" blasts can sound the loudest, especially when exploded near the ground.

Troubles, too, can boom through our hearts, minds, and homes. The "fireworks" of life—family struggles, relationship problems, work challenges, financial strain, even church division—can feel like explosions, rattling our emotional atmosphere.

Yet we know the One who lifts us over this uproar. Christ himself "is our peace," Paul wrote in Ephesians 2:14. When we abide in His presence, His peace is greater than any disruption, quieting the noise of any worry, hurt, or disunity.

This would have been powerful assurance to Jews and Gentiles alike. They'd once lived "without hope and without God in the world" (v. 12). Now they faced threats of persecution and internal threats of division. But in Christ, they'd been brought near to Him, and consequently to each other, by His blood. "For he himself is our peace, who has made the two groups one and has destroyed the barrier, the dividing wall of hostility" (v. 14).

As we start a new year, with threats of unrest and division ever rumbling on the horizon, let's turn from life's noisy trials to seek our ever-present Peace. He quiets the booms, healing us. *Patricia*

the writers

Alyson Kieda was an editor for Our Daily Bread Ministries for over a decade. Alyson has loved writing since she was a child and is thrilled to be writing for *Our Daily Bread*. She's married with three adult children and a growing number of grandchildren. Alyson loves reading, walking in the woods, and being with family. She feels blessed to be following in the footsteps of her mother, who wrote articles many years ago for another devotional.

Amy Boucher Pye is a writer, speaker, and retreat leader who lives in North London. She's the author of *A Loving Look at Life in Britain*, the award-winning *Finding Myself in Britain*, and an exploration of forgiveness, *The Living Cross*. She holds an MA in Christian spirituality from the University of London, runs the Woman Alive book club in the UK, and enjoys life with her family in their English vicarage. Find her at amyboucherpye.com or on Facebook, Twitter, and Instagram (@amyboucherpye).

Anne Cetas became a follower of Jesus in her late teens. She was given a copy of *Our Daily Bread* by a friend to help her read the Bible consistently and also studied the Discovery Series topical booklets. Several years later, she joined the editorial staff of *Our Daily Bread* as a proofreader. Anne began writing for the devotional booklet in 2004 and was a longtime editor for the publication. Anne and her husband, Carl, enjoy serving in the nursery and refugee ministries at their church. Anne's collection of *Our Daily Bread* articles, published by Our Daily Bread Publishing is called *Finding Jesus in Everyday Moments*.

Cindy Hess Kasper served for more than forty years at Our Daily Bread Ministries. During that time, she penned youth devotional articles for more than a decade before beginning to write for *Our Daily Bread* in 2006. She developed a passion for working with words because of her dad and favorite mentor and encourager—longtime senior editor Clair Hess. Cindy and her husband, Tom, have three grown children and—according to Cindy—several delightfully crazy grandchildren.

Elisa Morgan has authored over twenty-five books including *The NIV Mom's Devotional Bible*, *The Beauty of Broken*, *Hello, Beauty Full*, *She Did What She Could*, and *When We Pray Like Jesus*. For twenty years, Elisa Morgan served as CEO of MOPS International. In addition to writing for the *Our Daily Bread* devotional, she cohosts both the daily radio program *Discover the Word* and the podcast *God Hears Her* for Our Daily Bread Ministries. Elisa is married to Evan (vice-president of Online Learning for Our Daily Bread Ministries), and they have two grown children and two grandchildren who live near them in Denver, Colorado. Connect with Elisa and her blog *Really* at elisamorgan.com and follow her on Facebook and Instagram (@elisamorganauthor) and Twitter (@elisa_morgan).

Estera Pirosca Escobar is a Romanian with a heart for the world. After coming to the US as a college student, she experienced what it means to be lonely and homesick, but she also experienced the Christian community's love for internationals. She saw many international students become followers of Jesus through hospitality and love. In her role as National Field Director for International Friendships, Inc. (IFI), Estera helped IFI ministry leaders around the US strengthen and grow their local ministry. Estera and her Chilean husband, Francisco, live in Columbus, Ohio, where she is working on a doctorate in international education.

Jennifer Benson Schuldt has been writing professionally since 1997 when she graduated from Cedarville University and began her career as a technical writer. She's a graduate of the C.S. Lewis Institute Fellowship Program and is in the process of earning a master of fine arts degree in writing from Lindenwood University. Jennifer lives in the Chicago area with her husband, Bob, and their two children. When she isn't writing or serving at home and church, she enjoys painting, reading poetry and fiction, and taking walks with her family.

Julie Schwab holds a BA in creative writing and an MA in theological studies. She works as an editor and professor, but her love of learning has taken over, so she's a student (again), working on an MA in English. She lives in Michigan with her husband Jake (who frequently talks her out of adopting more cats), and their "zoo"—one labrashepherd (Shep) and two cats (Tabi and Tuxi). Jake and Julie love their life together and spend much of their free time going for walks, discussing vocation, story, and God's greatness as well as lovingly encouraging each other not to start too many house projects at once.

Kirsten Holmberg is a speaker, author, and coach based in the Pacific Northwest. She's the author of *Advent with the Word: Approaching Christmas Through the Inspired Language of God* and several Bible studies. She speaks regularly at business, church, and community events, encouraging others to step closer to Jesus and better know His love for them through His Word. Find her online at www.kirstenholmberg.com or on Facebook, Twitter, and Instagram (@kirholmberg).

Laura L. Smith is both an author and a speaker—and a lover of music. She grew up singing old hymns in her traditional church, then rushing home to count down the rest of the Top 40 on Billboard's music charts with Casey Kasem. Smith speaks around the country sharing the love of Christ with women at conferences and events. She lives in the college town of Oxford, Ohio, with her husband and four kids. Visit laurasmithauthor.com to learn more. Her book *How Sweet the Sound* is available through Our Daily Bread Publishing.

Linda Washington received a B.A. in English/Writing from Northwestern University in Evanston, Illinois, and an MFA from Vermont College of Fine Arts in Montpelier, Vermont. She has authored or coauthored fiction and nonfiction books for kids, teens, and adults, including *God and Me* (ages 10–12; Hendrickson Rose Publishing) and *The Soul of C.S. Lewis* (with Jerry Root, Wayne Martindale, and others; Tyndale House).

Lisa Samra desires to see Christ glorified in her life and in the ministries where she serves. Born and raised in Texas, Lisa is always on the lookout for sweet tea and brisket. She graduated with a Bachelor of Journalism from the University of Texas and earned a Master of Biblical Studies degree from Dallas Theological Seminary. Lisa now lives in Grand Rapids, Michigan, with her husband, Jim, and their four children. She is passionate about facilitating mentoring relationships for women and developing groups focused on spiritual formation and leadership development.

Lori Hatcher is a blogger, pastor's wife, and women's ministry speaker. She's the editor of South Carolina's *Reach Out, Columbia* magazine, president of Columbia Toastmasters, and regular contributor to magazines such as *Christian Living Today* and websites like Crosswalk.com. Her book *Hungry for God . . . Starving for Time*, won the Christian Small Publisher 2016 Book of the Year award. Her recent book *Refresh Your Faith* was published by Our Daily Bread Publishing. Find out more about Lori and her well-loved five-minute devotions at lorihatcher.com.

Monica La Rose studied English and theology at Trinity Christian College in Palos Heights, Illinois, and completed a Master of Theological Studies degree at Calvin Seminary in Grand Rapids, Michigan. In October 2019, she married Ben La Rose, a musician and electrical engineer. She and Ben live in St. Charles, Illinois, and they treasure time with friends, family, and their two crazy cats, Heathcliff and Mystique.

Patricia Raybon writes bridge-building books that help believers move big mountains. An award-winning author and journalist, she writes to encourage people in the Word, inspiring believers to love God and each other. A supporter of Bible-translation projects worldwide, she is author of *I Told the Mountain to Move*; *My First White Friend*; her One Year® devotional, *God's Great Blessings*; and *Undivided: A Muslim Daughter, Her Christian Mother, Their Path to Peace*. A mother and wife, she and her husband Dan, a retired educator, live in her beloved home state of Colorado. Join her on the journey at patriciaraybon.com.

Poh Fang Chia never dreamed of being in a language-related profession; chemistry was her first love. The turning point came when she received Jesus as her Savior as a 15-year-old and expressed to Jesus that she would like to create books that touch lives. She serves with Our Daily Bread Ministries at the Singapore office as director of English content development and is also a member of the Chinese editorial review committee. Poh Fang says: "I really enjoy exploring the Scripture and finding passages that bring a fresh viewpoint, answer a question that is burning in my mind, or deal with a life issue I'm facing. My prayer is to write so that readers will see how presently alive the Bible is and will respond to the life-transforming power of the Word."

Remi Oyedele is a finance professional and freelance writer with twin passions for God's word and children's books. Her ultimate life goal is to channel scriptural truths into stories for children and children at heart.

Needless to say, C.S. Lewis is a major inspiration! Remi has an MA in Writing for Children and has completed correspondence courses with the Christian Writer's Guild and the Institute of Children's Literature. A native of Nigeria, she currently resides in Central Florida where she spends her spare time reading and blogging at wordzpread.com. Remi is married to David, her number one blog fan.

Ruth O'Reilly Smith was born in South Africa and has lived in the UK since 1999. There she met and married her husband, and they have twins, a boy and a girl. Ruth started out in radio in 1995 while attending the University of Pretoria. She went on to work as presenter of a variety of music and talk-based shows, along with heading up the news desk at a Christian community radio station. She currently hosts a weekday show with United Christian Broadcasters. Her first book, *God Speaks: 40 Letters from the Father's Heart* was published in September 2021. Ruth and her family are part of a local church in Staffordshire, England.

Xochitl (soh-cheel) Dixon equips and encourages readers to embrace God's grace and grow deeper in their personal relationships with Christ and others. Serving as an author, speaker, and blogger at xedixon.com, she enjoys singing, reading, photography, motherhood, and being married to her best friend Dr. W. Alan Dixon Sr., a college professor. Xochitl has published two books with Our Daily Bread Publishing: *Waiting for God: Trusting Daily in God's Plan and Pace* and *Different Like Me*, a children's book that was a 2021 ECPA Christian Book Award finalist.

Help us get the word out!

Our Daily Bread Publishing exists to feed the soul with the Word of God.

If you appreciated this book, please let others know.

- Pick up another copy to give as a gift.
- Share a link to the book or mention it on social media.
- Write a review on your blog, on a bookseller's website, or at our own site (odb.org/store).
- Recommend this book for your church, book club, or small group.

Connect with us:

f @ourdailybread

⊙ @ourdailybread

𝕏 @ourdailybread

Our Daily Bread Publishing
PO Box 3566
Grand Rapids, Michigan 49501 USA

✉ books@odb.org